THE TRAUMA OF PSYCHOLOGICAL TORTURE

Edited by Almerindo E. Ojeda

WITHDRAWN

Disaster and Trauma Psychology

Gilbert Reyes, Series Editor

Westport, Connecticut
London

Library of Congress Cataloging-in-Publication Data

The trauma of psychological torture / edited by Almerindo E. Ojeda.
    p. ; cm. — (Disaster and trauma psychology, ISSN 1940–901X)
  Includes bibliographical references and index.
  ISBN 978–0–313–34514–2 (alk. paper)
1. Psychological torture—United States. 2. Torture—United States—Psychological aspects. 3. Torture victims—Mental health—United States. I. Ojeda, Almerindo E.
[DNLM: 1. Stress, Psychological—psychology—United States. 2. Torture—psychology—United States. 3. Prisoners—psychology—United States. 4. Psychological Warfare—United States. WM 172 T7772 2008]
HV8599.U6T73 2008
364.6'7—dc22   2008010131

British Library Cataloguing in Publication Data is available.

Library of Congress Catalog Card Number: 2008010131
ISBN: 978–0–313–34514–2
ISSN: 1940–901X

First published in 2008

Praeger Publishers, 88 Post Road West, Westport, CT 06881
An imprint of Greenwood Publishing Group, Inc.
www.praeger.com

Printed in the United States of America

The paper used in this book complies with the Permanent Paper Standard issued by the National Information Standards Organization (Z39.48–1984).

10 9 8 7 6 5 4 3 2 1

To all those who have undergone the trauma of psychological torture.

CONTENTS

SERIES FOREWORD

Praeger's series on Trauma and Disaster Psychology provides a forum for sharing thoughtful and progressive perspectives on some of the most compelling issues facing humanity today. Contributors to this series bring expertise from various disciplines, cultures, and backgrounds ranging across academia, clinical practice, public health, law, journalism, community activism, humanitarian agencies, human rights organizations, governmental intelligence agencies, and others too numerous to mention. The theme that aligns these volumes and their authors to form a meaningful series is the recognition that people's lives are profoundly and enduringly affected by disasters and other potentially traumatic events that are increasingly common and troubling in today's global community. Those who contribute to this series are engaged in more than an intellectual enterprise, and their efforts not only illuminate the darker recesses of the human experience, but also light the way toward preventing trauma and relieving suffering.

The newest entry in this series addresses an issue that is far from new, but which has until recently been neglected, ignored, minimized, euphemized, and rationalized until graphic evidence became available that has at least temporarily lifted the curtain of denial obscuring the fact that forms of torture are practiced even by democratic governments. These acts are performed in secrecy and in violation of these nations' espoused observance of human rights conventions and international law. Once they are exposed, the illicit practices are vehemently denied, piously denounced, and circuitously debated, while in practice they continue unabated.

The present volume is titled *The Trauma of Psychological Torture,* and it addresses a particular aspect of the broader issue of torture, that being the intentional infliction of psychological pain. As the authors demonstrate, this is a dark art that has been studied and practiced for centuries and that has only recently been designated as a crime against humanity, and thus the lines of demarcation between acceptable practices and those that amount to torture are not so well established as to prevent transgressions or preclude moral equivocation. What seems too often lost in both the agreements and the controversies is any recognition of the psychological trauma that is inflicted upon not only the guilty persons toward whom these techniques are ostensibly directed for the greater good, but also upon the innocently accused, their loved ones, and the communities that look on in horror and wonder at what is done to others of their kind and might next be visited upon them.

One line that is sometimes notoriously transgressed is one that would bar the involvement of health care professionals in torturous practices. Among the most horrendous and well documented of these transgressions were atrocities performed under the auspices of research or experimental treatment against prisoners during the Second World War by doctors who were later prosecuted at the Nuremberg Trials. Safeguards have since been put in place to protect prisoners and other highly vulnerable groups from this kind of exploitation in the name of science or progress, and other restrictions have been placed on what can be done under cover of war, but there is little in place to prevent practitioners of the healing professions within military or intelligence agencies from participating in aggressive practices that are tantamount to psychological torture.

Recent revelations regarding the participation of specialists in psychology, psychiatry, and behavioral sciences in interrogations described as coercive or abusive triggered a heated debate over the ethical, moral, and legal implications of the alleged activities. Professional organizations including the American Medical Association, the American Psychiatric Association, and the American Psychological Association weighed in on the subject and issued statements articulating their positions regarding the involvement of their members in interrogations where coercive or abusive tactics were involved, or in which other human rights protections were being violated.

Of particular note was the escalating and cyclical conflict among the members and leadership of the American Psychological Association, which became and continues to be strikingly polarized and contentious. News media coverage of the controversy has further fueled the conflict, and none of the ensuing negotiations and decisions has produced a satisfactory resolution of the central point of contention: To what, if any, extent may mental health professionals ethically participate in the interrogation of suspects when the methods or conditions of the interrogation are abusive, deceptive, or degrading? No book, including this one, can definitively and authoritatively resolve this issue to the satisfaction of all sides. But the authors and the editor have provided a foundation of knowledge and principles for understanding what psychological torture is and how it affects those upon whom it is inflicted and those who practice it, with case examples that illustrate what is or may be at stake.

Reading this book should prepare most anyone for reasoning critically about this very complicated and vexing set of issues and arguments. What is also made clear is that this is the furthest thing from a merely academic debate, because these actions are taken with great regularity across the entire spectrum of authoritarian to democratically elected governments in the name of their people, their values, and their security. Like it or not, we are all involved to some extent, and those of us living in the most privileged and democratic societies carry the highest obligation to stand accountable for what is done by those whom we authorized to use force on our behalf.

Gilbert Reyes, PhD
Series Editor
Praeger Series on Trauma and Disaster Psychology

INTRODUCTION

Psychological torture is generally construed as a set of practices used worldwide to inflict pain or suffering without resorting to direct physical violence. Psychological torture (henceforth *PT*) includes the use of sleep deprivation, sensory disorientation, the cultivation of anxiety, solitary confinement, mock execution, severe humiliation, mind-altering drugs, and threats of violence—as well as the exploitation of personal or cultural phobias (for a more precise definition of *PT*, see Ojeda, Chapter 1). *PT* thus contrasts with its physical counterpart in that the latter opts for physical violence and includes practices such as beating, whipping, burning, drowning, and electrocution (see Rejali, 2007). It is because it foregoes direct physical violence that *PT* is sometimes regarded as a distasteful but benign practice—*torture lite,* in fact. But there is nothing *lite* about *PT.*

The origins of *PT* can be traced back to the Middle Ages, where it was employed by the Spanish Inquisition and the witch hunt trials (see Streatfeild 2007, 356ff). Yet, the core techniques that now constitute it were isolated by the two totalitarian systems of the twentieth century—fascism and communism. During the Cold War, and particularly after the Korean War, *PT* experienced a veritable scientific revolution, as it benefited from hundreds of studies of "coercive behavior" that took place at leading research institutions in the United Kingdom, the United States, and Canada (see McCoy, 2006, and Chapter 3). Distilled and refined by this research, the techniques of *PT* were immediately applied worldwide—from Latin America to Ireland; from Jordan to Eritrea; from Turkey to Pakistan; from Vietnam to Guantánamo and Abu Ghraib (see Ojeda, Gildner, and Fields, Chapters 1, 2, and 8).

PT has undeniably traumatic psychological consequences. A recent cross-sectional study of 279 survivors of torture in the Balkans found, for example, that the effects of psychological torture were comparable to those of physical torture. In fact, it was discovered that physical torture and psychological torture were similar in terms of the severity of the mental suffering they caused (see Basoglu et al., 2007). But the psychiatric sequelae of *PT* are traumatic as well. They include delirium, psychosis, regression, self-mutilation, cognitive impairment, and anxiety disorders, including Posttraumatic Stress Disorder (see Physicians for Human Rights, 2005, and Grassian, Chapter 6; see Kupers, Chapter 7, for the social consequences of these sequelae). Neuroscience research on these and related mental disorders continues to establish their neurobiological underpinnings, thus challenging the view that *PT* is not physical, not serious, and perhaps not even torture at all (see Fields, Chapter 8, Jacobs, Chapter 9, and Catani, Chapter 10). It is these traumatic effects of *PT* that the present volume intends to chart.

In light of the traumatic nature of its effects, *PT* must be considered torture under the internationally recognized definitions of the practice. Two such definitions are currently in use. The first is that of the World Medical Association. It reads as follows.

> [Torture is] the deliberate, systematic, or wanton infliction of physical or mental suffering by one or more persons acting alone or on the orders of any authority, to force another person to yield information, to make a confession, or for any other reason. (World Medical Association, 1975)

The second is the definition advanced by the United Nations in the *Convention Against Torture and Other Cruel, Inhuman and Degrading Treatment or Punishment*:

> [Torture is] any act by which severe pain or suffering, whether physical or mental, is intentionally inflicted on a person for such purposes as obtaining from him or a third person information or a confession, punishing him for an act he or a third person has committed or is suspected of having committed, or intimidating or coercing him or a third person, or for any reason based on discrimination of any kind, when such pain or suffering is inflicted by, or at the instigation of, or with the consent or acquiescence of a public official or other person acting in an official capacity. (United Nations, 1988)

As the reader of this volume will be able to ascertain, *PT* is a practice by which official agents intend to inflict severe pain or suffering on their victims. Invariably, they succeed.

In the summer of 2006, The UC Davis Center for the Study of Human Rights in the Americas and the UCDavis Center for Mind and Brain initiated a long-term collaboration to investigate the neurobiology of psychological torture. The two centers launched their collaborative efforts by holding *The First UCDavis*

Workshop on the Neurobiology of Psychological Torture. The workshop was hosted by the Center for Mind and Brain on September 30, 2006. The goal of that workshop was to bring together researchers and practitioners from different specialties and research groups in order to set off a unified, long-term, research program on the ways in which *PT* affects the central nervous systems of its victims. All of this was done in an effort to understand *PT* in relation to the more traditional forms of physical torture, and to establish clearly articulated ethical, legal, and medical descriptions of this set of practices. We expected that these descriptions would help understand, document, treat, and deter *PT.* We still do.

The deliberations at *The First UC Davis Workshop on the Neurobiology of Psychological Torture* served as the basis of the publication we now offer to the reader. In addition to the presentations made at that workshop, the present volume includes another chapter on the expansion of *PT* (see Gildner, Chapter 2), and a number of chapters on the ethical issues raised by the participation of psychologists in settings where *PT* is known to have taken place (see both Soldz and Olson, Chapter 4, and Marks, Chapter 5). The volume closes with a couple of "case studies" of victims of psychological torture—those of Mohammed al Qahtani and Salim Hamdan. The former was written by the lead attorney in al Qahtani's case (see Gutierrez, Chapter 11); the latter is a declaration by a psychiatrist offering expert witness in the Hamdan case (see Matthews, Chapter 12).

REFERENCES

Basoglu, Metin, et al. (2007). "Torture vs other cruel, inhuman, and degrading treatment: is the distinction real or apparent?" *Archives of General Psychiatry* 64(3), 277–85.

McCoy, Alfred (2006). *A Question of Torture: CIA Interrogation from the Cold War to the War on Terror.* New York: Metropolitan Books, Henry Holt and Company.

Physicians for Human Rights (2005). *Break them Down. Systematic Use of Psychological Torture by US Forces.* Printed in the United States. Available at http://physiciansforhumanrights.org/torture/.

Rejali, Darius (2007). *Torture and Democracy.* Princeton, NJ: Princeton University Press.

Streatfeild, Dominic (2007). *Brainwash: The Secret History of Mind Control.* New York: Thomas Dunne Books, St. Martin's Press.

United Nations (1988) *Convention Against Torture and Other Cruel, Inhuman, or Degrading Treatment or Punishment.* Washington, DC: U.S. GPO.

World Medical Association (1975) *Guidelines for Medical Doctors Concerning Torture and Other Cruel, Inhuman, and Degrading Treatment or Punishment in Relation to Detention and Imprisonment* (Declaration of Tokyo).

CHAPTER 1

WHAT IS PSYCHOLOGICAL TORTURE?

Almerindo E. Ojeda

Psychological Torture (*PT*) is a practice that is often proscribed but seldom defined. This is to be expected, as a series of complex issues arise as soon as we take on the question of *PT*. What is psychological pain? How is it different from physical pain? And does not physical torture produce psychological pain as well? How much psychological pain should a practice induce in order to count as torture? And do not individuals vary as to the amount of pain they can tolerate? If so, how can we justify a universal threshold of torturous pain?

Finding a satisfying definition of *PT* is a challenge. It is also an imperative, as a clear, legally binding, definition of *PT* is essential for the detection, prosecution, and erradication of this pernicious practice.

Indeed, back in 1972, Lord Hubert Lister Parker, Baron of Waddington, was asked to review earlier inquiries into the abusive treatment of suspected members of the Irish Republican Army (see below). In his final report, Lord Parker of Waddington asked "where, however, does hardship and discomfort end and for instance humiliating treatment begin, and where does the latter end and torture begin? Whatever words of definition are used, opinions will inevitably differ as to whether the action under consideration falls within one or the other definition."[1]

More recently, on July 13, 2005, Lieutenant General Randall M. Schmidt appeared before the Armed Services Committee of the U.S. Senate to testify about the interrogation methods used at Guantánamo. There General Schmidt found that "the lines were hard to define. Humane treatment, torture I felt were the clear lines...anything else beyond that was fairly vague." He believed that "[s]omething might be degrading but not necessarily torture. And it may not be inhumane. It may be humiliating, but it may not be torture." General Schmidt felt that "the cumulative effect of simultaneous applications of numerous authorized techniques had an abusive and degrading impact on the detainee [with ISN 063]."

Yet, in the general's judgement, the application of those techniques "did not rise to the level . . . of inhumane treatment." Overall, "no torture occurred."[2]

In essence, the questions that arise when we attempt a definition of *PT* are two:

1. What is psychological pain (as opposed to physical pain)?
2. How much of it must torture produce (in order to count as such)?

We will call (1) the *qualitative* question, as it inquires about the nature of psychological pain. We will call (2) the *quantitative* question, as it asks about the amount thereof needed to qualify as *PT.* The purpose of this essay is to argue that neither one of these difficult questions needs to be answered in order to define *PT.* We will proceed constructively, by proposing a satisfying definition of *PT* that does not try to dispose of the thorny issues above.

AN EXTENSIONAL DEFINITION

In principle, there are two ways in which we could define *PT.* One of them is to list all (and only) the practices that constitute *PT.* The other is to identify the property or properties that practices must satisfy in order to count as instances of *PT.* The former is the *extensional* definition of the term; the latter is the *intensional* one.

Intuitively, when we think of *PT* we think of a set of practices that include:

A1. *Isolation:* solitary confinement (no human contact whatsoever) or semi-solitary confinement (contact only with interrogators, guards, and other personnel ancillary to the detention).

A2. *Psychological Debilitation:* the effect of deprivation of food, water, clothes, or sleep, the disruption of sleep cycles, prolonged standing, crouching, or kneeling, forced physical exertion, exposure to temperatures leading to stifling or hypothermia.

A3. *Spatial Disorientation:* confinement in small places; small, darkened or otherwise nonfunctional windows.

A4. *Temporal Disorientation:* denial of natural light; nighttime recreation time; erratic scheduling of meals, showers, or otherwise regular activities.

A5. *Sensory Disorientation:* use of *magic rooms,* i.e., holding facilities or interrogation chambers that induce misperceptions of sensory failure, narcosis, or hypnosis.

A6. *Sensory Deprivation:* use of hooding, blindfolding, opaque goggles, darkness, sound proofing/canceling headsets, nasal masks (possibly deodorized), gloves, arm covers, sensory deprivation tanks or vaults.

A7. *Sensory Assault (Overstimulation):* use of bright or stroboscopic lights; loud noise (or music); shouting or using public address equipment at close range.

A8. *Induced Desperation:* arbitrary arrest; indefinite detention; random punishment or reward; forced feeding; implanting sense of guilt, abandonment, or "learned helplessness."

A9. *Threats:* to self or to others; threats of death, physical torture, or rendition; mock executions; forced witnessing of torture (visually or aurally).

A10. *Feral Treatment:* berating victim to the subhuman level of wild animals; forced nakedness; denial of personal hygiene; overcrowding; forced interaction with pests; contact with blood or excreta; bestiality; incest.

A11. *Sexual Humiliation:* forcing the victim to witness or carry out masturbation, copulation, or other forms of sexual behavior.

A12. *Desecration:* forcing victims to witness or engage in the violation of religious practices (irreverence, blasphemy, profanity, defilement, sacrilege, incest, Satanism).

A13. *Pharmacological Manipulation:* nontherapeutic use of drugs or placebos.

We propose to define *PT,* extensionally, as the set of practices A1 through A13.

The instances of the practices in A1–A13 can be defined with an unusually high degree of precision. Forced nakedness and contact with pests or excreta are already precise. Isolation, sleep deprivation, temporal disorientation, and prolonged standing can be quantified in terms of time; sensory assault can be measured in terms of lumens, decibels, and standard equipment; food and water deprivation can be measured as ratios of caloric intake or volume of water taken per day; overcrowding can be defined as a ratio of detainees to area; sensory deprivation, forced feeding, spatial and sensory disorientation, and mock execution involve straightforwardly specifiable equipment or holding conditions; acts of sexual humiliation and desecration have been carefully codified by religion; pharmacological manipulation can be established through chemical analysis; arbitrary arrests and indefinite detention have perfectly clear legal meanings; verbal threats and berating involve linguistic expressions that can be tested for their effects on the victims' peers.

An extensional definition of *PT* as the set of practices in A1–A13 would thus inherit the high degree of precision with which their instances can be defined. Needless to say, the practices in A1–A13 could be revised (or supplemented by other equally well-defined practices). Given the *modular* nature of the proposed definition, these revisions can be done on one practice (or module) of the definition without compromising the others. The definition under consideration is, therefore, one that paves the way to its own improvement.

Now, it might be objected that some of the practices mentioned in A2 are forms of physical rather than psychological torture. There is no question that prolonged standing, kneeling, and crouching can produce pain and bodily harm that qualify as physical torture. Similarly, prolonged shackling in stressful or painful positions (as is always the case with "short-shackling"), and manipulation of bodily temperature (be it by exposure to inclement weather, by heating or cooling equipment, or by dousing with cold water), should be considered physical torture. Yet, A2 pertains not to them, but to the psychological debilitation they produce in their victims. This debilitation, which includes cognitive impairment, is what A2 is about.

It should be noted, finally, that the definition of *PT* under consideration is *phenomenological* rather than *teleological,* as it proceeds by defining a set of practices in themselves rather than in terms of the goals, intended or attained, of those who designed these practices or carried them out. This means that the pain these practices may produce plays no role in the definition of *PT.* Thus, no reference is necessary to a definition of psychological pain (as opposed to physical pain) nor to the necessary amount thereof (to establish torture). In short, we have arrived at an extensional definition of *PT* that voids, as desired, both the qualitative and the quantitative questions.

RELEVANCE OF THIS EXTENSIONAL DEFINITION

The set of practices embodied in the extensional definition of *PT* have been applied throughout the world for more than 50 years. They have also been widely characterized either as psychological torture or as another form of cruel, inhuman, or degrading treatment or punishment—as we will presently see.

Stunned by the unlikely confessions made at the Stalinist show trials of the 1930s, at the Hungarian trial of Cardinal Mindszenty in the 1940s, and at the American POW camps in the Korean War, hundreds of studies were published in the 1950s and 1960s to identify the methods whereby Communist regimes could exact implausible confessions from their enemies (and to understand, more broadly, the psychology of coercion).[3]

The methods in question, it was soon discovered, were psychological rather than physical in nature. Outlined in Biderman (1956, 6–13), the "basic communist techniques of coercive interrogation" were as follows.[4]

> **B1.** *Isolation:* complete solitary confinement (where prisoner has no social contact whatsoever); complete isolation (where prisoner lives only with interrogator or guard), semi-isolation (where two to four prisoners are isolated from the rest, frequently making sure that one of them is more inclined to capitulation than the rest); group isolation (where eight to 30 prisoners are isolated from the rest under extremely crowded and difficult conditions calculated to promote destructive competition and dissension).

> **B2.** *Monopolization of Attention:* physical isolation (small, bare, windowless cells, sometimes in complete darkness); other restrictions of sensory stimulation (denial of gratifying sensations or the pleasure of movement; forbidding deviations from a fixed posture; hearing real or feigned cries of anguish from another victim; receiving a visit from a "friendly" interrogator); prolonged interrogation and forced writing (regarding answers to very general questions).

> **B3.** *Induced Debilitation and Exhaustion:* semi-starvation (survival rations); exposure (intense cold, intense heat, or dampness); exploitation of wounds and chronic illness

(which are not immediately life-threatening; offering medical treatment after interrogations are completed); sleep deprivation (through uncomfortable positions, with minimal protection from the cold, and on hard or vermin-infested surfaces; waking prisoners up for interrogation or "bed-checks"); prolonged constraint (forced sitting, standing at attention, or in other forced positions; confinement to a hole or box; shackles permitting only painful, unnatural postures); prolonged interrogation and forced writing (lasting many hours a day and over weeks or months, and carried out by successive interrogators).

B4. *Cultivation of Anxiety and Despair:* threats of death (verbal threats, grave digging, fake executions, death sentences in fake trials); threats of non-repatriation (absent compliance); threats of punishment as a "war criminal" (possibly at civilian hands); threats of endless isolation (or interrogation; prisoners are told that "interrogators are not in a hurry"); vague threats (either by veiling threats in order to fake a benevolent interest in the prisoner, or by threatening with "a fate more terrible than words can express"); threats against prisoner's family; mysterious changes of treatment or place of confinement (of the prisoner and his "belongings"), changes in questioning and interrogators.

B5. *Alternating Punishments and Rewards:* occasional "favors" (to plant the belief that the interrogators are "good people," to remind the prisoner of how pleasant things can be, and to prevent him to adjust to doing without comforts); extreme fluctuations of interrogator's attitudes (either within a single interrogator or within a team playing the good cop/bad cop routine, where the interrogator with higher authority plays the good cop and pretends not to approve of the methods of his subordinate); promises of improved conditions (including POW status, given compliance), special promises (jobs, status, or other rewards in exchange for cooperation), rewards given for partial compliance (all of which would be trivial), tantalizing (displaying prisoners receiving better treatment; offering cigarettes with no matches or appetizing food in miniscule quantities).

B6. *Demonstrating "Omnipotence" and "Omniscience" of Captor:* omniscience (by painstakingly gathering detailed facts about the prisoner, interrogators attempt to create the impression that they know all about him, including the answers to the questions they ask, so that the interrogation is only "a test of the cooperativeness and veracity of the prisoner," who is constantly accused of lying and being caught in lies); omnipotence (displaying overwhelming force, repeated mention of the captor's might; taking cooperativeness for granted and resistance as a foolish aberration; presenting "evidence" that other prisoners, especially acquaintances of his, have capitulated).

B7. *Degradation:* personal hygiene prevented (withholding of combs, and shaving equipment; individual may even be forced to live in his own filth); filthy or infested surroundings (prisoners are kept in filthy, vermin- or rodent-infested places of confinement), demeaning punishments (slapping, ear-twisting, and other degrading but physically mild punishments may be inflicted); insults and taunts (repeating insults that seem to affect the prisoner; casting aspersions about wife's morality; issuing false diagnoses of venereal diseases), denial of privacy (subjection to constant surveillance;

if vulnerable to embarrassment, prisoners may be forced to perform private functions in public).

B8. *Enforcing Trivial and Absurd Demands:* forced writing (and rewriting answers to numerous, exceedingly trivial questions; very general instructions are given out, but prisoners are forced to rewrite their answers over and over again until an "acceptable" answer is completed), enforcing rules (numerous rules are handed out; punishments are meted for unstated rules; rules may include the positions to be assumed when sleeping, with the prisoner awakened if he changes position; permission is required to perform almost any act, including washing or going to the latrine), "upping the ante" (pretending that only a relatively trivial demand needs to be met, only to place increasingly taxing demands afterwards; the interrogator may demand, for example, that the prisoner write a denial of the accusations levelled against him, then go on to ask him to break down those denials into increasingly detailed denials, and then convince him to eliminate each of these denials—thus turning the denial of an accusation into a confession of guilt).

After outlining these techniques authoritatively, Biderman (1956, 16) goes on to qualify them as "abominable outrages," adding that "[p]robably no other aspect of communism reveals more thoroughly its disrespect for truth and the individuals than its resort to these techniques" (Biderman 1956, 3f). Yet, by 1963, several of these techniques had become recommended CIA practice.

In July 1963, the CIA drafted a comprehensive interrogation manual titled *KUBARK Counterintelligence Interrogation.*[5] It is a systematic presentation of successful and unsuccessful interrogation techniques drawn from the author's review of the literature on the psychology of coercion produced between 1950 and 1961. Originally secret, the handbook was declassified in 1997 through a Freedom of Information Act (*FOIA*) request initiated by the *Baltimore Sun.*[6]

The *KUBARK Counterintelligence Interrogation* manual recommends a number of the interrogation techniques identified in Biderman (1956), namely:

C1. *Monopolization of Attention:* The more completely the place of confinement eliminates sensory stimuli, the more rapidly and deeply will the interrogatee be affected...An early effect of such an environment is anxiety...The interrogator can benefit from the subject's anxiety...The deprivation of stimuli induces regression [of the interrogatee's to his childhood] by depriving the subject's mind of contact with an outer world and thus forcing it upon itself (90).

C2. *Induced Debilitation and Exhaustion:* An over-stuffed chair for the use of the interrogatee is sometimes preferable to a straight-backed, wooden chair because *if he is made to stand for a lengthy period or is otherwise deprived of physical comfort,* the contrast is intensified and increased disorientation results (45, *emphasis supplied*) | *When the individual is told to stand at attention for long periods*...[t]he immediate source of pain is not the interrogator but the victim himself. The motivational strength of the individual is likely to exhaust itself in this internal encounter (94, *emphasis supplied*).

C3. *Cultivation of Anxiety and Despair:* The interrogator can and does make the subject's world not only unlike the world to which he had been accustomed but also strange in itself—a world in which familiar patterns of time, space, and sensory perception are overthrown (52). | A pale face indicates fear and usually shows that the interrogator is hitting close to the mark (55). | What we aim to do is to ensure that the manner of arrest achieves, if possible, surprise, and *the maximum amount of mental discomfort*...The ideal time at which to arrest a person is in the early hours of the morning because surprise is achieved then (85, emphasis in the original). | The circumstances of detention are arranged to enhance within the subject his feelings of being cut off from the known and the reassuring, and of being plunged into the strange. Usually his own clothes are immediately taken away, because familiar clothing reinforces identity and thus the capacity for resistance....Detention permits the interrogator to cut through these links and throw the interrogatee back upon his own unaided internal resources....Control of source's environment permits the interrogator to determine his diet, sleep pattern, and other fundamentals. Manipulating these into irregularities, so that the subject becomes disorientated, is very likely to create feelings of fear and helplessness...In any event, it is advisable to keep the subject upset by constant disruptions of patterns (86f). | It is usually useful to intensify [the subject's feelings of guilt] (103). | (see also *Monopolization of Attention*).

C4. *Alternating Punishments and Rewards:* The commonest of the joint interrogator techniques is the Mutt-and-Jeff routine: the brutal, angry, domineering type contrasted with the friendly, quiet type. This routine works best with women, teenagers, and timid men...An interrogator working alone can also use the Mutt-and-Jeff technique...(72f). | Half-hearted efforts to cooperate can be ignored, and conversely he can be rewarded for non-cooperation. (For example, a successfully resisting source may become distraught if given some reward for the "valuable contribution" that he has made.) (77) | Meals and sleep granted irregularly, in more than abundance or less than adequacy, the shifts occurring on no discernible time pattern, will normally disorient an interrogatee and sap his will to resist more effectively than a sustained deprivation leading to debility (93).

C5. *Demonstrating "Omniscience" of Captor:* [The interrogator] can create and amplify an effect of omniscience in a number of ways. For example, he can show the interrogatee a thick file bearing his own name. Even if the file contains little or nothing but blank paper, the air of familiarity with which the interrogator refers to the subject's background can convince some sources that all is known and that resistance is futile (52) | The interrogator...explains to the source that the purpose of the questioning is not to gain information; the interrogator knows everything already. His real purpose is to test the sincerity (reliability, honor, etc.) of the source. The interrogator then asks a few questions to which he knows the answers. If the subject lies, he is informed firmly and dispassionately that he has lied. By skilled manipulation of the known, the questioner can convince a naive subject that all his secrets are out (67).

C6. *Demonstrating "Omnipotence" of Captor:* [The interrogator] exercises the powers of an all-powerful parent, determining when the source will be sent to bed, when and what he will eat, whether he will be rewarded for good behavior or punished for being bad (52).

In addition, it recommended four of the practices listed in A1–A13 above, namely:

C7. *Temporal Disorientation:* The subject may be left alone for days; and he may be returned to his cell, allowed to sleep for five minutes, and brought back to an interrogation which is conducted as though eight hours had intervened. The principle is that sessions should be so planned as to disrupt the source's sense of chronological order (49f). | There are a number of non-coercive techniques for inducing regression... Some interrogatees can be re[g]ressed by persistent manipulation of time, by retarding and advancing clocks and serving meals at odd times—ten minutes or ten hours after the last food was given. Day and night are jumbled. Interrogation sessions are similarly unpatterned[;] the subject may be brought back for more questioning just a few minutes after being dismissed for the night (76f).

C8. *Sensory Disorientation:* The confusion [or *Alice-in-Wonderland*] technique is designed not only to obliterate the familiar, but to replace it with the weird...When the subject enters the room, the first interrogator asks a double talk question—one which seems straightforward but is essentially nonsensical...the second interrogator follows up...with a wholly unrelated and equally illogical query...No pattern of questions and answers is permitted to develop...as the process continues, day after day if necessary, the subject begins to try to make sense of the situation, which becomes mentally intolerable (76). | [As an example of the *magic room* technique,] the prisoner...is given a hypnotic suggestion that his hand is growing warm. However, in this instance, the prisoner's hand actually does become warm, a problem easily resolved by the use of a concealed diathermy machine. Or it might be suggested... that...a cigarette will taste bitter. Here again, he could be given a cigarette prepared to have a slight but noticeably bitter taste (77f).

C9. *Threats:* The threat of coercion usually weakens or destroys resistance more effectively than coercion itself. The threat to inflict pain, for example, can trigger fears more damaging than the immediate sensation of pain...The same principle holds for other fears: sustained long enough, a strong fear of anything vague or unknown induces regression, whereas the materialization of the fear, the infliction of some form of punishment, is likely to come as a relief...Threats delivered coldly are more effective than those shouted in rage (90f).

C10. *Pharmacological Manipulation:* Persons burdened with feelings of shame or guilt are likely to unburden themselves when drugged, especially if these feelings have been reinforced by the interrogator...drugs (and the other aids discussed in this section) should not be used persistently to facilitate the interrogative debriefing that follows capitulation. Their function is to cause capitulation, to aid in the shift from resistance to cooperation (100).

Many of the techniques advocated in *KUBARK Counterintelligence Interrogation* were applied, within the United States, in the "hostile interrogation" of Soviet defector Yuri Nosenko—an affair that lasted 1,277 days from 1964 to 1967.[7] At the same time, the CIA "set about disseminating the new practices worldwide, first through U.S. AID's Office of Public Safety to police departments in Asia and Latin America and later, after 1975, through the U.S. Army Mobile Training Teams active in Central America during the 1980s" (McCoy 2006, 10f). A detailed account of the application of these techniques in Latin America can be found in Timerman (1981).

But the practices spread to Europe as well. In 1971, the Royal Ulster Constabulary (the Belfast police) resorted to the combined application of five particular techniques during the "interrogation in depth" of 14 alleged members of the Irish Republican Army. Based on facts established by the European Commission of Human Rights, the European Court of Human Rights described these techniques as follows.[8]

> **D1.** *Wall-standing:* Forcing the detainees to remain for periods of some hours in a "stress position," described by those who underwent it as being "spread eagled against the wall, with their fingers put high above the head against the wall, the legs spread apart and the feet back, causing them to stand on their toes with the weight of the body mainly on the fingers."
>
> **D2.** *Hooding:* Putting a black or [navy-colored] bag over the detainees' heads and, at least initially, keeping it there all the time except during interrogation.
>
> **D3.** *Subjection to Noise:* Pending their interrogations, holding the detainees in a room where there was a continuous loud and hissing noise.
>
> **D4.** *Deprivation of Sleep:* Pending their interrogations, depriving the detainees of sleep.
>
> **D5.** *Deprivation of Food and Drink:* Subjecting the detainees to a reduced diet during their stay at the centre and pending interrogations.

These five techniques were soon regarded as instances of torture, inhuman or degrading treatment or punishment. Thus, in their report on the case surrounding these techniques, the European Commission of Human Rights concluded, unanimously, that the combined use of the five techniques in the cases before it constituted a practice of inhuman treatment and of torture in breach of Article 3 of the *Council of Europe Convention for the Protection of Human Rights and Fundamental Freedoms.*[9] Similarly, in its judgment of the case, the European Court of Human Rights concluded that recourse to the five techniques amounted to a practice of inhuman and degrading treatment (though not torture), which practice was in breach of Article 3 of the said Convention.[10] Within the United Kingdom, both the prime minister and the attorney-general spoke for the Government, saying that the five techniques would not be reintroduced, under any circumstances, as an aid to interrogation.[11]

Intelligence training to Latin American military officers was also offered at the U.S. Army School of the Americas. This training took place from 1965 to 1976, when it was halted by the Carter administration and by a Congressional panel that witnessed the training. But training soon resumed under the Reagan administration. Indeed, according to Sergeant Florencio Caballero from the

Honduran army, he was taken to Texas with 24 others for six months between 1979 and 1980. There, Americans

> taught me interrogation, in order to end physical torture in Honduras. They taught us psychological methods—to study the fears and weaknesses of a prisoner. [E1] Make him stand up, [E2] don't let him sleep, [E3] keep him naked, [E4] and isolated, [E5] put rats and cockroaches in his cell, [E6] give him bad food, [E7] serve him dead animals, [E8] throw cold water on him, [E9] change the temperature. (James LeMoyne, "Testifying to Torture," *New York Times Magazine,* June 5, 1988)

And these lessons did not fall on deaf ears. Both Sergeant Caballero and Ms. Inés Murillo (one of his victims at a clandestine prison near Tegucigalpa, Honduras) say that, while she was in captivity in 1983, "Mr. Caballero and other interrogators gave her raw dead birds and rats for dinner, threw freezing water on her naked body every half hour for extended periods and made her stand for hours without sleep and without being allowed to urinate" (James LeMoyne, "Testifying to Torture," *New York Times Magazine,* June 5, 1988).

In 1983, another CIA manual was produced.[12] It was the *Human Resource Exploitation Training Manual-1983.* It drew heavily—if not *verbatim*—from the *KUBARK* manual. Yet it elaborated upon many of the techniques found there and in the Biderman outline. These elaborations bear citing in some detail (see below). Like the *KUBARK* manual, the *Human Resource Exploitation Training Manual-1983* was declassified under a *FOIA* request initiated by the *Baltimore Sun.*[13] Curiously, the version declassified for this newspaper was amended by hand in ways that invariably soften the more objectionable passages of the original. In the selections found below, passages crossed out by hand are indicated by ~~strikethrough~~ characters, while the material added by hand is given in *italics.* Parenthesized references of the form *Y-X* are to page *X* of section *Y* of the manual. Throughout the manual, all the derivatives of the verb *to question* appear in quotes.

> **F1.** *Isolation:* Total isolation should be maintained until after the first "questioning" session (F-4).

> **F2.** *Monopolization of Attention:* [Cell] window should be set high in the wall with the capability of blocking out light. (This allows the "questioner" to be able to disrupt the subject's sense of time, day and night.) (E-3) | [The "questioning" room should have] no windows, or windows that can be completely blacked out (E-5). | Deprivation of Sensory Stimuli. Solitary confinement acts on most persons as a powerful stress. A person cut off from external stimuli turns his awareness inward and projects his unconscious [*sic*] outward. The symptoms most commonly produced by solitary confinement are superstition, intense love of any other living thing, perceiving inanimate objects as alive, hallucinations, and delusions. *Deliberately causing these symtoms [sic] is a serious impropriety and to use prolonged solitary confinement for the purpose of extracting information in questioning violates policy* (K-6).

F3. *Induced Debilitation and Exhaustion:* Heat, air and light ~~should~~ *may* be externally controlled [~~fullstop~~], *but not to the point of torture* (E-3).

F4. *Cultivation of Anxiety and Despair:* Cell doors should be of heavy steel...The slamming of a heavy steel door impresses upon the subjct [*sic*] that he is cut off from the rest of the world (E-3). | Bedding should be minimal—cot and blanket—no mattress. (The idea is to prevent the subject from relaxing ~~and recovering from shock~~.) (E-3). | The ideal time at which to make an arrest is in the early hours of the morning. When arrested at this time, most subjects experience intense feelings of shock, insecurity, and psychological stress and for the most part have great difficulty adjusting to the situation (F-1). | Subject should be made to believe that he has been forsaken by his comrades (F-4). | The effectiveness of most "questioning" techniques depends upon their unsettling effect. The "questioning" process itself is unsettling to most people encountering it for the first time. The "questioner" tries to enhance this effect, to disrupt radically the familiar emotional and psychological associations of the subject. Once this disruption is achieved. The subject's resistance is seriously impaired. He experiences a kind of psychological shock...during which he is far more open to suggestion and far likelier to comply, than he was before he experiences the shock. Frequently the subject will experience a feeling of guilt. If the "questioner" can intensify these guilt feelings, it will increase the subject's anxiety and his urge to cooperate as a means of escape (J-1 and J-2). | [The "questioner"] is able to manipulate the subject's environment, to create unpleasant ~~or intolerable~~ situations, ~~to disrupt patterns of time, space, and sensory perception~~ (J-2).

F5. *Demonstrating "Omnipotence" and "Omniscience" of Captor:* Throughout his detention, subject must be convinced that his "questioner" controls his ultimate destiny, and that his absolute cooperation is essential to survival (F-4).

F6. *Degradation:* ~~There should be no~~ *If there are no* built-in toilet facilities, ~~the subject should have to ask to relieve himself then~~ he should either be given a bucket or escorted by a guard to a latrine. The guard stays at his side the entire time he is in the latrine (E-3).

With a nation traumatized from the terrorist attacks of September 11, 2001, President George W. Bush announces, a month later, the initiation of military strikes against al Qaeda and Taliban positions in Afghanistan. On January 16, 2006, the first suspected al Qaeda and Taliban prisoners arrive at the detention facilities of the Naval Base at Guantánamo Bay, Cuba. Nine months later, on October 11, 2002, LTC Jerald Phifer sent a memorandum to the commander of Joint Task Force 170 (Guantánamo) claiming that current guidelines for interrogation procedures at the detention facilities were limiting the ability of the interrogators to counter "advanced resistance" from the detainees. He therefore requested the base commander to approve the use of the following "counter-resistance strategies" at the base (if the "direct approach" to interrogation failed).[14]

G1. Yelling at the detainee (not directly in his ear or to the level that it would cause physical pain or hearing problems).

G2. Techniques of deception (multiple interrogator techniques; the interviewer may identify himself as an interrogator from a country with a reputation for harsh treatment of detainees).

G3. Use of stress positions (like standing), for a maximum of four hours.

G4. The use of falsified documents or reports.

G5. Use of isolation facility for up to thirty days (permission may be requested for isolation to cover medical visits of a non-emergent nature and extend beyond the initial thirty days).

G6. Interrogation of the detainee in an environment other than the standard interrogation booth.

G7. Deprivation of light and auditory stimuli.

G8. Detainee may also have a hood placed over his head during transportation and questioning. The hood should not restrict breathing in any way and the detainee should be under direct observation when hooded.

G9. Use of twenty-hour interrogations.

G10. Removal of all comfort items (including religious items).

G11. Switching the detainee from hot rations to MRE.

G12. Removal of clothing.

G13. Forced grooming (shaving of facial hair, etc.).

G14. Using detainees' individual phobias (such as fear of dogs) to induce stress.

G15. The use of scenarios designed to convince the detainee that death or severely painful consequences are imminent for him and/or his family.

G16. Exposure to cold weather or water (with appropriate medical monitoring).

G17. Use of a wet towel and dripping water to induce the misperception of suffocation [or waterboarding].

G18. Use of mild, non-injurious physical contact such as grabbing, poking in the chest with the finger and light pushing.

These 18 techniques were put into three categories in the Phifer memo. Category I included techniques G1 and G2. Category II techniques covered techniques G3 through G14 and required permission of the OIC, Interrogation Section. Category III techniques involved G15 through G18 and required approval of the commanding general and information to the commander of U.S. Southern Command.[15] Category III techniques "and other aversive techniques, such as those used in U.S. military interrogation resistance training or by other U.S. government agencies, may be utilized," the memo proposed, "to help interrogate exceptionally resistant detainees." Thus, defensive programs designed for the *resistance* to interrogation would become offensive programs for the *enhancement* of interrogation. As detailed in an August 25, 2006, report from the Department of Defense Inspector General, one of these defensive-turned-offensive training programs was *SERE* (for Survival-Evasion-Resistance-Escape). This is a program that incorporates physical and psychological pressures that "replicate harsh conditions that the Service member might encounter if he or she is held by forces that do not abide by the Geneva Conventions."

Indeed, a month prior to LTC Phifer's memo, a SERE psychologist conference was organized in Fort Bragg, North Carolina, for Guantánamo interrogation personnel. At that conference, Guantánamo personnel understood

> that they were to become familiar with SERE training and be capable of determining which SERE information and techniques might be useful in interrogations at Guantanamo. Guantanamo Behavioral Science Consultation Team personnel understood that they were to review documentation and standard operating procedures for SERE training in developing the standard operating procedure for the JTF-170 [Guantanamo], if the command approved those practices.

And, on at least two occasions, "SERE instructors from Fort Bragg responded to Guantanamo requests for instructors trained in the use of SERE interrogation resistance techniques."[16]

On December 2, 2002, Secretary of Defense Donald Rumsfeld approved all the techniques G1 through G14, as well as G18. On that very month, Dr. Michael Gelles, chief psychologist at the Naval Criminal Investigative Service, said that Guantánamo interrogators were using "abusive techniques" and "coercive psychological procedures" on one of the Guantánamo prisoners (Mohammed al Qahtani; on his interrogation, see Gutierrez, Chapter 11). Furthermore, Alberto Mora, general counsel for the U.S. Navy, told his superiors at the Pentagon that these methods were "unlawful and unworthy of the military services," and that the use of "coercive techniques" placed all involved in risk of prosecution (McCoy 2006, 128).

Six weeks later, on January 15, 2003, Mr. Rumsfeld rescinded his blanket permission to use previously approved categories G3 through G14, and category G18 (but allowed their use on a case-by-case basis and with approval of the secretary of defense). He also convenes a working group of top legal advisors from the U.S. Armed Forces to assess legal, policy, and operational issues relating to the interrogation of detainees. On April 4, 2003, this working group issued a report recommending the following 35 techniques "for use with unlawful combatants outside the U.S."[17]

H1. *Direct:* Asking straightforward questions.

H2. *Incentive/Removal of Incentive:* Providing a reward or removing a privilege, above and beyond those [POW privileges] required by the Geneva Convention, from detainees....

H3. *Emotional Love:* Playing on the love a detainee has for an individual or group.

H4. *Emotional Hate:* Playing on the hatred a detainee has for an individual or group.

H5. *Fear Up Harsh:* Significantly increasing the fear level in a detainee.

H6. *Fear Up Mild:* Moderately increasing the fear level in a detainee.

H7. *Reduced Fear:* Reducing the fear level of a detainee.

H8. *Pride and Ego Up:* Boosting the ego of a detainee.

H9. *Pride and Ego Down:* Attacking or insulting the ego of a detainee, not beyond the limits that would apply to a POW.

H10. *Futility:* Invoking the feeling of futility of a detainee.

H11. *We Know All:* Convincing the detainee that the interrogator knows the answer to questions he asks the detainee.

H12. *Establish Your Identity:* Convincing the detainee that the interrogator has mistaken the detainee for someone else.

H13. *Repetition Approach:* Continuously repeating the same question to the detainee within interrogation periods of normal duration.

H14. *File and Dossier:* Convincing the detainee that the interrogator has a damning and inaccurate file that must be fixed.

H15. *Mutt and Jeff:* A team consisting of a friendly and harsh interrogator. The harsh interrogator might employ the Pride and Ego Down technique.

H16. *Rapid Fire:* Questioning in rapid succession without allowing the detainee to answer.

H17. *Silence:* Staring at the detainee to encourage discomfort.

H18. *Change of Scenery Up:* Removing the detainee from the standard interrogation setting (generally to a location more pleasant, but no worse).

H19. *Change of Scenery Down:* Removing the detainee from the standard interrogation setting and placing him in a setting that may be less comfortable; would not constitute a substantial change in environmental quality.

H20. *Hooding:* This technique is questioning the detainee with a blindfold in place. For interrogation purposes, the blindfold is not on other than during the interrogation.

H21. *Mild Physical Contact:* Lightly touching a detainee or lightly poking the detainee in a completely non-injurious manner. This also includes softly grabbing of shoulders to get the detainee's attention or to comfort the detainee.

H22. *Dietary Manipulation:* Changing the diet of a detainee; no intended deprivation of food or water; no adverse medical or cultural effect and without intent to deprive subject of food or water; e.g. hot rations to MREs.

H23. *Environmental Manipulation:* Altering the environment to create moderate discomfort (e.g. adjusting temperature or introducing an unpleasant smell). Conditions would not be such that they would injure the detainee.

H24. *Sleep Adjustment:* Adjusting the sleeping times of the detainee (e.g. reversing sleep cycles from night to day). This technique is NOT sleep deprivation [sleep deprivation is a separate technique; see H31 below].

H25. *False Flag:* Convincing the detainee that individuals from a country other than the United States are interrogating him.

H26. *Threat of Transfer:* Threatening to transfer the subject to a third country that subject is likely to fear would subject him to torture or death. (The threat would not be acted upon nor would the threat include any information beyond the naming of the receiving country.)

H27. *Isolation:* Isolating the detainee from other detainees while still complying with basic standards of treatment.

H28. *Use of Prolonged Interrogations:* The continued use of a series of approaches that extend over a long period of time (e.g. 20 hours per day per interrogation).

H29. *Forced Grooming:* Forcing a detainee to shave hair or beard. (Force applied with intention to avoid injury. Would not use force that would cause serious injury.)

H30. *Prolonged Standing:* Lengthy standing in a "normal" position (nonstress). This has been successful, but should never make the detainee exhausted to the point of weakness or collapse. Not enforced by physical restraints. Not to exceed four hours in a 24-hour period.

H31. *Sleep Deprivation:* Keeping the detainee awake for an extended period of time (Allowing the individual to rest and then awakening him, repeatedly). Not to exceed four days in succession.

H32. *Physical Training:* Requiring detainees to exercise (perform ordinary physical exercises actions) (e.g., running, jumping jacks); not to exceed 15 minutes in a two-hour period; not more than two cycles, per 24-hour periods). Assists in generating compliance and fatiguing the detainees. No enforced compliance.

H33. *Face Slap/Stomach Slap:* A quick glancing slap to the fleshy part of the cheek or stomach. These techniques are used strictly as shock measures and do not cause pain or injury. They are only effective if used once or twice together. After the second time on a detainee, it will lose the shock effect. Limited to two slaps per application; no more than two applications per interrogation.

H34. *Removal of Clothing:* Potential removal of all clothing; removal to be done by military police if not agreed to by the subject. Creating a feeling of helplessness and dependence. This technique must be monitored to ensure the environmental conditions are such that this technique does not injure the detainee.

H35. *Increasing Anxiety by Use of Aversions:* Introducing factors that of themselves create anxiety but do not create terror or mental trauma (e.g. simple presence of dog without directly threatening action). This technique requires the commander to develop specific and detailed safeguards to insure the detainee's safety.

Several of the Phifer/Working Group techniques have been considered torture in the U.S. State Department *Country Reports on Human Rights Practices* (*CRHRP*). Consider, for instance, the following.[18]

The Constitution prohibits torture; however, the security service routinely and systematically tortured detainees. According to former prisoners, torture techniques included...denial of food and water, extended solitary confinement in dark and extremely small compartments [G3, G7], and threats to rape or otherwise harm family members and relatives [G15] (*CRHRP* 2001, *Iraq,* §1.c).

The most frequently alleged methods of torture include sleep deprivation [H31]...and extended solitary confinement [G5, H27] (*CRHRP* 2001, *Jordan,* §1.c).

Common torture methods include:...prolonged isolation [G5, H27]...denial of food or sleep [H31]...and public humiliation [H9, H34] (*CRHRP* 2001, *Pakistan,* §1.c).

[S]ecurity officials mainly used torture methods that did not leave physical traces, including repeated slapping [G18, H33], exposure to cold [G16, H23], stripping [G12, H34] and blindfolding [G8, H20], food and sleep deprivation [H31], threats to detainees or family members [G15], dripping water on the head, squeezing of the testicles, and mock executions [G15] (*CRHRP* 2004, *Turkey,* §1.c).

[I]n recent years, government officials have inflicted severe prisoner abuse and torture in a series of "unofficial" secret prisons and detention centers outside the national prison system. Common methods included prolonged solitary confinement [G5, H27] with sensory deprivation [G7, H20]...long confinement in contorted positions [G3]...threats of execution if individuals refused to confess [G15]...sleep deprivation [H31] (*CRHRP* 2004, *Iran,* §1.c).

During the year there continued to be reports that security forces used extreme physical abuse such as bondage, heat exposure [H23] (*CRHRP* 2005, *Eritrea,* §2.c).

But criticisms would not come only from the State Department. An early draft of the April 2004 report circulated by the Working Group had elicited objections from top legal advisers in the military. Deputy judge advocate general for the Air Force, Major General Jack Rives, observed that "the more extreme interrogation techniques, on their face, amount to violations of domestic law and the UCMJ [Uniform Code of Military Justice]," placing interrogators "at risk of criminal accusations." Similarly, the Navy's chief lawyer, Rear Admiral Michael F. Lohr, expressed concern that the American people would condemn the military for "condoning practices that, while technically legal, are inconsistent with our most fundamental values" (McCoy 2006, 128f).

All these objections would be cast aside. In a memo issued on April 16, 2003, Secretary Rumsfeld approved techniques H1–H19, H22–H25, and H27 (Greenberg and Dratel 2005, Memo 27). Beyond this, all of these techniques (plus two others) would be eventually authorized for use in the interrogation of Iraqi prisoners.

In the summer of 2003, at a Pentagon briefing on the growing Iraqi resistance to American forces in Iraq, Secretary Rumsfeld gave oral orders for the Guantánamo commander, Major General Geoffrey Miller, to "Gitmoize" Iraqi intelligence. Traveling to Iraq, the general issued a report for army headquarters in Iraq. In it he argued for a radical restructuring of detainee policy, to make Iraq's prisons the front line for information warfare (McCoy 2005, 133). Five days after General Miller's departure from Iraq, on September 14, 2003, Lt. General Ricardo S. Sanchez, commander of the Coalition forces in Iraq, issued a memo authorizing an interrogation policy for Iraq "modeled on the one implemented for interrogations conducted at Guantanamo Bay, but modified for applicability to a theater of war in which the Geneva Conventions apply."[19]

The techniques recommended in this memo were H1–H19, H22–H25, H27, H31,[20] and a particular instance of H35, namely

> *Presence of Military Working Dog:* Exploits Arab fear of dogs while maintaining security during interrogations. Dogs will be muzzled and under control of MWD handler at all times to prevent contact with detainee.

In addition, it recommended an expansion of the Phifer techniques G1 and G3, and a blend of techniques G2 and G4:

- *Yelling, Loud Music, and Light Control:* Used to create fear, disorient the detainee, and prolong capture shock. Volume controlled to prevent injury.
- *Deception:* Use of falsified representations including documents and reports.
- *Stress Positions:* Use of physical postures (sitting, standing, kneeling, prone, etc.) for no more than 1 hour per use. Use of technique will not exceed 4 hours and adequate rest between use of each position will be provided.

In a subsequent memo General Sanchez limited his recommendations to techniques H1–H17, but justified isolation (called there *segregation*) of "security detainees" for up to 30 days (or longer if his permission was granted).[21]

In February 2004, the International Committee of the Red Cross (ICRC) presented a *Report on the Treatment by the Coalition Forces of Prisoners of War and other Protected Persons by the Geneva Conventions in Iraq During Arrest, Internment and Interrogation.*[22] This report, which was based on visits made by the ICRC to Iraqi places of detention between March and November 2003, found that the methods of ill treatment most frequently alleged during interrogation included:

> **J1.** Hooding, used to prevent people from seeing and to disorient them, and also to prevent them from breathing freely...Hooding was sometimes used in conjunction with beating thus increasing anxiety as to when blows would come...Hooding could last for periods from a few hours to up to two or four consecutive days.
>
> **J2.** Threats (of ill-treatment, reprisals against family members, imminent execution, or transfer to Guantanamo).
>
> **J3.** Being stripped naked for several days while held in solitary confinement in an empty and completely dark cell that included a latrine.
>
> **J4.** Being held in solitary confinement combined with threats (to intern the individual indefinitely, to arrest other family members, or transfer the individual to Guantanamo) insufficient sleep, food or water deprivation, minimal access to showers...denial of access to open air and prohibition of contacts with other persons deprived of their liberty.

J5. Being paraded naked outside cells...sometimes hooded or with women's under-wear over the head.

J6. Acts of humiliation such as being made to stand naked against the wall of the cell with arms raised or with women's underwear over the head...while being laughed at by guards, including female guards, and sometimes photographed in this position.

J7. Being attached repeatedly over several days, for several hours each time, with handcuffs to the bars of their cell door in humiliating (i.e. naked or in underwear) and/or uncomfortable position causing physical pain.

J8. Exposure while hooded to loud noise or music, prolonged exposure while hooded to the sun over several hours, including during the hottest time of the day, when temperatures could reach 50 degrees Celsius (122 degrees Fahrenheit) or higher.

J9. Being forced to remain for prolonged periods in stress positions such as squatting, or standing, with or without the arms lifted.

On April 28, 2004, pictures of abuse at Abu Ghraib exploded into the public consciousness. Response to this was swift. In 2005, Physicians for Human Rights issued a scathing report, which found that "there is sufficient evidence available now to show a consistent pattern of the use of psychological torture as a key element in the interrogation of detainees by US personnel" during the War on Terror.[23] The report furthermore identified four techniques of "a regime of psychological torture," sometimes used in combination:

K1. Prolonged Isolation

K2. Sleep Deprivation

K3. Severe Sexual and Cultural Humiliation

K4. Use of Threats and Dogs to Induce Fear of Death or Injury

COMPREHENSIVENESS OF THE DEFINITION

The extensional definition of *PT* embodied in A1–A13 is quite comprehensive. As shown in Table 1.1, it encompasses all of the well-defined techniques of *PT* described in the preceding section.

The practices included in this table span a period of fifty years and spread over three continents. They are taken from descriptions composed by victims (cf. Biderman and ICRC), perpetrators (Caballero), training manuals (KUBARK, HRETM 83), military officers (Phifer), military lawyers (Working Group), and human rights judges (Ulster) or physicians (PHR). The fact that they are encompassed by our extensional definition thus attests to its comprehensiveness.

But the proposed definition is at the same time discriminating. Excluded by it are techniques which should not count as torture—i.e., direct interrogation (H1), comfort item removal (G10, G11, H2, H22), misleading the detainee into believing there is false information about him (G4, H12, H14), or the ostensibly inane interrogation "in an environment other the interrogation booth" (G6).

Table 1.1
Comprehensiveness of the Extensional Definition

Extensional Definition Practices	Biderman	Kubark	Ulster	Caballero	HRETM 83	Phifer/GTMO	Working Group	ICRC/Iraq	PHR
A1. Isolation	B1			E4	F1	G5	H27	J4a	K1
A2. Psychological Debilitation	B2a, B3a	C2	D1, D 4, D5	E1, E2, E6, E8, E9	F3	G3, G16	H23-24, 28, 30-32	J4c,6b, 7a,8c,9	K2
A3. Spatial Disorientation	B2b				F4a				
A4. Temporal Disorientation	B2c	C7			F2a, F4b			J3	
A5. Sensory Disorientation		C3a, C8			F4c				
A6. Sensory Deprivation	B2d	C1	D2		F2b	G7, G8	H20	J1, 3, 5b, 8a	
A7. Sensory Assault (Overstimulation)			D3			G1		J8b	
A8. Induced Desperation	B4a, B5-6, B8	C3b, 4-6			F4d, F5	G9, G14a, G17	H3-11,13, 15-19,35		
A9. Threats	B2e, B4b	C9				G2, G14b, G15	H25-H26	J2, J4b	K4
A10. Feral Treatment	B3b, B7			E3, E5, E7	F6			J3, J4d	
A11. Sexual Humiliation						G12	H34	J5a, J6a, J7b	K3a
A12. Desecration						G13	H29		K3b
A13. Pharmacological Manipulation		C10							

Note: Well-documented practices of cruel, inhuman, degrading psychological treatment (or torture) fit within the proposed extensional definition of psychological torture. See preceding text for an explanation of the codes to the practices. Multifaceted practices like B2 are entered separately into the table as B2a, B2b, etc.

Excluded also are forms of physical contact like pushing, poking, or slapping, which may or may not fall within the parameters of physical torture (G18, H21, H33).

CONCLUSION

I have presented an extensional definition of *PT* that avoids settling the complex quantitative and the qualitative questions raised by *PT*. This definition is precise, modular, phenomenological, relevant, comprehensive, and discriminating. Thus, it is, in many respects, satisfying.

Yet, it might be thought that the proposed definition is wanting in some respects. One may wonder, for example, whether the definition is fully exhaustive. To settle this issue, one should test the definition against more data. Although the data from official sources is notoriously difficult to come by, testimony from victims is, unfortunately, abundant. Testimony found in the online *Guantánamo Testimonials Project* currently being developed by the UC Davis Center for the Study of Human Rights in the Americas may be a good place to turn to in this regard. Other collections of testimony gathered by human rights groups and truth commissions are rich sources as well.

But beyond exhaustiveness, it might be thought that we should have an understanding of the practices in A1–A13 that will *explain* why they constitute *PT*. In other words, we should have an intensional definition of *PT*. One approach that will not work is to define it by the psychological pain (or mental suffering) it produces, as all forms of torture produce it. A more promising approach in this regard is to define *PT* by its *modus operandi*—i.e., by the fact that it does not involve direct physical violence (beating, lashing, slashing, burning, electrocuting, hanging, pulling, or twisting, to name a few). Whether *PT* can indeed be defined as "no-touch torture" (McCoy 2006) is an issue that must be left for future research.

NOTES

I am indebted to Nelson Martínez Berríos, Jonathan Marks, and Alfred McCoy for comments to earlier versions of this chapter.

1. See the *Report of the Committee of Privy Counsellors Appointed to Consider Authorized Procedures for the Interrogation of Persons Suspected of Terrorism* (The Parker Report), Section I, paragraph 9. Available at http://cain.ulst.ac.uk/hmso/parker.htm

2. U.S. Senate Armed Services Committee, Hearing on Treatment of Guantanamo Bay Detainees, July 13, 2005.

3. See Streatfeild (2007) for a gripping account of the mindset of the period. According to the *KUBARK Counterintelligence Interrogation Manual* to be discussed below, more than a thousand works were published on the counterintelligence interrogation of resistant sources by 1963. See *KUBARK* 1963, 103.

4. Like all bracketed material in this chapter, the codes heading the various practices cited throughout the chapter have been supplied by the author in order to ease future reference to them.

5. KUBARK is widely thought to be an old cryptonym for CIA Headquarters.

6. See Gary Cohn, Ginger Thompson, and Mark Matthews, "Torture was taught by CIA. Declassified manual details the methods used in Honduras. Agency denials refuted," *Baltimore Sun,* January 27, 1997. The manual can be downloaded from the Web site of the National Security Archive at George Washington University. See http://www.gwu.edu/~nsarchiv/.

7. See the testimony of John Hart at the Hearings of the House Select Committee on Assassinations (HSCA), September 15, 1978. *HSCA Hearings,* Volume II, September 11–15, 1978, pp. 497–504 and 508. Available at: http://history-matters.com/archive/jfk/hsca/reportvols/vol2/contents.htm. According to these hearings, John Hart was a career agent with the CIA, where he served for 24 years. He was the chief of station in Korea, Thailand, Morocco, and Vietnam. He also held senior posts at CIA headquarters in Virginia. In 1976, he authored an extensive study of the handling of Yuri Nosenko by the CIA. See also *The CIA Family Jewels Report,* p. 522, available at http://www.gwu.edu/~nsarchiv/NSAEBB/NSAEBB222/index.htm.

8. European Court of Human Rights, *Case of Ireland v. The United Kingdom,* Application No. 5310/71, paragraph 96.

9. European Court of Human Rights, *Case of Ireland v. The United Kingdom,* Application No. 5310/71, paragraph 147. Article 3 of the *Convention for the Protection of Human Rights and Fundamental Freedoms* reads, in its entirety, as follows: *No one shall be subjected to torture or to inhuman or degrading treatment or punishment.*

10. European Court of Human Rights, *Case of Ireland v. The United Kingdom,* Application No. 5310/71, paragraph 168.

11. European Court of Human Rights, *Case of Ireland v. The United Kingdom,* Application No. 5310/71, paragraphs 101–2.

12. See *DOD, SOUTHCOM CI Training-Supplemental Information, 31 July 1991.* This document can be downloaded from the National Security Archive at http://www.gwu.edu/~nsarchiv/NSAEBB/NSAEBB122/index.htm#southcom.

13. See Cohn, Thompson, and Mark Matthews, "Torture was taught by CIA."

14. This memorandum can be downloaded from the Human Rights Watch Web site at http://hrw.org/english/docs/2004/08/19/usdom9248_txt.htm.

15. See Greenberg and Dratel (2005, xxvii). According to a November 27, 2002, memo from an FBI agent to his superiors, there was also a Category IV technique by which "Detainee will be sent off GTMO, either temporarily or permanently, to Jordan, Egypt, or another third country to allow those countries to employ interrogation techniques that will enable them to obtain the requisite information." See Margulies (2006, 98).

16. The report from the Department of Defense Inspector General can be obtained from the Web site of the Center for the Study of Human Rights in the Americas at http://humanrights.ucdavis.edu/projects/the-guantanamo-testimonials-project/testimonies/testimonies-of-the-defense-department/review-of-dod-directed-investigations-of-detainee-abuse/.

17. This report can be downloaded from the Human Rights Watch Web site at http://hrw.org/english/docs/2004/08/19/usdom9248_txt.htm.

18. Cited in Human Rights Watch (2006) and Margulies (2006, 106).

19. This memo was made public by the ACLU. See: http://www.aclu.org/safefree/general/17562prs20050329.html.

20. Except that the technique is called "Sleep Management," rather than "Sleep Deprivation," here.

21. This memo was made public by the ACLU. See http://www.aclu.org/safefree/general/17562prs20050329.html.

22. This report can be found in Greenberg and Dratel (2005, 383–404).

23. See Physicians for Human Rights (2005, 2). Available at: http://physiciansfor humanrights.org/torture/.

BIBLIOGRAPHY

Anonymous (1983). *Human Resource Exploitation Training Manual.* Mimeographed?

Anonymous (1963). *KUBARK Counterintelligence Interrogation Manual.* Mimeographed?

Biderman, Albert (1956). *Communist Techniques of Coercive Interrogation.* Air Force Personnel & Training Research Center, Lackland Air Force Base, San Antonio, Texas. AFPTRC-TN-56–132. ASTIA Document No. 098908.

Greenberg, Karen J., and Dratel, Joshua L. (2005). *The Torture Papers. The Road to Abu Ghraib.* Cambridge: Cambridge University Press.

Human Rights Watch (2006). *Descriptions of Techniques Allegedly Authorized by the CIA.* Available online at http://hrw.org/english/docs/2005/11/21/usdom12071.htm.

Margulies, Joseph (2006). *Guantánamo and the Abuse of Presidential Power.* New York: Simon and Shuster.

McCoy, Alfred (2006). *A Question of Torture: CIA Interrogation from the Cold War to the War on Terror.* New York: Metropolitan Books, Henry Holt and Company.

Physicians for Human Rights (2005). *Break Them Down: Systematic Use of Psychological Torture by US Forces.* Printed in the United States.

Streatfeild, Dominic (2007). *Brainwash.* New York: Thomas Dunne Books, St. Martin's Press.

Timerman, Jacobo (1981). *Preso sin Nombre Celda sin Número.* New York: Random. Translated from Spanish to English by Toby Talbot as *Prisoner without a Name, Cell without a Number.* New York: Knopf, 1981.

CHAPTER 2

PSYCHOLOGICAL TORTURE AS A COLD WAR IMPERATIVE

R. Matthew Gildner

In 1950, the U.S. Central Intelligence Agency (CIA) initiated extensive, often-clandestine research into the behavioral and cognitive sciences to develop more effective methods of counterintelligence interrogation. By 1963, this research yielded a novel approach to torture that eschewed physical duress and instead targeted the human mind.[1] Isolation, degradation, threats, sleep deprivation, temporal disorientation, sensory manipulation, and narcosis were each part of a systematic psychological torture paradigm that the CIA codified in the KUBARK *Counterintelligence Interrogation* manual (KUBARK) and then deployed as a secret weapon in Washington's global struggle to suppress local communist subversion. Focusing on the CIA's efforts to develop and propagate the KUBARK paradigm, this chapter seeks to illuminate the central role that psychological torture played in the containment strategy that guided U.S. foreign policy for the duration of the Cold War. Introduced by the Truman administration, the containment strategy was intended to consolidate the free-market capitalism and liberal democracy that underlie the so-called "American system" by preventing the expansion of communism in general and the Soviet Union in particular.[2] While shrewd diplomacy, alliance formation, and nuclear brinkmanship established "the long peace" that characterized relations between the two superpowers, the Cold War increasingly became a geopolitical struggle over the Third World.[3] And during the 1960s, as Washington and Moscow increasingly competed to expand their political influence and attendant economic reach, psychological torture emerged as a crucial component of U.S. efforts to establish a bulwark against communist expansion into Africa, Asia, Latin America and the Middle East.

For 25 years, the CIA disseminated psychological torture techniques to foreign internal security forces as part of a broader containment initiative aimed at fortifying Third World governments against local communist subversion. First operating through the Office of Public Safety (OPS), a U.S. foreign police training program, between 1963 and 1975, and then collaborating with U.S. Army Green Berets Mobile Training Teams from 1982 to 1987, the CIA's efforts to propagate psychological torture attended to the specific challenges posed by communist subversion. Similar to the War on Terror that the United States is today waging against a stateless enemy extending from metropolitan Europe to the remote jungles of the Philippine archipelago, during the Cold War, Washington confronted in Third World communist subversion, underground networks of ideologically motivated militants seeking to subvert U.S. interests abroad. Of course, during the Cold War, those ideological motivations were not religious, but secular—particularly Communist, Socialist, Maoist, Trotskyite, or some local derivative thereof. In the Cold War, moreover, U.S. interests abroad were typically manifest in anticommunist governments whose maintenance was an absolutely essential objective of American foreign policy. The greatest commonality between the two conflicts then lies in the nature of the enemy: the "non-state actor"—immortalized in the being of Ernesto "Che" Guevara during the Cold War and, today, in that of Osama bin Laden—who, abandoning national allegiance for ideology, operates in clandestine, often transnational networks that rely on propaganda and terrorism to realize their objectives. And with this common enemy, another, perhaps more significant, though infinitely more troubling similarity between the two conflicts becomes especially salient: the CIA's continued reliance on psychological torture to acquire the intelligence necessary to identify, infiltrate, and ultimately defeat this invisible adversary.

RESEARCH AND DEVELOPMENT

The U.S. government initiated the vast research and development program that would later produce the CIA's psychological torture paradigm in response to increasing reports of communist success in brainwashing, hypnosis, and the use of drugs in interrogation. Already bewildered by Stalin's show trials of the 1930s, U.S. officials were transfixed by the "bizarre" and trance-like confession of Hungarian dissident Cardinal Joseph Mindszenty in his February 1949 trial.[4] U.S. officials were further perplexed by the implausible confessions of American Korean War POWs. Upon being released, former POW Colonel Frank H. Schwable, reflected on his confession, stating, "the words were mine, but the thoughts were theirs."[5] Indicating the extent to which such cases made the study of more effective interrogation methods a top priority within the U.S. intelligence community, the CIA chief of medical staff observed in a 1952 memo that "there is ample evidence in the reports of innumerable interrogations that the Communists were utilizing drugs, physical duress, electric shock and possibly hypnosis against their enemies." Lamenting America's "apparent laxity" in pursuing such methods, he contended that "we are forced by this mounting evidence to assume a more aggressive role in the development of these techniques"[6]

Further compelling U.S. policymakers to pursue more effective interrogation methods were broader foreign policy concerns regarding the Soviet Union's "design for world domination."[7] The 1954 Hoover Report on Government Operations (worth quoting at length below) illustrates the perceptions crystallizing within the U.S. foreign policy and intelligence communities:

> It is now clear that we are facing an implacable enemy whose avowed objective is world domination by whatever means and at whatever cost. There are no rules in such a game. Hitherto acceptable norms of human conduct do not apply. If the U.S. is to survive, long-standing American concepts of "fair play" must be reconsidered. We must develop effective espionage and counterespionage services. We must learn to subvert, sabotage and destroy our enemies by more clever [sic], more sophisticated, and more effective methods than those used against us. It may become necessary that the American people will be made aquatinted with, understand and support this fundamentally repugnant philosophy.[8]

Policymakers no longer deemed conventional methods of realizing foreign policy objectives as entirely effective against an adversary that would seemingly use any means necessary to subvert U.S. influence abroad.

By the time this report was written, both the Pentagon and the CIA had already been exploring the effectiveness of drugs, hypnosis, electric shock, and polygraph techniques in interrogation for the better part of five years. In 1949, the Navy—maintaining liaisons with the Army, the CIA, and the FBI—initiated Project CHATTER to research "the identification and testing of truth drugs for use in interrogation and in the recruitment of agents."[9] The CIA launched a similar effort in 1950, Project BLUEBIRD, to determine the efficacy of "unconventional" interrogation techniques such as hypnosis and a variety of drugs, including sodium pentothal, mescaline, LSD, THC, and heroin.[10] In August 1951, the CIA shifted the focus of the project from experimental to operational and renamed it ARTICHOKE. The renewed focus underlying ARTICHOKE "included in-house experiments on interrogation techniques, conducted under medical and security controls which would ensure that no damage was done to individuals volunteering for the experiments."[11] However, these techniques were also tested on unwitting human subjects—a trend that would continue in later CIA projects. With the creation of ARTICHOKE, moreover, all U.S. government research and development programs in interrogation techniques—being simultaneously carried out by the Army, Navy, and Air Force—were increasingly placed under the operational jurisdiction of the CIA.

In 1953, the CIA folded ARTICHOKE into a much larger, more ambitious new project studying human behavior modification, MKULTRA. Between its creation in 1953 and dismantlement on 1964, MKULTRA researched, among other things, the effects of behavioral drugs and/or alcohol on witting and unwitting human subjects; hypnosis; the effect of combinations of hypnosis and drugs; sleep deprivation; behavioral changes during psychotherapy; polygraphs; brainwashing; and the effects of electroshock and sensory deprivation.[12] Classified top secret, MKULTRA was placed under the direction of the CIA's Technical Services Division (TSD), where it was headed by Dr. Sidney Gottlieb. Besides the obvious Cold War espionage concerns, the secrecy was also due to the nature of the research. Many people "both within and outside the Agency" found human testing and the manipulation of human behavior—in the words of the CIA—"unethical and distasteful."[13] While Gottlieb oversaw all of the "in-house" research and development programs of MKULTRA at the TSD in Langley, most of the projects were "externally contracted" through various covert funding conduits, including the Josiah J. Macy Foundation, the Geschickter Fund for Medical Research, Psychological Assessment Associates, the Scientific Engineering Institute, and perhaps most importantly, the Society for the Investigation of Human Ecology (SIHE).[14]

The SIHE was founded by two renowned neurologists, Dr. Harold Wolff and Dr. Lawrence Hinkle, at Cornell Medical College in 1955 as what John Marks has described as a clandestine "CIA controlled funding mechanism for studies and experiments into the behavioral sciences."[15] The Agency had originally contracted Wolff and Hinkle in 1953 to study communist brainwashing and, at Cornell, they greatly expanded their research—specifically exploring the relative usefulness of brainwashing in interrogation.[16] Yet by 1958, the CIA severed the SIHE's relationship with the medical college, as the university was becoming critical of the organization's more questionable research. The separation ultimately benefited the Agency. Not only did its cover remain intact, but with the SIHE independent from the Cornell bureaucracy, the CIA had greater discretion over the direction of the research. Proposals continued to flood in from some of the most prestigious research institutions in the United States. Even world-renowned psychologists Carl Rodgers and B.F. Skinner received grants from the SIHE for their work during the late 1950s and early 1960s.[17] The SIHE awarded Albert Biderman of the Bureau of Social Science Research (BSSR) at American University a grant to study prisoner interrogation methods.[18] According to Christopher Simpson, the BSSR also received SIHE funding to research "the relative usefulness of drugs, electroshock, violence and other coercive techniques during interrogation of prisoners."[19] The SIHE also awarded a grant to Dr. D. Ewen Cameron of the Allen Memorial Institute at McGill University in Montreal to study the effects of extended sensory deprivation, electroshock, and drugs on human subjects. Both Dr. John Lilly and Dr. Maitland Baldwin of the National Institute of Health also studied the impact of sensory deprivation with SIHE funding.[20]

By July 1963, 10 years of research into the behavioral and cognitive sciences carried out by MKULTRA's team of scientists, doctors, and academics had yielded a systematic psychological torture paradigm that the CIA codified in *KUBARK Counterintelligence Interrogation*. According to the manual itself, the interrogation methods contained within are "based largely upon the published results of extensive research, including scientific inquiries conducted by specialists in closely related subjects."[21] Indeed, most of this research was made possible with SIHE funding. While Hinkle's research is cited most often, the work of Biderman, Lilly, and Cameron is also noted with frequency.

The objective of this new psychological torture paradigm was to break down the interrogation subject by inducing psychological regression. Through various projects underwritten by the SIHE, MKULTRA researchers concluded that psychological regression causes the interrogation subject's "mature defenses" to crumble "and he becomes more childlike."[22] Having regressed into this childlike state, the subject's will to resist will have deteriorated, and he will be more likely to yield information. The CIA's most significant contribution to this "cruel science" was that it renounced regression by way of physical pain and instead stressed human psychology.[23] MKULTRA researchers had deemed physical torture as an ineffective means of inducing regression because it generates pain externally and often intensifies the subject's resistance. The application of psychological methods, on the other hand, causes the victim's pain and discomfort to be generated from within. Quoting the research of Albert Biderman, KUBARK states:

> It has been plausibly suggested that, whereas pain inflicted on a person from outside himself may actually focus or intensify his will to resist, his resistance is likelier to be sapped by pain which he seems to inflict upon himself. "In the simple torture situation the contest is one between an individual and his tormentor (...and he can frequently endure). When the individual is told to stand at attention for long periods, an intervening factor is introduced. The immediate source of pain is not the interrogator but the victim himself."[24]

KUBARK presents several methods to generate internalized pain and psychological regression, including "arrest, detention, deprivation of sensory stimuli through solitary confinement or similar methods, threats and fear, debility, pain, heightened suggestibility and hypnosis, and induced regression."[25] The exact method (or combination of methods) to be employed is dependent upon several variables such as the personality of the prisoner, their psychological health, their personal history, the interrogation setting, and local laws regarding prisoner detention and treatment. Some techniques are more severe than others, but all can unquestionably be considered psychological torture. For example, as

SIHE researcher Lawrence Hinkle notes, isolation techniques such as sensory deprivation

> seemed to be the ideal way of "breaking down" a prisoner, because, to the unsophis-
> ticated, it seems to create precisely the state that the interrogator desires: malleability
> and the desire to talk, with the added advantage that one can delude himself that
> he is using no force or coercion...However, the effect of isolation on the brain
> function of the prisoner is much like that which occurs if he is beaten, starved, or
> deprived of sleep.[26]

Augmenting isolation, KUBARK outlines the specific practices an interrogator should employ to take advantage of his complete control over the environment to weaken the subject:

> The interrogator should use his power over the resistant subject's physical environ-
> ment to disrupt patterns of response, not to create them. Meals and sleep granted
> irregularly, in more than abundance or less than adequacy, the shifts occurring on
> no discernable time pattern, will normally disorient an interrogatee and sap his will
> to resist more effectively than a sustained deprivation leading to debility.[27]

KUBARK may also allude to electroshock as a means of acquiescence—a method to which foreign internal security forces would later become especially partial. "If a new safehouse is to be used as the interrogation site," KUBARK states, "the electric current should be known in advance, so that transformers or other modifying devices will be on hand if needed."[28] The manual clearly advises, however, that prior approval from headquarters was necessary, "if medical, chemical, or electrical methods are going to be used to induce acquiescence."[29]

THE INTERNAL SECURITY IMPERATIVE AND FOREIGN POLICE TRAINING

As the CIA secretly worked to develop more effective methods of interrogation during the 1950s, the dynamics of the Cold War were changing. While by no means subsiding, Cold War tensions had at least stabilized in Europe. The Marshall Plan was providing development capital to the free-market economies in the West. NATO had been ratified. The United States had successfully aided in the suppression of communist movements in both Greece and Turkey. And, with NSC-68, the United States had put into play a viable containment strategy that confronted the broader Soviet military and nuclear threats. Yet, with decolonization in Africa, Asia, and the Middle East, and poverty and so-called "underdevelopment" in Latin America, the danger of communist subversion in the Third World loomed larger than ever. What was even more troubling to policymakers was the fact that the United States lacked the adequate means to confront this growing threat. Eisenhower had already twice dispatched the CIA to overthrow moderate leftist governments—Iran in 1953 and Guatemala in

1954. And with the French losing ground in Southeast Asia, the need for U.S. intervention seemed imminent. In short, by the mid-1950s, foreign internal security was fast becoming a paramount concern among U.S. policymakers.

In December 1954, Eisenhower adapted the existing containment strategy to confront the threat of communist subversion by strengthening the internal security capabilities of Third World governments. Given the clandestine nature of subversion and the specific challenges it presented, National Security Council Action Memorandum 1290d (NSC-1290d) identified local police as the key to maintaining foreign internal security.[30] Intimately linked to the community and familiar with its residents, local police were best suited to identify, and ultimately "prevent," subversion before it developed into a full-scale insurgency that would necessitate costly military intervention. Accordingly, in 1955, Eisenhower launched a not-inconsiderable foreign police training program, the Civil Police Administration (CPA). The Defense Department had already been administering similar programs in postwar Japan, Korea, and the Philippines, as had the CIA in Turkey.[31] Yet with the creation of the CPA, Eisenhower began coordinating these existing—albeit bureaucratically disjointed—efforts within the State Department to more effectively mitigate Third World internal security deficiencies.

Upon taking office in 1961, Kennedy made foreign internal security the number one priority of his foreign policy agenda. In light of the 1959 Cuban Revolution and an escalating military commitment to contain communism in Southeast Asia, the administration developed an aggressive new counterinsurgency strategy to confront the global threat of communist subversion.[32] According foreign police training a central role in this new initiative, Kennedy and his Special Group (Counterinsurgency)—General Maxwell Taylor, CIA director John McCone, and National Security Adviser McGeorge Bundy—both expanded and centralized Eisenhower's foreign police training program, creating the Office of Public Safety (OPS) in November 1962. Although housed within the Agency for International Development (AID) bureaucracy, OPS was a hybrid agency that incorporated personnel and training from the CIA's Counterintelligence Division. A top secret Kennedy administration report from June 1962 underscored the important assistance the CIA could render to U.S. foreign police training efforts. Not only did the CIA provide "the latest information on developments in Sino-Soviet strategy and techniques to its personnel in the AID police programs who are working as advisors in the counterinsurgency, counterespionage, counterguerrilla, and other countersubversive fields." But the Agency was also particularly knowledgeable of the "investigative mechanisms capable of detecting subversive individuals and organizations, collecting and collating information...and neutralizing their effort."[33]

To lead this new hybrid agency, Kennedy's Special Group handpicked Byron Engle, a career CIA officer who, while working in the Counterintelligence

Division, had trained and advised foreign police forces since 1950.[34] Upon settling into his new position (which he held until 1972), Engle began formulating policy and recruiting personnel. His first move, according to historian David Lobe, was to obtain "the transfer of CIA officers who had worked with foreign police in the past, and who had an understanding of the intelligence objectives to be promoted among Third World police."[35] Once hired, CIA officers were trained and sent abroad, where they worked alongside legitimate OPS advisors to provide "technical assistance, using training aids and equipment demonstrations," to serve "as guest instructors in the police academies and schools of the host country," and to "direct training in AID sponsored courses and seminars."[36]

Augmenting the OPS in-country training programs, Kennedy founded the Inter-American Police Academy (IAPA), a police training school at Fort Davis in the Panama Canal Zone. Here, OPS trained over 700 police officials from throughout Latin America in counterinsurgency methods with a curriculum largely formulated by the CIA's Counterintelligence Division between 1962 and 1963.[37] Yet, before long, reports began filtering back to Washington that "the training in Panama was rougher than the United States would tolerate on its own shores."[38] As a result, the White House began gradually transferring the IAPA to Washington, DC, in December 1963, renaming it the International Police Academy (IPA). IPA instructors taught basic courses in "internal security, riot control, scientific aids, firearms, narcotics, border control, and counterinsurgency" while CIA officers offered more "specialized courses" on bomb making, investigation, and interrogation.[39]

THE OFFICE OF PUBLIC SAFETY AND PSYCHOLOGICAL TORTURE

Interrogation training was a crucial component of both OPS in-country and IPA curriculum. In communist subversive movements such as the Tupamaros National Liberation Movement (Uruguay), The Movement 8th of October (Brazil), and the National Liberation Front (South Vietnam), for example, local police and security forces confronted clandestine networks of ideologically motivated militants operating under furtive command structures. The ability of local security forces to successfully identify, infiltrate, and suppress these movements depended not only on the acquisition of reliable intelligence, but also on interrogation methods that could effectively extract that intelligence. It was here that OPS's relationship with the CIA's Counterintelligence Division began to bear fruit. After completing KUBARK in July 1963, the CIA began collaborating with OPS to disseminate its practices to foreign internal security forces—specifically, through OPS "Technical Interrogation" and IPA "Interviews and Interrogation" courses.[40]

In Uruguay, for instance, OPS advisors introduced psychological torture techniques to police and internal security forces to help crush the left-wing Tupamaros National Liberal Movement (Tupamaros). One former CIA officer working under OPS cover recalled that the "academic, almost clinical atmosphere" of OPS interrogation courses in Uruguay emphasized "the use of electric shocks, special chemicals, and modern psychological techniques."[41] While OPS advisors "advocated psychological methods to create despair," Uruguayan police forces became especially partial to electric shock.[42] Using field telephones supplied by the United States—and oftentimes allegedly bearing the U.S. AID crest—to generate a powerful electric current, Uruguayan interrogators would electrocute their Tupamaro prisoners until they divulged the names of other members of the secret organization.[43] Oftentimes, while a prisoner was being held in solitary confinement, tapes of screaming women and children would be played in an adjacent room to simulate the torture of that prisoner's family— the desired outcome being increased feelings of helplessness and despair.[44]

Not only had MKULTRA researchers discovered that psychological torture was more effective than physical torture, but it seems that U.S. policymakers believed OPS was doing the host countries a service by dissuading the use of brutality and force, and instead instructing what they considered as more "humane" or "humanitarian" psychological interrogation techniques (what Alfred McCoy has keenly dubbed "no-touch torture").[45] Yet, despite the emphasis OPS placed on psychological techniques in its training curriculum, some foreign police officials initially rejected the new methodology and continued to rely on physical torture. Incidents of physical torture carried out by local police and security forces caused alarm among State Department officials—particularly if those incidents involved OPS trainees. Being associated with the instruction of such methods could potentially jeopardize the public perception of an already sensitive U.S. program.

In response to two separate cases of "misconduct in police interrogation" in Latin America in March 1964, Secretary of State Dean Rusk circulated a memo to all OPS in-country advisors regarding the effectiveness of interrogation training. He recognized that "training programs in the application of modern humanitarian methods of police interrogation have been stressed" and that, "the effectiveness of these new methods has been demonstrated whenever possible to police officials at every level." Rusk expressed concern, however, that "many Public Safety Advisors have encountered much difficulty in getting these humanitarian concepts accepted by police officials who have grown up in an environment which has been insensitive to human rights or human dignity." Seeking to improve the effectiveness of OPS interrogation training, he requested instructive information from bureaus that had successfully inculcated "modern humanitarian interrogation techniques." The information would not only benefit in-country advisors, Rusk stressed, but it would also be "valuable for lecture or reading material at the OPS International Police Academy in Washington and the Inter-American Police Academy in the Panama Canal Zone."[46]

Successful OPS advisors apparently provided valuable counsel to the organization and, in subsequent years, instruction in "modern humanitarian interrogation techniques" seems to have become more effective. At the IPA, for example, the lesson plans for the "Interviews and Interrogation" course discouraged physical torture, emphasizing instead psychological methods similar to those contained within KUBARK: solitary confinement, sensory deprivation, "'emotional appeals,' 'exaggerated fears,' and psychological 'jolts.'"[47] The theses of IPA graduates demonstrate that the instruction stuck. Nickolas V. Fotinfpfulos of Greece, who attended the IPA in 1968, wrote in his thesis that "the interrogation of reluctant witnesses is devoted to a discussion of the psychological tactics and techniques of an effective interrogation of reluctant witness by means of instrumental aids or drugs."[48] A thesis entitled "The Use of Force and Threat in Interrogation" by Lam Van Huu of South Vietnam concluded, "we have four sorts of torture: use of force as such; use of threats; physical suffering, imposed indirectly; and mental or psychological torture."[49] The thesis of Nguyen Van Thieu, also from South Vietnam, outlines "three ways of interrogation" one of which included the "utilization of threats and scaring the prisoner: (a) by using torture; (b) by denying food and water; (c) by causing moral tension so that the prisoner's mind is so depressed the prisoner seems to be out of mind and recognizes his imaginary faults."[50] Thieu further revealed that "thanks to foreign aid from other countries in the freed [sic] world, the U.S. most of all, has assisted the national police in technical and equipments aid [sic] to help an interrogator in his interrogation of communist prisoners to be more effective."[51]

The interrogation courses were effective—perhaps too effective—and by 1970, allegations of OPS complicity in torture training began circulating in the international media. The accusations were triggered by the kidnapping and subsequent execution of OPS advisor Dan Mitrione by Tupamaros in Montevideo, Uruguay, in August 1970. Particularly damning was a *Jornal do Brazil* article quoting Uruguay's Chief of Police Intelligence, Alejandro Otero, that Mitrione had instructed Uruguayan police in "violent techniques of torture and repression."[52] Although the U.S. Embassy in Uruguay dismissed Otero's allegations as "absolutely false," the incident not only raised suspicion among U.S. lawmakers and the public alike, but cast a sinister legacy for the OPS program—most saliently exemplified by the 1972 Costa Gavras film, *State of Siege.*[53]

With OPS interrogation training already mired in suspicion, increasing reports of the widespread use of torture in Brazil sparked a congressional investigation into U.S. assistance programs there.[54] Brazil was the largest recipient of OPS assistance in a Latin America—and the second largest in the world, behind South Vietnam. During its 13-year tenure in Brazil, OPS trained over 100,000 police in the country, and a total of 691 in the United States and other third-country programs.[55] OPS operations in Brazil were especially peculiar, however. In March 1964, when the military deposed the democratically elected populist president, João Goulart, OPS advisors had suddenly found themselves training the security apparatus of a repressive dictatorship. By 1971, Brazil had one of the most dismal human rights records in the hemisphere and liberal U.S. Senators, already critical of the Vietnam War, sought to explore the connection, if any, between the repression and U.S. assistance programs. When the Subcommittee on Western Hemisphere Affairs of the Senate Foreign Relations Committee convened to discuss U.S. assistance programs in Brazil on May 4, 1971, Chairman Frank Church turned almost immediately to allegations of OPS torture training. After remarking on the "continuous" reports of "the widespread use of torture" by Brazilian police and security forces, Senator Church questioned Theodore Brown, Chief Public Safety Advisor on OPS's role in police torture.[56] Brown acknowledged that he was aware of the use of torture by Brazilian security forces. He assured Church, however, that OPS "emphasized humane methods" in interrogation training, reminding the senator that, "as with any organization, there is always the possibility that there might be isolated cases of unnecessary use of force."[57]

Despite the controversy surrounding OPS, it was not until 1973 that Congress began to take the torture allegations seriously. James Abourezk, an otherwise obscure liberal freshman senator from South Dakota, launched a sweeping investigation into OPS torture allegations. Abourezk and his staff dredged up IPA theses reflecting instruction in psychological torture, uncovered "fragmentary but persuasive evidence" that OPS had been culpable in training torture to Brazilian, Bolivian, Iranian, South Vietnamese, and Uruguayan internal security forces, and provided mounting evidence "that representatives of U.S. agencies are even involved in torture with some of the national police forces in some underdeveloped countries."[58] Although the CIA launched what Jack Anderson of the *Washington Post* described as a "discrete but intense lobbying effort to keep alive U.S. support for foreign police programs," Abourezk succeeded in persuading his fellow lawmakers to shut down both OPS and IPA.[59] By prohibiting funds for foreign police training in the Foreign Assistance Acts of 1973 and 1974, Congress terminated the primary conduit for CIA psychological torture training.[60]

PSYCHOLOGICAL TORTURE AND CONTAINMENT IN CENTRAL AMERICA

Yet the effort ultimately failed against the CIA, which continued to deploy its psychological torture paradigm according to the exigencies of Cold War containment. In the early 1980s, the CIA teamed up with U.S. Army Green Berets Mobile Training Teams to disseminate psychological torture techniques to anticommunist forces in Central and South America. On June 5, 1988, the *New York Times*

Magazine published a piece by James LeMoyne entitled "Testifying to Torture," alleging that between 1980 and 1984, the CIA had trained an elite Honduran Army Intelligence Unit, Battalion 316, in psychological torture techniques as part of Washington's broader effort to destabilize the leftist Sandinista regime in neighboring Nicaragua. Florencio Caballero, a former sergeant in Battalion 316, told LeMoyne, that the CIA "taught me interrogation, in order to end physical torture in Honduras."[61] As Caballero's testimony unfolded, his experience as a CIA-trained interrogator echoed the psychological techniques introduced 20 years earlier with KUBARK: "They taught us psychological methods—to study the fears and weaknesses of a prisoner. Make him stand up, don't let him sleep, keep him naked and isolated, put rats and cockroaches in his cell, give him bad food, serve him dead animals, throw cold water on him, change the temperature."[62]

When the Senate Select Committee on Intelligence (SSCI) convened a closed session to look into the allegations on June 16, 1988, the CIA's Deputy Director for Operations (DDO) Richard Stoltz revealed that an internal investigation into LeMoyne's allegations uncovered "a program for instruction; that is, a guide for instructors to use when teaching interrogation techniques" that dated back as far back as 1982. A Freedom of Information Act request subsequently filed by the *Baltimore Sun* later revealed documents demonstrating that Mobile Training Teams and the CIA had used this "program for instruction"—that is, an interrogation manual entitled *Human Resource Exploitation Training Manual-1983*—to teach interrogation not only in Honduras, but throughout Central and South America.[63] Stoltz confirmed that LeMoyne's article was accurate: "Caballero did indeed attend a CIA human resources exploitation or interrogation course [excised] from February 8 to March 13, 1983."[64]

According to the CIA Inspector General, Mobile Training Teams provided at least seven Human Resources Exploitation interrogation courses to security forces in an undisclosed number of countries in Central and South America between 1982 and 1987.[65] Not coincidentally, the CIA's 1983 *Human Resources Exploitation Training Manual* advocated the same psychological torture methodology outlined in KUBARK—in fact, some passages are identical. Notably, the new manual also included more recent material that had resulted from "Project X"—which, according to a 1991 Department of Defense memo, was a U.S. Army program intended "to develop an exportable foreign intelligence training package to provide counterinsurgency techniques learned in Vietnam to Latin American countries."[66]

CONCLUSION

For the duration of the Cold War, officials from the CIA, the State Department, the Department of Defense, and the White House compromised fundamental U.S. ideals for what they perceived as a necessary, even virtuous, global anticommunist campaign. Often cast in simple though infinitely problematic binaries of good versus evil, freedom versus slavery, civilization versus barbarity, and, of course, capitalism versus communism, the Cold War was, for U.S. officials, a struggle for the very survival of the United States and what it represented: free-market capitalism and liberal democracy, as well as the more lofty, albeit subjective, ideals of freedom, liberty, and justice. By containing communism in general and the Soviet Union in particular, U.S. policymakers sought to secure the republic and its ideals. And, in what is a remarkable stroke of irony, psychological torture played a crucial role in that effort.

The CIA's continued, even recalcitrant, deployment of the KUBARK paradigm in itself underscores the crucial role played by psychological torture in Cold War containment. For 25 years, psychological torture was the CIA's secret weapon in establishing a bulwark against communist expansion into the Third World. First operating through the Office of Public Safety and then collaborating with Green Berets Mobile Training Teams, the CIA's dissemination of psychological torture to foreign police and military forces corresponded to the overseas internal security imperative that emerged as a defining characteristic of the containment strategy with the Eisenhower and Kennedy administrations. As the Uruguay case briefly illustrates, psychological torture attended to the specific challenges that communist subversion posed to foreign internal security forces. By providing what U.S. officials considered more "humane" or even "humanitarian" interrogation techniques, CIA/OPS sought to strengthen the capacity of Uruguayan national police to identify and infiltrate the clandestine cells of the Tupamaros, thus suppressing the subversive threat and preventing the spread of communism. Working through Mobile Training Teams, the CIA pursued a similar goal in Honduras as the specter of communism loomed in Central and South America during the 1980s.

As the U.S. government redeploys the KUBARK paradigm as a central weapon in the War on Terror, it becomes particularly urgent to reflect on the consequences of Cold War psychological torture training. In much of the Third World, the psychological torture methods disseminated to contain communism during the 1960s were, by the 1970s, folded into more elaborate state-terror systems by the dictatorships that emerged as states failed to effectively reconcile democratic institutions with national security concerns. Although those states have since made the difficult transition back to democracy, the trauma of psychological torture—individual and collective—lingers as a painful reminder of the authoritarian past, often hindering the processes of truth and reconciliation critical to democratization. Today, the War on Terror corresponds to a broader U.S. foreign policy objective characterized by an unprecedented effort to promote democracy worldwide. Yet, the central role played by psychological torture in Washington's global antiterrorist campaign threatens to subvert that objective. The Cold War consequences of psychological torture reveal that current U.S.

practices—from the CIA's secret interrogation program to condoning the use of physical torture by foreign intelligence services through "extraordinary renditions"—have the potential to derail democratic institutions in both the United States and abroad and to lower international standards of human rights. Moreover, concerted efforts within the Bush administration to redefine torture in order to both legally and ethically justify coercive interrogation practices provoke international derision while further eroding U.S. moral authority. In a moment when the American public is becoming increasingly anesthetized to the horrors of psychological torture, we must consider the potent threat that the unapologetic promotion of this brutal practice poses not only to our long-term diplomatic objectives, but to our own democratic ideals.

NOTES

1. U.S. Central Intelligence Agency (hereafter cited as CIA), "KUBARK Counterintelligence Interrogation," manual/handbook, Secret (declassified), July 1963, p. 103, CIA Training Manuals, Box 1: "KUBARK," The National Security Archive, Washington, DC (NSA). Hereafter cited as KUBARK. For more on both the novelty and significance of this new psychological torture paradigm in the long history of this "cruel science," see Alfred W. McCoy, *A Question of Torture: CIA Interrogation from the Cold War to the War on Terror* (New York: Metropolitan Books, Henry Holt and Company, 2006).

2. "NSC 68: United States Objectives and Programs for National Security. A Report to the President Pursuant to the President's Directive of January 31, 1950," April 14, 1950, *Foreign Relations of the Unites States (FRUS),* 1950, Vol. 1, National Security Affairs; Foreign Economic Policy.

3. John Lewis Gaddis, *The Long Peace: Inquiries in the History of the Cold War* (New York: Oxford University Press, 1987).

4. CIA, "Behavioral Drugs and Testing," draft, memorandum, February 5, 1975, contained in U.S., Congress, Senate, Joint Hearing before the Subcommittee on Health of the Committee on Labor and Public Welfare and the Subcommittee on Administrative Practice and Procedure of the Committee on the Judiciary, *Biomedical and Behavioral Research* (Government Printing Office, 1975), 909. (Hereafter cited as *Biomedical and Behavioral Research*.)

5. Quoted in Joost A.M. Meerloo, MD, *The Rape of the Mind: The Psychology of Thought Control, Menticide, and Brainwashing* (Cleveland, OH: World Publishing Co., 1956), 20.

6. CIA, "Memorandum from the Chief of the Medical Staff, 1/25/52," reproduced in U.S., Congress, Senate, Select Committee to Study Governmental Operations with Respect to Intelligence Activities, *Final Report on Intelligence Activities, Book I: Foreign and Military Intelligence* (Government Printing Office, 1975), 393. (Hereafter cited as *Church Committee—Final Report*.)

7. NSC-68, *FRUS,* 1950, Vol. 1.

8. Report reproduced in *Church Committee—Final Report,* 9.

9. "Project CHATTER," draft, memorandum, November, 1950, *Behavioral and Biomedical Research,* 988; *Church Committee—Final Report,* 387.

10. *Church Committee—Final Report,* 387; John Marks, *The Search for the Manchurian Candidate* (Times Books, 1979), 38–40.

11. *Church Committee—Final Report,* 387–388.

12. Ibid., 6; Marks, *Manchurian Candidate,* 134–56.

13. CIA, "Report on Inspection of MKULTRA," memorandum, July 26, 1963, in *Behavioral and Biomedical Research,* 880.

14. CIA, "MKULTRA," memorandum for the record, January 17, 1975, in *Behavioral and Biomedical Research,* 298.

15. Ibid., 159.

16. Marks, *Manchurian Candidate,* 135.

17. Ibid.

18. Christopher Simpson, *Science of Coercion* (New York: Oxford University Press, 1994), 72.

19. Ibid.

20. Marks, *Manchurian Candidate,* 157.

21. Ibid., 1.

22. KUBARK, 103.

23. McCoy, *A Question of Torture.*

24. KUBARK, 94.

25. Ibid., 85.

26. Albert D. Biderman and Herbert Zimmer, eds., *The Manipulation of Human Behavior* (New York: John Wiley & Sons, Inc., 1961), 29.

27. KUBARK, p. 93.

28. Ibid., p. 46.

29. Ibid., p. 8.

30. "Report of the NSC 1290d Working Group," February 16, 1955, *FRUS,* 1955–1957, Vol. 10, Foreign Aid and Economic Defense Policy, 1–5.

31. Michael McClintock, *Instruments of Statecraft: U.S. Guerrilla Warfare, Counterinsurgency, and Counter-terrorism, 1940–1990* (New York: Pantheon Books, 1992).

32. On August 24, 1962, the White House approved the "national counterinsurgency doctrine" manifest in the paper, "U.S. Overseas Internal Defense Policy" with National Security Action Memorandum No. 182. See *FRUS,* 1961–63, Vol. 8, National Security Policy.

33. U.S. Department of State, Agency for International Development, Office of Public Safety, *Report of Interdepartmental Technical Subcommittee on Police Advisory Assistance Programs,* June 11, 1962, secret (declassified), pp. 16–17, RG 286, Entry 18, Box 2, Folder 2, National Archives and Records Administration II, College Park, MD (NARA II).

34. Thomas David Lobe, "U.S. Police Assistance for the Third World" (PhD diss., University of Michigan, 1975), 56.

35. Ibid., 60.

36. U.S. Department of State, Agency for International Development, Office of Public Safety, *Program Guide—Public Safety Training* (Washington, DC, 1968), 1.

37. Lobe, "U.S. Police Assistance," 62.

38. A.J. Langguth, *Hidden Terrors: The Truth about U.S. Police Operations in Latin America* (New York: Pantheon Books, 1978), 53.

39. Otwin Marenin, "From IPA to ILEA: Change and Continuity in U.S. International Police Training Programs," *Police Quarterly* 1, no. 4 (1998): 99. U.S. Congress, Government Accounting Office, "Stopping U.S. Assistance to Foreign Police and Prisons" (Washington, DC: USGAO, 1976), p. 15; "CIA's 'Family Jewels,'" pp. 605–14, 613, available at http://www.gwu.edu/~nsarchiv/NSAEBB/NSAEBB222/index.htm.

40. Several declassified cables from the OPS station in Rio de Janeiro refer to "Technical Interrogation" courses taught by in-country advisors. Jack Anderson's investigative reporting on OPS in 1974 revealed that the IPA interrogation course was entitled "Interviews and Interrogation." See Jack Anderson, "Questionable Means of Interrogation," *Washington Post,* August 3, 1974, C15. To this author's knowledge, all OPS/IPA training manuals remain classified.

41. Alan Riding, "Cuban 'Agent' Says U.S. Police Aides Urged Torture," *New York Times,* August 5, 1978.

42. Langguth, *Hidden Terrors,* 286.

43. Ibid., 125. See also Amnesty International, *Report on Torture,* 2nd ed. (London: Duckworth, 1975), 217–18.

44. Langguth, *Hidden Terrors,* 286–87.

45. McCoy, *A Question of Torture,* 10.

46. See U.S. Department of State, Agency for International Development, *AID Circular: Misconduct in Police Interrogation,* March 25, 1964, RG 286, OPS/IAPA Subject Files, 1956–1964, Box 8, Folder: "IAPA—Training (General Correspondence, 1962–64)," NARA, College Park, MD.

47. Anderson, "Questionable Means of Interrogation," C15.

48. "Report of Nickolas V. Fotinfpfulos, Greece, February 10, 1968" contained in U.S. Congress, Senate, *Congressional Record,* 93rd Cong., 2d sess., 1974, vol. 120, pt. 25: 33474.

49. Lam Van Huu, "The Use of Force and Threats in Interrogation" contained in *Congressional Record,* 93rd Cong., 2d sess., vol. 120, pt. 25.

50. "Report of Nguyen Van Thieu, SVN, August 10, 1965" contained in *Congressional Record,* 93rd Cong., 2d sess., vol. 120, pt. 25.

51. *Congressional Record,* 93rd Cong., 2d sess., vol. 120, pt. 25.

52. UPI, "U.S. Denies Slain Advisor Tortured Latin Prisoners," *New York Times,* August 16, 1970; Reuters, "Jailed Guerrilla Chiefs Confer, Raising Hope of Deal," *New York Times,* August 15, 1970.

53. UPI, "U.S. Denies Slain Advisor Tortured Latin Prisoners."

54. Associated Press, "Brazil Aide Says Torture Is Used—Minister Makes First Such Government Admission," *New York Times,* December 4, 1970; Dan Griffin, "Tortures in Brazil Leak Out Despite Rebuff of OAS Probe," *Washington Post,* March 7, 1971.

55. Michael T. Klare, *Supplying Repression: U.S. Support for Authoritarian Regimes Abroad* (Washington, DC: Institute for Policy Studies, 1977), 20; U.S. Congress, Senate, Subcommittee on Western Hemisphere Affairs, Committee on Foreign Relations,

Hearing, *United States Policies and Programs in Brazil,* 92nd Cong., 1st sess., May 4, 5, and 11, 1971, 19.

56. U.S., *Policies and Programs in Brazil,* 18; Martha K. Huggins offers an in-depth study on the Senate investigation into OPS and torture. See *Political Policing: The United States and Latin America* (Durham, NC: Duke University Press, 1998).

57. Subcommittee on Western Hemisphere Affairs, *United States Policies and Programs in Brazil,* 17–18. Richard Helms, director of Central Intelligence, also testified, however, the entire transcript is redacted (FOIA request pending).

58. U.S. Congress, Senate, *Congressional Record,* 93rd Cong., 1st Sess., 1973, vol. 119, pt. 25: 32259; James Abourezk, telephone interview by author, September 11, 2000.

59. Jack Anderson, "CIA Admits Using Foreign Police," *Washington Post,* August 19, 1974.

60. See detailed discussion in Matthew Gildner, "Torture and U.S. Foreign Policy: An Examination of the Development, Propagation, and Congressional Termination of the CIA's Psychological Torture Model" (senior honors thesis, University of Wisconsin at Madison, 2001).

61. James LeMoyne, "Testifying to Torture," *New York Times Magazine,* June 5, 1988, 45.

62. Ibid., 62

63. Congressional Fact Sheet, June 8, 1988, contained as an introduction in the revised Human Resources Exploitation Training Manual: U.S., CIA, "Human Resources Exploitation Training Manual—1983," manual/handbook (declassified), 1983, p. 1, CIA Training Manuals, Box 1: Human Resources Exploitation, NSA.

64. U.S. Senate, Select Committee on Intelligence, "Honduran Interrogation Manual Hearing," June 16, 1988, 14, CIA Training Manuals, Box 1, Interrogation Manual Hearings, NSA.

65. Congressional Fact Sheet, June 8, 1988, p. 1, NSA.

66. U.S. Department of Defense, *USSOUTHCOM CI Training-Supplemental Information,* July 31, 1991, available at http://www.gwu.edu/~nsarchiv/NSAEBB/NSA EBB122/910801%20USSOUTHCOM%20CI%20Training%20(U).pdf

CHAPTER 3

LEGACY OF A DARK DECADE: CIA MIND CONTROL, CLASSIFIED BEHAVIORAL RESEARCH, AND THE ORIGINS OF MODERN MEDICAL ETHICS

Alfred W. McCoy

In August 2006, U.S. Army surgeon general Kevin Kiley, dressed in full combat uniform, appeared before the national convention of the American Psychological Association (APA) to defend the participation of psychologists in interrogation. "Psychology," he declared, invoking a military maxim that many present may have found unsettling, "is an important weapons system."[1]

Indeed, for over half a century psychology has served the U.S. intelligence community as a secret weapon in wars against its ideological enemies, first communism and now Islamic fundamentalism. From the start of the Cold War, several generations of select psychologists have served U.S. intelligence in the discovery and development of new interrogation methods whose extreme forms constitute nothing less than psychological torture. During the War on Terror, psychologists have designed "enhanced" CIA interrogation methods, including a cruel technique called "waterboarding," and participated in military interrogations at Guantanamo Bay condemned by the International Red Cross as "tantamount to torture."[2] In exchange, the U.S. intelligence community has lavished rewards upon the psychology profession, in terms of both generous funding for experimental researchers and employment for clinical specialists.

Psychology's service to U.S. national security has produced a variant of what psychiatrist Robert Lifton has called, in his study the Nazi doctors, a "Faustian bargain." In this case, the price paid has been the APA's collective silence, ethical "numbing," and, over time, historical amnesia.[3] In understanding how state imperatives can corrupt medical ethics, Lifton notes that "the Nazis were not the only ones to involve doctors in evil," citing the Cold War "role of... American physicians and psychologists employed by the Central Intelligence Agency...for unethical medical and psychological experiments involving drugs and mind manipulation."[4]

During the early years of the Cold War, the CIA in fact developed, through this secret behavioral research, a new form of torture that relied on psychological rather than physical pain. If genius is the discovery of the obvious, then the Agency's development of this "no-touch torture" was a counterintuitive break-through, the first real revolution in the cruel science of pain in centuries. Through more than 2,000 years of Western judicial torture using harsh physical methods, the same problem persisted—the strong defied pain while the weak blurted out whatever was necessary to stop it. By contrast, the CIA's psychological paradigm fused two new techniques, "sensory disorientation" and "self-inflicted pain," whose combination would cause victims to feel responsible for their own suffering and, in theory, capitulate more readily to their torturers. Refined through years of practice, the Agency's psychological paradigm relies on a mix of sensory overload and sensory deprivation for a systematic attack on all human stimuli via seemingly banal, even benign procedures—heat and cold, light and dark, noise and silence, isolation and then intense interrogation.

In early 2007, a full half-century after the CIA first codified these methods, we have the first convincing clinical evidence that psychological torture is just as traumatic as its physical variant. "Ill treatment during captivity, such as psychological manipulations...and forced stress positions," Dr. Metin Basoglu reports in the *Archives of General Psychiatry* after interviews with 279 Bosnian victims, "does not seem to be substantially different from physical torture in terms of the severity of mental suffering...and their long-term psychological outcome."[5] From the perspective of intelligence and interrogation, the development of a method that could inflict severe suffering from psychological, rather than physical methods, was a discovery of considerable import.

If this breakthrough had conventional instead of covert uses, then the search for new forms of interrogation might have become one of those heroic, history-of-science narratives of the brilliant scientist, working alone and besting rivals known or unknown, to capture the crown of discovery with all its recognition and reward. Just as the discovery of natural selection supposedly became a race between Charles Darwin and Alfred Wallace, or the development of the polio vaccine a rivalry between Jonas Salk and Albert Sabin, so the CIA's development of psychological torture can be reduced, in all its complexity, to a narrative of competing approaches by two titans of twentieth-century medical science—Donald O. Hebb's behavioral methods versus Henry K. Beecher's drug experimentation.[6] Their eminence should not be underestimated: Hebb is a towering figure in cognitive science whose 1949 book is regarded by some as second only to Darwin's *Origin of the Species* in scientific significance;[7] while Beecher is remembered as a pioneer in American anesthesiology and, above all, clinical ethics.[8] Yet for both, there was a fortuitous convergence between the CIA's mind-control project and their own professional trajectories, providing them, at the cost of the ethical compromises inherent in classified work, needed funding for the human experimentation central to their research and rising reputations —hence the Faustian bargain.

Though research into psychological torture was indeed a dark science, it was science nonetheless, and has a significant history that commands close attention rather than willful amnesia or spurious denials. For probing this covert confluence between CIA research and cognitive science reveals not only the discovery of a virulent form of psychological torture that has persisted to the present, but the development of its antidote in the form of modern medical ethics. In one of history's supreme ironies, this secret CIA research, with its harsh treatment of human subjects, also seemed to produce its own correction, making Dr. Beecher the ultimate victor in this silent, scientific competition.

THE DUAL LEGACY OF DACHAU

At the dawn of the Cold War, the human mind became a covert battleground in the deployment of new weapons for mass persuasion and individual interrogation. From 1950 to 1962, the CIA led a massive, secret effort to crack the code of human consciousness, a veritable Manhattan project of the mind with costs for psychological research and operations that reached, at peak, a billion dollars a year.[9]

In 1950, after just a few months of this investigation, the CIA decided to "transfer the psychological part of the [research] program to an outside agency, where more adequate facilities...and volunteers could be utilized as subjects." One of the first of these new contracts was for $300,000, through the Navy, to a "Department of Psychology" at an unnamed university. Within two years, the Office of Naval Research (ONR), with an unknown portion of its grants from the CIA, would become an influential patron for experimental psychology by funding 117 contracts at 58 universities.[10] More broadly, as Christopher Simpson explains, "The Department of Defense and the Central Intelligence Agency helped bankroll substantially all of the post–World War II generation's research into techniques of persuasion, opinion measurement, [and] interrogation."[11]

In understanding this Cold War mobilization of behavioral science, Lifton's study of the Nazi doctors offers a useful analogue. Soon after taking power, Nazi appeals to the German medical profession's ingrained conservatism persuaded 45 percent, led by a few prominent physicians, to join the party; a smaller number, about 350 doctors, later participated in "medical crimes" through a process of psychological "numbing" and "doubling." Just as Lifton asked how these German doctors could betray their Hippocratic oath, so we might ask how American psychologists dedicated to healing pain might instead choose to inflict it through medical experiments or interrogation.[12]

But the Nazi doctors are much more than mere metaphor or analogue in the history of CIA torture research. Just as the U.S. space program benefited from the work of Werner von Braun's rocket scientists at Peenemuende and the Luftwaffe's murderous medical experiments at Dachau, so this CIA mind-control effort continued the research of the Nazi doctors, both their specific findings and innovative use of human subjects. In 1942, the Luftwaffe had done pioneering research into altitude sickness and hypothermia on some 200 prisoners at the Dachau death camp, documenting their agonizing deaths in graphic films shown at the 1942 Nazi aviation medical conference. After the war, the U.S. Air Force, enticed by the scientific significance of this work, recruited 34 of these Nazi doctors who had eluded Nuremberg's net to establish its School of Aviation Medicine at Randolph Field, Texas—bringing the Reich's research esprit into the heart of U.S. military medicine.[13] In 1950, the U.S. Air Force effectively expunged these crimes from the historical record by publishing *German Aviation Medicine: World War II,* a hagiographic account of these Nazi doctors as heroic men who "showed great scientific understanding...and personal concern in aeromedical research."[14]

More broadly, the Nazi use of human subjects, which shattered long-standing clinical restraints, had contradictory effects—cautioning medical science about the need for ethics embodied in the 1947 Nuremberg medical code, while simultaneously alerting the U.S. national security community to the yield from inhumane treatment.[15] "The Nuremberg Code has remained official American policy ever since 1946," wrote John Marks in his landmark study of CIA mind-control research, "but, even before the verdicts were in, special U.S. investigating teams were sifting through the experimental records at Dachau for information of military value."[16] In sum, medical science was repulsed by Dachau's inhumanity, but U.S. national security was intrigued.

Consequently, Washington's postwar defense research was soon infected by the Dachau model, whose methods it mimed across a broad spectrum of Cold War experiments on, literally, tens of thousands of unwitting human subjects—for atomic, chemical, biological, and psychological warfare.[17] To cite just a few examples, atomic experiments exposed over 200,000 U.S. servicemen to radiation and used 3,000 more as human subjects; a range of "psychoactive chemicals," particularly LSD, were tested on some 6,700 unwitting subjects, including a thousand soldiers; virulent biological warfare agents were administered to some 2,300 Seven Day Adventist volunteers; and chemicals were tested on thousands of soldiers, including 1,366 exposed to CS riot-control gas.[18]

Behavioral scientists who collaborated with the CIA's mind-control research soon drew from Dachau's poisoned well. Reflecting this era's ethical ethos, all the behavioral researchers cited in this paper with ties to secret research—Baldwin, Beecher, Hebb, Milgram, Wexler, Mendelson, Leiderman, and Solomon—conducted experiments whose success entailed infliction of psychological pain upon human subjects in violation of the Nuremberg Code of medical ethics.

THE TWO ROADS TO MIND CONTROL

In contrast to command-economy models for scientific mobilization in the Soviet Union or the Third Reich, the CIA employed financial incentives and collegial manipulation to effect a subtle redirection of the cognitive science community, making its mind-control effort a dominant research objective during this troubled Cold War decade. As the *New York Times* reported after a major investigation into this "secret, 25-year, $25 million effort by the Central Intelligence Agency to learn how to control the human mind," the Agency "was able to assemble an extensive network of non-government scientists and facilities—apparently without the knowledge of the institutions where the facilities were located." As the CIA's Inspector General noted in 1957, the Agency "had added difficulty in obtaining expert services" since some experiments "are considered to be professionally unethical and in some instances border on the illegal." Hence, as one member of the CIA's Technical Services Division told the *Times,* "secrecy has been used to protect the researchers from peer group pressure should it be known that they were working for the Agency."[19] Apart from a few lead researchers who were knowing collaborators, most of those implicated—their colleagues, junior faculty, and graduate assistants—were likely unaware of the covert agenda, and often pursued research remote from the Agency's goals. Nonetheless, the CIA presided over a scientific research effort that made important gains—elimination of exotic methods such as hypnosis and LSD, and, above all, discovery of innovative behavioral techniques. While the Agency's exotic drug testing led nowhere except to endless lawsuits by its Canadian victims, obscure CIA-funded behavioral experiments, outsourced to leading American and Canadian universities, soon made key contributions to the development of psychological torture.[20]

OUR MAN IN MONTREAL: DR. HEBB OF MCGILL

Although the CIA's project was initially a defensive reaction to apparent Soviet mind-control at communist show trials in Eastern Europe during 1948–49, the Agency's effort quickly shifted from defense to offense. As the *New York Times* reported after reviewing 5,000 pages of documents and interviewing CIA veterans, the program's aims had initially been defensive, a search for " a way to insulate its agents from brain-washing attempts." But "by the early 1950s... the program's goals became offensive."[21] In 1951, the CIA launched a determined search for offensive mind-control methods in close collaboration with its British and Canadian allies. In March, the Agency initiated what it called, in a classified memo, a "top secret" research program into "all aspects of special interrogation" through "exchange of information and coordination of related programs."[22]

Consequently, in the words of a Canadian inquiry by George Cooper, QC, "a high-level meeting took place at the Ritz Carlton Hotel in Montreal on June 1, 1951." Attending were Sir Henry T. Tizard, the influential senior scientist from the UK Ministry of Defense; Dr. Omond Solandt, head of Canada's Defense Research Board (DRB); Dr. Donald O. Hebb, head of the DRB's Behavioral Research and chair of psychology at McGill; and two Americans, Dr. Caryl Haskins and Commander R. J. Williams. These latter two were identified, in a "handwritten note" found in DRB files, as "CIA."[23]

Indicative of the import of this meeting, Dr. Tizard's earlier trans-Atlantic voyage at the start of World War II had mobilized thousands of physicists to make radar a key weapon in the Allied defeat of the Axis powers.[24] And indicative of the extent of CIA penetration of the U.S. scientific establishment, Dr. Haskins became, five years after this meeting, president of the influential Carnegie Institution of Washington, a position he held for 15 years until his retirement in 1971.[25]

According to the board's minutes of this Montreal mind-control summit, "Dr. Hebb suggested that an approach based upon the situation of sensory isolation might lead to some clues" to answering "the central problem" which interested this covert research coalition: i.e., "'confession,' 'menticide,' 'intervention in the individual mind,'—together with methods concerned in psychological coercion." Speaking at length, Hebb suggested that by "cutting off all sensory stimulation...the individual could be led into a situation whereby ideas, etc. might be implanted." In response, Sir Henry Tizard concurred, stating that these issues "had become a matter of concern in the U.K.," and adding that "the methods of psychological coercion...had been well developed by the inquisition."[26]

As consensus formed about "research methods and design," the group adopted Hebb's suggestion that "experimental isolation in various forms for the production of *sensory isolation*" might place subjects "in such a position psychologically that they would be susceptible to implantation of new or different ideas." Despite the DRB's later claims to the contrary, its minutes indicate clearly that their priority in backing Hebb's brainwashing work was not defensive but *offensive* operations against communist enemies. "With respect to...useful results," the Montreal principals agreed, "present methods of offence had moved over into the psychological field and that the whole area of change in public opinion and individual attitude was assuming rapidly increasing importance." Then, as an afterthought and distinctly secondary concern, the group noted: "In addition, the project itself would serve to open up this general area for research by those concerned with defence."[27]

The CIA's own minutes concur with the DRB's emphasis on offensive aims, recording that the Montreal group agreed there was "no conclusive evidence" that the Soviets had made anything akin to "revolutionary progress," and dismissed their interrogation as "remarkably similar...to the age-old methods." Behind closed doors, therefore, the defensive pretence evaporated, and these cold warriors decided to pursue control over human consciousness for offensive "cold war operations": i.e., ideological conversion and coerced interrogation.[28]

"Medical science," reads a February 1952 CIA memo that seems to echo this Montreal meeting, "particularly...psychiatry and psychotherapy, has developed various techniques by means of which some external control can be imposed on the mind/or will of an individual, such as drugs, hypnosis, electric shock and neurosurgery."[29] In another memo dated January 25, 1952, the Agency summarized the overarching offensive aims of its mind control effort, now coordinated under Project Artichoke, as "the evaluation and development of any method by which we can get information from a person against his will and without his knowledge," allowing "control of an individual where he will do our bidding against his will and even against such fundamental laws of nature as self-preservation."[30]

Within just a few years, this allied scientific offensive would pursue classified research concealed within public and private facilities in at least four major nations—including, a British "intelligence research unit" at Maresfield, Sussex; an Anglo-American facility near Frankfurt for lethal experiments on captured Soviet-bloc "expendables"; CIA-funded psychology research at leading U.S. hospitals and universities; periodic allied conferences to exchange results; and, above all, classified Canadian studies of sensory deprivation at McGill University.[31] In marked contrast to the surprisingly poor yield from the CIA's drug experiments, three behavioral projects, among the hundreds outsourced to academics, produced important results.

Three months after the Montreal meeting, in one of the most significant steps for the gestation of the CIA's psychological paradigm, the DRB awarded Dr. Hebb a "secret" grant, under Contract DRB-X38 from 1951 to 1954, for experiments that discovered the devastating psychological impact of sensory isolation. As Hebb explained in his classified 1952 report, this experiment was measuring "whether *slight* changes of attitude might be effected" by shorter periods of isolation intensified by "wearing (a) light-diffusing goggles, (b) earphones through which white noise may be constantly delivered...and (c) cardboard tubes over his [the subject's] forearms so that his hands...cannot be used for tactual perception of the environment." In contrast to the modest impact anticipated, Hebb reported that "motivational disturbance appears great," and that among 22 subjects, "four remarked spontaneously that being in the apparatus was a form of torture." Evidently encouraged, Hebb concluded, "the contract is opening up a field of study that is of both theoretical and practical significance."[32]

With a growing sense of this project's scientific importance, and concerned that his McGill colleague Dr. Ewan Cameron "is now undertaking some work with this method," Hebb pressed the DRB for permission to publicize his results. But the board resisted by insisting on secrecy and, if necessary, deceptive cover stories.[33] A year later, Hebb argued that a full presentation, albeit one masked by a cover story to conceal the project's real aim, for Dr. Cameron's psychiatry conference at McGill's Allen Memorial Institute "would be useful to me, for the furtherance of our work and for getting financed." After reminding the board that "I *have* worked hard for you people, with no other pay than getting these experimental results," Hebb concluded his impassioned, ultimately unsuccessful appeal by sketching, at the bottom of his letter, a kneeling figure with arms raised in supplication.[34] While public disclosures were thus restricted, Hebb's 1952 annual report was distributed to all three branches of the U.S. military along with "1 copy to Central Intelligence Agency (USA)."[35]

After three years of secret research, the story finally leaked to the *Toronto Star* in January 1954. In a background memo for the minister, the DRB's Dr. Solandt explained that Hebb's research had "originated from a discussion among Sir Henry Tizard, representatives of the US Central Intelligence Agency, Dr. Hebb...and myself in June 1951." Hebb's subsequent research has "given some indication that significant changes in attitude can be brought about by use of propaganda under conditions of isolation." With a misleading cover story that the project was preventing monotony by those monitoring a radar display, the DRB soon silenced the press.[36]

Even so, questions were raised in Canada's Parliament, and the Cabinet decided, on "questions of principle," that "the contract with Hebb at McGill be cancelled." In an internal memo to Solandt, a Defense official noted that "there continues to be interest from U.S. in this project...Hebb has previously had several official US visitations."[37] In his report for the Cabinet, Dr. Solandt, hinting at continuing CIA contacts, noted Hebb's work has been of "appreciable interest to U.S. research agencies, representatives of which have by arrangement visited Hebb."[38]

While Canada was cutting Hebb loose, the CIA continued its regular contacts. In September 1954, as more than 6,000 psychologists filled New York City's Statler Hotel for the APA convention, an anonymous CIA scientist met Hebb's close colleague, Dr. Edward C. Webster, later chair of psychology at McGill, for a detailed briefing on the sensory deprivation experiment.[39] At some point as well, according to Hebb's colleague Dr. Peter M. Milner, "The project...did receive money from a research foundation that was later revealed to be a front for the C.I.A."[40]

Two years later, the director of the U.S. National Institutes of Health, Dr. Robert H. Felix, demolished Hebb's carefully constructed cover when he told Congress about a study by "Dr. Donald Hebb, Professor of Psychology, McGill University," using 60 students "who stayed as long as they could on a bed in an air conditioned box." Asked if "this is a form of brainwashing," Dr. Felix replied: "You can break down anyone with this, I don't care what their background." After coverage in the *New York Times* of April 15, 1956, prompted "Brainwashing" headlines in the Montreal *Gazette*, Dr. Hebb insisted, inaccurately, on the "defensive" nature of his research: "We were not trying to find bigger and better ways of torturing others, but to find out how to protect our own men."[41]

There is good reason to doubt the credence of Dr. Hebb's assertion that the prime aim of his mind-control research was defensive. As evident in extant CIA memoranda and the DRB minutes of the 1951 Montreal meeting, his research was done in a period, 1951–54, when the paramount objective of the Agency and its Canadian allies was the development of mind-control methods for offensive operations—interrogation of communist captives, turning enemy agents into double-agents, and imposing alien beliefs on target assets. Admittedly, there was later a renewed interest in the defensive uses of mind control in 1954–55 when news of the "brain washing" of American prisoners in North Korea was confirmed, upon their release, by debriefings and military inquires, producing a number of popular and scholarly publications.[42] After a yearlong Defense Department inquiry, President Dwight Eisenhower issued an executive order, dated August 17, 1955, that every soldier be given "specific training and instruction designed to better equip him to counter and withstand all enemy efforts against him." Consequently, the Air Force developed its SERE program (Survival, Evasion, Resistance, Escape) to train its pilots in resistance to psychological torture.[43] As the military consulted psychologists and psychiatrists to diagnose past POW treatment in Korea and propose an antidote, there developed two related strands in mind-control research—offensive for CIA interrogation of enemy agents, and defensive for training American pilots to resist enemy interrogators.[44] Significantly, almost all this interest in defensive measures came in 1954–56, well after Hebb had completed his four years of offensive mind control research for the CIA from 1951–54.

Paralleling Hebb's exculpatory press statement in response to those 1956 "brainwashing" headlines, the DRB insisted that "the scientists...were extremely careful to limit the research techniques so that there was no possibility of damage to the subjects who volunteered."[45] Once again, there are grounds for a contrary view. An experiment that discovered the driver in CIA psychological torture may well have subjected students to this same torture—a complaint, in fact, made by four of Hebb's original volunteers. So extreme was this sensory deprivation that Hebb's subjects had unanticipated hallucinations akin to mescaline. In his 1992 epic poem, "Listening to the Candle," one of these student subjects, Professor Peter Dale Scott, described how he, not Hebb, first noticed the vivid hallucinations and, in a follow-up interview, recalled the researchers' initial incredulity at his report.[46]

> yet the very aimlessness
> preconditioning my mind...
> for blank lucrative hours
> of sensory deprivation
> as a paid volunteer
> in the McGill experiment...
> my ears sore from their earphones'
> amniotic hum my eyes
> under two bulging halves of pingpong balls
> *arms covered to the tips with cardboard tubes*
> those familiar hallucinations
> I was the first to report
> as for example the string
> of cut-out paper men
> emerging from a manhole
> in the side of a snow-white hill
> distinctly two-dimensional

Many of Hebb's subjects were McGill medical students. Through phone interviews, I have learned that, a few months after participating in the experiment, one subject, who had no prior history of such hysteria, suffered a complete breakdown, collapsing on the floor during lecture in a paroxysm of weeping so uncontrollable and protracted that the professor was forced to clear the classroom.[47] Although repeating the DRB's claim that Hebb had "the highest regard for the welfare of the volunteer students," Cooper's inquiry did note "an unconfirmed report that one student developed a form of mental illness following the experiment." But he dismissed the matter after hearing an unsubstantiated "suggestion... that the illness was incipient in any event, and would have resulted regardless of Dr. Hebb's experiments."[48]

By contrast, Hebb himself admitted that he did not screen his subjects for instability and was not prepared for the extreme hallucinations. "For subjects," he recalled in a memoir written before his death in 1985, "we simply called the employment office at McGill and hired the student they sent us. Presently we found that...the subjects, some of them, were seeing things in the experimental conditions, and feeling things. One felt his head was disconnected from his body, another had two bodies." Hebb was also shocked at the devastating impact of his experiments: "It scared the hell out of us to see how completely dependent the mind is on a close connection with the ordinary sensory environment, and how disorganizing to be cut off from that support."[49]

The implications of Hebb's experiment for both cognitive science and CIA interrogation were, in retrospect, profound. As Hebb himself later put it, "the experiment did give support for my theory of behavior" first propounded, without experimental confirmation, in his landmark 1949 book, *The Organization of Behaviour,* and got him "recognized abroad."[50] Within seven years of his team's first publications, over 230 articles on sensory deprivation appeared in leading scientific journals, citing Hebb's work and contributing to his rising reputation.[51] In June 1958, for example, ONR funded a symposium on sensory deprivation at Harvard Medical School, featuring Hebb and some of the leading cognitive scientists of his generation, that confirmed the significance of his discovery and further explored the devastating impact of sensory deprivation on the human mind.[52]

TESTING THE HEBB HYPOTHESIS

Significantly, several follow-up experiments inflicted similarly dangerous trauma on their human subjects. In 1955, one of Hebb's former students now at the National Institute of Mental Health, Dr. Maitland Baldwin, confined an Army volunteer inside a Hebbian sensory deprivation box. After 40 hours, the subject began "an hour of crying loudly and sobbing in a most heartrending fashion" before kicking his way out. At the prompting of Morse Allen, chief of the CIA's Artichoke Project, Dr. Baldwin agreed to push the experiment further into "terminal type" tests if the Agency would provide expendable human subjects—a proposal that a CIA medical officer rejected as "immoral and inhuman."[53]

Similarly, in 1957 a team of four Harvard University psychiatrists, funded by the ONR, confined 17 paid volunteers "in a tank-type respirator" arranged "to inhibit movement and tactile contact." After 17 hours, one subject, a 25-year-old dental student, "began to punch and shake the respirator," his "eyes full of tears, and his voice shaking." Four volunteers terminated from "anxiety and panic," and all suffered "degrees of anxiety."[54] We have no way of knowing whether such trauma did lasting damage, for none of these researchers—Hebb, Baldwin, or the Harvard psychiatrists—reported any follow-up treatment.

Just a few months later, an active CIA contractor, Dr. Lawrence Hinkle of Cornell University Medical Center, conducted a comprehensive review of "interrogation . . . for the purposes of intelligence," finding Hebb's isolation "the ideal way of 'breaking down' a prisoner, because . . . it seems to create precisely the state that the interrogator desires: malleability and the desire to talk, with the added advantage that one can delude himself that he is using no force or coercion."[55]

Finally, in 1963, the CIA synthesized this decade of mind-control research in its "Kubark Counter Intelligence Interrogation" manual that emphasized the important implications of Hebb's work for effective interrogation. Citing "experiments conducted at McGill University," this Agency report explained that sensory deprivation was effective because "the calculated provision of stimuli during interrogation tends to make the regressed subject view the interrogator as a father-figure...strengthening...the subject's tendencies toward compliance."[56]

PARADIGM'S CLANDESTINE JOURNEY

In its clandestine journey across continents and decades, the CIA's form of psychological torture would prove elusive, resilient, adaptable, powerfully seductive, and devastatingly destructive—attributes that have permitted it to persist to the present and may well allow it to continue into the future. To understand the character and the resilience of this distinctively American form of torture, we need to review each attribute in some detail.

Unlike its physical variant, psychological torture lacks clear signs of abuse and easily *eludes* detection, greatly complicating any investigation, prosecution, or attempt at prohibition. After British intelligence applied these CIA techniques on IRA suspects arrested at Belfast in 1971, an inquiry headed by Lord Parker of Waddington found that psychological methods complicated any determination of torture. "Where," Lord Parker asked in his report to Parliament, "does hardship and discomfort end and for instance humiliating treatment begin, and where does the latter end and torture begin?" The answer, he said, turns on "words of definition" and thus "opinions will inevitably differ."[57] Note Lord Parker's curiously precise and eerily prescient phrase—"words of definition."

When Dublin sued London over this issue in 1977, the European Court of Human Rights found Britain guilty of "inhuman and degrading treatment," but not torture. Alone among the 17 justices, Judge Demetrios Evrigenis of Greece understood that there are "new forms of suffering that have little in common with the physical pain caused by conventional torture," whose sum "must have caused...extremely intense physical, mental and psychological suffering, inevitably covered by the strictest definition of torture."[58]

Perpetrators and their protectors have a strong stake in maintaining the elusive quality of this psychological paradigm by muddying definitions of psychological torture or resisting them all together. For example, at the APA convention in August 2006, Lieutenant General Kevin Kiley, the U.S. Army's surgeon general, asked in an intimidating, almost mocking manner: "How loud does a scream have to be? How many angels can dance on the head of a pin?"[59] Indeed, definitions of terms such as "severe mental pain," "degrading," "cruel," and even "torture" have played a central role in both the protection and prosecution of perpetrators, making these terms a central focus in the political struggle over torture at home and abroad.

Psychological torture is shrouded in a scientific patina that appeals to policy markers and avoids the obvious physical brutality unpalatable to the American public, lending an extraordinary *resilience* to the practice. In the 40 years since its discovery, the Agency's psychological paradigm has, moreover, proved surprisingly *adaptable,* with each sustained application producing innovations. For both the perpetrators and the powerful who command them, torture has, I suspect, a darkly erotic appeal, lending a *seductive* quality to its practice. Even when torture is initially intended for a few Soviet spies or top al Qaeda commanders, it soon spreads in two directions—rapid proliferation to the torture of many, and an inexorable escalation in the scale of brutality. So seductive is torture's appeal that the powerful often concoct rationales to preserve their prerogative of torture, in defiance of all evidence of ineffectiveness in interrogation and the enormously high political costs.

Although seemingly less brutal than physical methods, the CIA's "no touch" torture has proved emotionally *destructive,* inflicting trauma that leaves searing psychological scars. Victims often need long treatment to recover from a trauma many experts, such as those at the Center for Torture Victims in Minneapolis, consider more crippling than physical pain. And, as noted above, Dr. Metin Basoglu's research has recently established, through convincing research, that these psychological techniques are just as traumatic as physical methods.

THE CIA AND CANADA

Controversy over McGill's mind-control experiments flared anew in the mid-1980s, when nine victims of Dr. Cameron's CIA-funded research at Allen Memorial Institute sued the Agency in Washington, DC, sparking important revelations. With annual CIA payments of $20,000 from 1957 to 1963, Dr. Cameron had used approximately a hundred patients, many admitted to his institute with moderate problems, as involuntary subjects to test a three-stage method for "brain washing" or "depatterning"—first, a drug-induced coma, spiked with LSD for up to 86 days; next, extreme electroshock treatment three times daily for 30 days; and, finally, a football helmet clamped to the head with a looped tape repeating, up to a half-million times, messages like "my mother hates me."[60]

Despite the horrific abuse, the Canadian establishment closed ranks behind Washington—with Cooper's report dismissing the Agency's role as a "side issue" or "red herring"; medical deans finding Cameron's research ethical by the standards of the day; Ottawa's Justice Department denying legal responsibility; the Canadian Psychiatric Association, unlike its American counterpart, refusing any apology; and Prime Minister Brian Mulroney's government offering each victim a nugatory $20,000 "nuisance" payment even though Ottawa had provided most of the funding ($495,000 versus the CIA's $64,000).[61] After years of denials from Ottawa and Langley, the ultimate defendants in the lawsuit, the CIA director and the former DRB chief Dr. Solandt, finally admitted the truth—admissions that, in conjunction with CIA documents extracted in the trial's discovery phase, cast considerable light on the dark side of Canada's Cold War relations with the CIA.

Throughout the litigation, Dr. Solandt spoke frankly about Ottawa's close cooperation with the CIA during his tenure as DRB's head from 1946 to 1957. "During the 1950's," Solandt stated in a sworn affidavit, "the United States Central Intelligence Agency had a resident representative at the United States Embassy in Ottawa who was publicly introduced as such...and was free to attend Defense Research Board...meetings where defence research programs were discussed."[62] In an interview with the *Toronto Star*, Solandt revealed his board's secret protocol with the CIA: "If they wanted classified research they came to the board and if we thought it was suitable we paid for it and then passed it on to the U.S. We never knowingly let the U.S. place a contract with any agency in Canada."[63] After similar communications with Solandt, Cooper reported that this protocol let Canadian researchers like Hebb work for the CIA or Pentagon without being paid by Washington. In lieu of direct payments, there was a "rough *quid pro quo* in that, when Canada requested the U.S. to do certain work in exchange, the work would be done south of the border." In defense of Ottawa's "open policy with the CIA," Dr. Solandt told the press that "we got five times the information from them that [*sic*] they received from us."[64]

Despite later denials by McGill colleagues that Dr. Hebb had any U.S. contacts, this litigation documented his close, continuing relationship with the CIA.[65] According to the plaintiff's attorney Joseph L. Rauh Jr., in pretrial discovery "the CIA formally admitted in court papers...its close ties with Dr. Hebb"— specifically, that Hebb received an Agency briefing in 1963 and was issued "a special CIA security clearance" on April 10, 1964—a decade after Canada had terminated its participation in the CIA mind-control project.[66]

Significantly, Ottawa's denials ended only when the Agency, after eight years of litigation, finally admitted its culpability. As Prime Minister Mulroney's conservative, pro-American government became "an active and hostile opponent" of this suit by its own citizens, Rauh, a Washington insider, noted with growing dismay that its nominally "independent study" was chaired by George Cooper, "a former M.P. who maintained close ties with the Tory machine." His staffers took key assessments "from the lips of the CIA's lawyers," and their 1986 report was "a complete whitewash."[67] Corroborating Rauh's critique, Cooper's report described Dr. Cameron as "a good man...trying to do the best he could for his patients" and even speculated that he "did not know of CIA involvement" in his funding.[68]

Ironically, Cooper's exculpation of the CIA was rendered risible just two years later when the Agency itself paid the Canadian victims $750,000, the maximum allowable under U.S. law. After evaluating the evidence, CIA director William Webster ordered the settlement, saying: "Sometimes you see the right thing to do, and you do it."[69] As for Dr. Cameron's treatment of his patients, the eminent psychiatrist Robert Lifton stated, in an affidavit for the plaintiffs, that his depatterning experiments had "deviated from standard and customary psychiatric therapies in use during the 1950s"; and instead "represent a mechanized extension of... 'brainwashing' methods."[70] As for Cooper's speculation about Cameron's ignorance of the Agency's role, other sources show that the McGill psychiatrist was a close personal friend of spymaster Allen Dulles from their days at the Nuremberg tribunal. Years later, when Dulles was CIA director, Cameron met with him in Washington to arrange the Agency's covert funding for his McGill experiments.[71] Indeed, this Nuremberg experience and his exposure to the Nazi medical experiments there might explain why Cameron later conducted his own research with a cruelty that none, including Cooper, can explain.[72]

Although acknowledging that Hebb was "a very fine scientist" and "Canada's foremost psychologist," the Cooper report still implied that his work had contributed to the dark art of interrogation: "By 'softening up' a prisoner through the use of sensory isolation techniques, a captor is indeed able to bring about a state of mind in which the prisoner is receptive to the implantation of ideas contrary to previously held beliefs."[73] For his discovery of the key principle in the CIA's new paradigm and his long collaboration with the Agency's research, it seems appropriate to regard Dr. Hebb today as the "progenitor of psychological torture."[74]

DR. MILGRAM'S OBEDIENCE EXPERIMENTS

As Lifton reminds us in his study of the Nazi doctors, we must explore these ethical compromises in the context of the response by a wider professional cohort to state pressures. Indeed, other leading scientists contributed to the CIA's evolving psychological paradigm—notably, Cornell neurologists Lawrence Hinkle and Harold Wolff, who, while working under a CIA contract to test "useful secret drugs (and various brain damaging procedures)," identified self-inflicted pain as the most effective Soviet interrogation technique—a second, key contribution to the Agency's emerging psychological paradigm.[75]

In retrospect, Stanley Milgram seems like an example of a junior researcher whose work was incorporated into this larger mind-control project. At key points in his career, Milgram benefited from patronage of behavioral scientists connected to the national security apparatus. After a review of his proposal for his obedience experiments by the head of Group Psychology at ONR, a key CIA conduit for covert funding, the National Science Foundation (NSF) gave Milgram a $24,700 grant—a substantial award when compared to Hebb's $40,000 over four years and Cameron's $64,000 over seven years. In later years, as the field shed the CIA's once pervasive influence, Milgram never received another NSF grant—even though he later proposed a project that made similar use of a mechanical device to test human behavior.[76]

Like others linked to this mind-control project, Milgram showed an apparent disregard for his subjects. After recruiting participants without serious screening by innocuous advertisements in the local newspaper, he then manipulated them, through deceptive instructions, to participate in apparent torture. With the exception of some exit interviews for the camera, he then dismissed his subjects without significant counseling, bearing the unsettling knowledge that they were, like the Gestapo, moral monsters who could inflict calibrated cruelty upon fellow humans. Indeed, one subject, a military veteran named William Menold, recalled feeling "an emotional wreck," a "basket case," from the realization "that somebody could get me to do that stuff." Privately, Milgram himself viewed the experiment as "ethically questionable" since "it is not nice to lure people into the laboratory and snare them into a situation that is stressful and unpleasant to them."[77] In this sense, Milgram clearly violated the first principle of the 1947 Nuremberg Code, requiring that subjects should "be able to exercise free power of choice, without...force, fraud, deceit."[78]

While Hebb was a great scientist whose work had lasting importance far beyond the CIA's agenda, Milgram was a technician whose single finding, that anyone can torture, was more appropriate for historical research. Milgram's research was driven, as a close colleague explained, "by deep personal concerns about how readily the Nazis had killed Jews during the Holocaust." But Milgram's torture experiments do not address this historical issue as directly or, arguably, as effectively as Christopher Browning did in his more relevant and revealing archival study, *Ordinary Men*—and did so, lest we forget, without inflicting trauma on anyone.[79] In this sense, Milgram failed to abide by article two of the Nuremberg Code: "The experiment should be such as to yield fruitful results for the good of society, unprocurable by other methods or means of study."[80]

Yet Milgram was a skilled publicist, filming the experiment for a documentary whose allure soon expunged the ethical reservations of his contemporaries. Whatever his motivations, which may have been admirable, Milgram also provided the intelligence community, in this Cold War context, with useful information as it began global propagation of its new psychological torture paradigm—i.e., anyone could be trained to torture.[81] In retrospect, Milgram's work might be best studied as another Faustian quest for knowledge and power that led, during a dark decade in the history of behavioral science, to ethical compromises in the treatment of human subjects.

THE NAZI DOCTOR'S APPRENTICE: HENRY BEECHER OF HARVARD

In September 1951, just three months after the CIA's secret Montreal meeting, Dr. Henry K. Beecher, the Dorr Professor of Anesthesiology at Harvard University, crossed the Atlantic in a determined search for drugs that would pry open the human mind for interrogation. At home and abroad for over a decade, Beecher pursued this secret military research, testing powerful psychotropic drugs, mescaline and LSD, on unwitting human subjects, and thus drinking deep from Dachau's poisoned well.

Our earliest indication of Beecher's interest in interrogation is a letter, dated February 7, 1947, from Dr. Arthur R. Turner, chief of the U.S. Army's Medical Intelligence Branch, reading: "Inclosed for your retention is a brochure, dealing with the Dachau Concentration Camp, which has just arrived. I...thought it might be of interest to you." This brochure, by the German aviation medical research unit, detailed thirty mescaline experiments on Dachau inmates by SS-Hauptsturmfuhrer Dr. Kurt Ploetner aimed "to eliminate the will of the person examined...by the Gestapo." In enticing words that promised to unlock the mind for interrogation, the report concluded: "If the Messkalin had an effect on the mental state of the P.E.'s, the examining person succeeded in every case in drawing even the most intimate secrets from the P.E. when the questions were cleverly put."[82]

In an apparent effort to encourage Beecher's research in this area, the U.S. Army's surgeon general sent him other reports on the Mauthausen Concentration Camp and LSD research at the Swiss Sandoz Company.[83] To assist the Army's Medical Research Board in its search for drugs that might serve as "truth sera" in interrogation, Beecher reported in June 1950 that he had consulted colleagues about the "considerable problem here in the use of healthy young volunteers" to test "synthetic agents in the mescaline group." Soon, though, he found that at Massachusetts General Hospital, "we have an almost ideal set-up here in Boston for study of this problem."[84]

Though we cannot be certain that SS-Hauptsturmfuhrer Ploetner's report inspired his quest, in September 1951, Dr. Beecher set off on a scientific odyssey, criss-crossing Europe to search for research "on the subject of the 'ego-depressant' drugs, usually called truth serum in the newspapers," paying particular attention to the Gestapo's drug of choice, mescaline. As he explained to the U.S. Army surgeon general, this search was an extension of their "orderly examination of the merits of various drugs" for use "as part of a broad attack on the central nervous system"—offensively "on prisoners (civil and military)," and defensively "to know if by the use of such agents a man of integrity and discretion can be altered without his knowledge."[85] In other words, Beecher was pursuing the very same offensive uses of mind control that the CIA had discussed at its June 1951 Montreal meeting.

Reflecting the Anglo-American cooperation forged at Montreal, Dr. Beecher had access to dozens of top scientists in his first stop, England. At the Ministry of Defense, Dr. B.A.R. Gater gave him a "bibliography on several drugs considered as promising," with eight citations for mescaline and 14 for LSD. In Stratford-upon-Avon, Sir Frederick Bartlett, professor of experimental psychology at Cambridge, agreed "that data are probably more readily obtainable with drugs than without and hence of special value if many men are to be interrogated." By stages, however, Dr. Beecher's hunt for appropriate collaborators led him full circle back to the Nazi war criminals he had encountered in reading Dr. Ploetner's report on Gestapo drug tests at Dachau.[86]

Moving on to the Allied Headquarters (SHAPE) at Marley-le Roi, Beecher learned, in discussions with U.S. officers, he could best expand his secret drug research by going beyond the medical corps to military intelligence, since "the Central Intelligence Agency has representatives...on the Joint Intelligence Committee."[87] Indeed, at Heidelberg, Dr. Beecher was sharply reminded of the immorality of his research, from a medical perspective, when the Chief U.S. Surgeon for Europe, General Guy B. Denit, advised him "that as a physician under the Geneva Convention he [Denit] could have nothing officially to do with the use of drugs for the purposes in mind and turned me over to G-II." Consequently, U.S. Army G-II, or Military Intelligence, transferred Dr. Beecher from the moral realm of military medicine to "Oberursel, to the European Command Interrogation Center," the dark center of the Allied interrogation effort.[88]

Outside Frankfurt, site of the CIA's German headquarters, the rolling Taunus Hills concealed two of the most secret U.S. intelligence facilities. Once site of the Luftwaffe's famed "Durchgangslage Luft" interrogation center, Oberursel had become Camp King, the home of the European Command Interrogation Center where, after 1948, a staff of ex-Gestapo soldiers and former Nazi doctors, including the notorious deputy Reich health leader Kurt Blome, were employed in inhumane interrogations of Soviet defectors and double agents. Nearby, in the town of Kronberg, the CIA used Haus Waldhof, a former country estate, as a safe house for drug testing, brutal torture, and lethal experiments on Soviet bloc expendables. In 1952, for example, the head the CIA's Project Artichoke, Morse Allen—assisted by Dr. Samuel V. Thompson, a Navy psychiatrist, and Professor G. Richard Wendt, a University of Rochester psychologist—would use the site to test dangerous combinations of drugs such as Benzedrin and Pentothal-Natrium on Russian captives, under the protocol that "disposal of the body is not a problem."[89]

At Oberursel, Dr. Beecher discussed possible drug uses for interrogation with six staffers including a Major Hart, head of a "brutal interrogation team" known as the "rough boys," and Captain Malcolm Hilty, chief interrogator. All agreed: "It would be desirable for me to return, perhaps in a year, when we know better the signs and symptoms of the newer derivatives of mescaline and lysergic acid [LSD], to interrogate especially high level escapees from Russian interrogation." In the interim, they recommended he work with a Dr. Schreiber, Camp King's former staff doctor, whom Beecher described as "a physician and former German general who is now on his way to the States, will be at the School of Aviation Medicine...Schreiber is intelligent and helpful."[90]

Who was Dr. Schreiber, this "intelligent and helpful" partner for Professor Beecher's secret drug research? He was, in fact, General Walter Schreiber, former medical chief for the Wehrmacht command who had presided over Nazi "concentration camp...experiments on inmates that usually resulted in a slow and agonizing death." After Camp King commended his "high efficiency," the Pentagon sent him to Texas, where he joined other Nazi doctors at the School of Aviation Medicine, albeit only until May 1952, when complaints about his war crimes forced a sudden departure for Argentina.[91]

Moving on to Berlin, Dr. Beecher met with a military intelligence officer and "Mr. Peter Sichel, C.I.A." to discuss acquisition of human subjects for his plans "to interrogate as many high-level escapees as possible as to the presence of significant signs and symptoms [of drugs] during periods of interrogation." All agreed that "the best sources of material for me are high level refugees and ranking political figures of the Eastern Zone who may defect." When Dr. Beecher's report on his voyage into this intelligence netherworld reached the Pentagon in October 1951, it was, at his recommendation, stamped "TOP SECRET" and not declassified until 1977, only months after his death.[92]

A year later in August 1952, Dr. Beecher, discarding Dr. Ploetner's preference for mescaline, returned to Europe where he now focused solely, almost obsessively, on the threat and promise of LSD 25. In the year between his visits, Beecher had joined the U.S. intelligence community's interrogation project with a "top secret" security clearance and a Pentagon grant to study the "Response of Normal Men to Lysergic Acid Derivatives."[93] Just as Dr. Ploetner's results had once heralded the promise of mescaline, so the Sandoz Company's report, provided earlier by the Pentagon, hinted this new drug might open the human mind for interrogation: "LSD 25 can bring thoughts from the subconscious into the conscious, can increase associative activity and, by removing inhibitions, can also improve the ekphoric ability." But Sandoz had also warned that the new drug produced "a peculiar personality disturbance similar to 'split personality,'" and induced a "tendency to pathological reactions (hysterical attacks, trances, epileptic fits)."[94] Evidently intrigued, Beecher wrote its chief pharmacologist in Basel, Dr. Ernst Rothlin, to arrange a meeting, explaining that "we have been doing some work in man with...LSD 25, which was kindly furnished us by your company."[95]

Consequently, Dr. Beecher returned from his second European sojourn warning about LSD's effect of "severe imbalance, hysteria" on, say, "a battleship's crew." In a secret report to the U.S. Army's surgeon general, he advised that this drug should be studied "(1) as aids to obtain suppressed information...(2) as threats to security when used by an enemy agent...(3) as tools of biological warfare." Above all, he urged the research into the use "of these agents as offensive weapons" since "the water supply of a large city could probably be disastrously and undetectably (until too late) contaminated." Determined that "the United

States...not get behind in this field for want of an organized plan of attack," he now planned to intensify dosages in his Boston LSD experiments, saying: "We need to know the effects of larger doses, of prolonged administration of small doses and so on." Fortunately for Beecher's plans, a professor he had met in Europe "has promised to send me for study the new L.A.E. (a mono ethyl amide of lysergic acid). This is said to be more excitant to normal individuals than is L.S.D. 25."[96]

Over the next two years, Dr. Beecher carried out these LSD tests using the unwitting human subjects he now believed, through his conventional work, essential to serious pharmacological research—creating, for Beecher, a productive confluence of his covert and conventional work.[97] In his final report on these tests to the Pentagon, Beecher noted that after administering LSD doses "as unknowns" four among the nine subjects given the stronger LAE variant became "mildly hostile and paranoid; another experienced acute panic."[98]

In his decade of secret drug testing, Dr. Beecher thus sacrificed his subjects to the cause of national security. During his European travels in 1951–52, he had sought expendable subjects for secret interrogation experiments. Back home at Harvard, Beecher, though aware of the drug's painful effects from the Sandoz report, tested powerful LSD and LAE doses that inflicted the trauma of "paranoid" reaction and "acute panic" on his unknowing human subjects—a "psychosis in miniature" that, he said coolly in his published report, "offers interesting possibilities." In sum, knowing in advance the serious trauma these drugs would cause, Beecher placed his unwitting subjects at risk by giving them dangerous doses dictated by the demands of secret research—all in violation of the Nuremberg Code. Yet he also maintained a perfect cover, minimizing public knowledge of his military research by publishing only one LSD study as third author—and even that was packaged innocuously as last in a series of drug tests. Throughout these years of secret drug research on unwitting human subjects, he sat on influential biomedical bodies, such as the National Research Council, setting the U.S. research agenda.[99]

During the period of his classified drug research, which clearly violated the principles of the Nuremberg Code, Dr. Beecher was, not surprisingly, vocal in his opposition to the federal government's attempt to impose the Code's ethical restraints on clinical researchers. In a 1959 article for the *Journal of the American Medical Association*, Beecher conducted an extended critique of the Nuremberg Code, arguing that a "rigid interpretation" of its first rule for "the voluntary consent of the human subject" would "effectively cripple, if not eliminate, most research in the field of mental disease" and bar the use of placebos which he called, not surprisingly given his own prominence in this area, "essential to progress in which judgment is involved in decision." Beecher was equally critical of Nuremberg's second rule requiring that experiments be "not random and unnecessary in nature," and dismissed it with the flat assertion that "most of the epoch-making discoveries in science have been unexpected." Effectively dismissing the importance of the Nuremberg Code, he concluded that "the problems of human experimentation do not lend themselves to a series of rigid rules."[100]

Two years later, Dr. Beecher applied these criticisms, forcefully and effectively, when the U.S. Army's surgeon general tried to impose its version of the Nuremberg Code on new university research contracts. On behalf of Harvard Medical School, Beecher drafted new clauses that set aside the "rigid rules" he so disdained in favor of loose guidelines to be interpreted by the "virtuous investigator." In July 1962, a university delegation won Pentagon approval for this less restrictive approach.[101]

MODERN MEDICAL ETHICS

This past, particularly its more public chapter, has some important lessons for the present debate over ethical standards within the APA. By the early 1960s, as the CIA's secret drug research wound down and his lucrative defense contracts thus dwindled, Beecher seems to have been freed from conflicts that may have heretofore prevented his moral regeneration.[102] Suddenly, he put aside his nuanced opposition to federal restraints on clinical research and became an impassioned advocate of ethical standards. In 1965, Beecher first voiced his new concerns in a lecture to journalists titled "Ethics and the Explosion of Human Experimentation," which contained his only hint of mea culpa. "Lest I seem to stand aside from these matters," he said without providing any details, "I am obliged to say that in years gone by work in my laboratory could have been criticized."[103]

A year later, Beecher published his famous essay, "Ethics and Clinical Research" in the *New England Journal of Medicine,* citing 22 instances of medical research whose human subjects "never had the risk satisfactorily explained to them" and thus suffered "grave consequences...as a direct result of experiments." After reviewing these cases in which clinical researchers had sacrificed their subjects to advance science, Beecher concluded that the "ethical approach to experimentation" had two clear components: first, a genuine effort to obtain fully "informed consent" for "moral, sociologic and legal reasons"; and second, "the presence of an intelligent, informed, conscientious, compassionate, responsible investigator." He warned that these unethical practices "will do great harm to medicine unless soon corrected," and questioned whether "data obtained unethically should be published even with stern editorial comment."[104]

With his reputation as an ethical paragon growing, Dr. Beecher did not elaborate further on his opaque mea culpa and began voicing a stern moral opposition to counterculture LSD experimentation that seems, in light of his earlier classified drug research, stunningly hypocritical. When controversy erupted over utopian LSD experimentation at Harvard in the late 1960s, Dr. Beecher played the moralist, roundly condemning one of Timothy Leary's colleagues, Dr. Walter N. Pahnke, for using the drug to ease the pain of dying. "There is an abundance of evidence," intoned Dr. Beecher, condemning such experiments, "that LSD can produce, has produced, lasting, serious damage to young people."[105]

Initially controversial, Dr. Beecher's 1966 article soon made his name synonymous with "informed consent" and ethical treatment of human subjects—a legacy commemorated today with the annual award of the Henry K. Beecher Prize in Medical Ethics at Harvard Medical School.[106] The award's 1993 recipient, Yale bioethics professor Jay Katz, praised Beecher for "the moral passion that punctuated his every word" in that 1966 essay.[107] Typical of this laudatory treatment, a 2001 article in the *Bulletin of the World Health Organization* describes how Beecher drew upon his "deep Christian faith" to produce "the most influential single paper ever written about experimentation involving human subjects" and thereby "played a significant role" in enacting strict federal regulations that precluded future abuse of human subjects.[108]

Apart from Beecher's own oblique references to his lab's ethical lapses, the literature seems ignorant of his darker side. Even aggressive exposés of government abuses have hailed him a "hero" of medical ethics, while investigations of the CIA's scandalous drug experiments make but cursory references to his early LSD research.[109] Today, every academic researcher in America and Canada lives under Dr. Beecher's long shadow, forced to submit all research to institutional review boards that would certainly ban the experiments once done by Hebb, Cameron, Milgram, and, ironically, Beecher himself.

So, what lesson might we draw from the career of Dr. Henry K. Beecher, other than the importance of dying before your secret reports are declassified? If members of the APA feel tainted by the work of colleagues at Guantánamo and their association's inaction, then Dr. Beecher provides a clear path to ethical reform. Just as he transformed himself from Dachau disciple and CIA drug researcher into moral paragon by embracing ethical standards, so the APA can expunge the stigma of its association with psychological torture. By using its professional standing to endorse ethical standards for its members and, more broadly, to restrain future abuse by defining "severe mental pain" and "psychological torture" in, for example, a future edition of the authoritative *DSM-IV* (*Diagnostic and Statistical Manual of Mental Disorders*), the APA can readily recover its moral leadership.

More broadly, biographers and historians alike should be cautious, in light of this troubled past, before rushing to canonize cognitive scientists who worked during the Cold War. If we do not investigate this past and the ways that it has shaped our present, then we cannot critique and correct. Clearly, history is too important to become mere hagiography.

NOTES

1. Arthur Levine, "Collective Unconscionable," *Washington Monthly,* January–February 2007, http://www.washingtonmonthly.com/features/2007/0701.levine.html (accessed May 28, 2007).

2. David Glenn, "A Policy on Torture Roils Psychologists Annual Meeting," *Chronicle of Higher Education,* September 7, 2007, A14–17; "Red Cross Finds Detainee Abuse in Guantanamo," *New York Times,* November 30, 2004, 1; "Report Warned C.I.A. on Tactics in Interrogation," *New York Times,* November 9, 2005, 1.

3. Robert Jay Lifton, *The Nazi Doctors: Medical Killing and the Psychology of Genocide* (New York: Basic Books, 1986), 418–19.

4. Lifton, *The Nazi Doctors,* xii; M. Gregg Bloche and Jonathan H. Marks, "Doctors and Interrogators at Guantanamo Bay," *New England Journal of Medicine* 353, no. 1 (July 7, 2005), http://www.nejm.org (accessed October 23, 2007).

5. Metin Basoglu, Maria Livanou, and Cvetana Crnobaric, "Torture vs Other Cruel, Inhuman, and Degrading Treatment: Is the Distinction Real or Apparent?" *Archives of General Psychiatry* 64, no. 3 (2007): 277–85.

6. David M. Oshinsky, *Polio: An American Story* (New York: Oxford University Press, 2005), 4–7, 174–87; Ross A. Slotten, *The Heretic in Darwin's Court: The Life of Alfred Russel Wallace* (New York: Columbia University Press, 2004), 1–9; Michael Shotland and Richard Yeo, "Introduction," in *Telling Lives In Science: Essays on Scientific Biography* (Cambridge: Cambridge University Press, 1996), 1–44; Thomas Söderqvist, "Existential Projects and Existential Choice in Science: Science Biography as an Edifying Genre," in *Telling Lives In Science: Essays on Scientific Biography,* 46; Hal Hellman, *Great Feuds in Science: Ten of the Liveliest Disputes Ever* (New York: John Wiley & Sons, 1998), xii–xv; Grove Wilson, *Great Men of Science: Their Lives and Discoveries* (New York: The New Home Library, 1929).

7. R.E. Brown and P.M. Milner, "The Legacy of Donald O. Hebb: more than the Hebb Synapse," *Nature Reviews/Neuroscience* 4 (2003): 1013–19.

8. C.E.W., "Henry K. Beecher, M.D.," *New England Journal of Medicine* 295, no. 13 (September 23, 1976): 730; Vincent J. Kopp, MD, "Henry K. Beecher, M.D.: Contrarian (1904–1976)," *ASA Newsletter* 63, no. 9 (September 1999), http://www.asahq.org/Newsletters/l999/09_99/beecher0999.html (accessed June 5, 2007); Nicholas M. Greene, MD, "Henry Knowles Beecher, 1904–1976," *Anesthesiology* 45, no. 4 (October 1976): 377–78.

9. Christopher Simpson, *Science of Coercion: Communication Research & Psychological Warfare 1945–1960* (New York: Oxford University Press, 1994), 9.

10. Central Intelligence Agency, Project NM 001 056.0, May 1, 1952, File: Naval Research, Box 8, CIA Behavior Control Experiments Collection (John Marks Donation), National Security Archive, Washington, DC; H.E. Page, "The Role of Psychology in ONR," *American Psychologist* 9, no. 10 (1954): 621–22.

11. Simpson, *Science of Coercion,* 4, 25–30, 127–32.

12. Lifton, *The Nazi Doctors,* 4, 16–17, 34–35, 37–39, 42–44, 269–78, 418–29.

13. Tom Bower, *The Paperclip Conspiracy: The Hunt for Nazi Scientists* (Boston: Little, Brown and Company, 1987), 3, 214–32; Philippine Coste, "Cette prison ou

l'Amérique recyclait des savants Nazis," *L'Express,* no. 2898 (January 18, 2007), 60–65.

14. Linda Hunt, *Secret Agenda: The United States Government, Nazi Scientists, and Project Paperclip, 1945 to 1990* (New York: St. Martin's Press, 1991), 89–93, 287.

15. Telford Taylor, "Opening Statement for the Prosecution December 9, 1946," in *The Nazi Doctors and the Nuremberg Code: Human Rights in Human Experimentation,* ed. George J. Annas and Michael A. Grodin (New York: Oxford University Press, 1992), 71–75, 77–78; Sharon Perley et al., "The Nuremberg Code: An International Overview," in *The Nazi Doctors and the Nuremberg Code,* 149–68.

16. John Marks, *The Search for the "Manchurian Candidate": The CIA and Mind Control* (New York: Times Books, 1979), 9–11.

17. Jonathan D. Moreno, *Undue Risk: Secret State Experiments on Humans* (New York: W. H. Freeman, 2000), 119–55, 189–297; Andrew Goliszek, *In the Name of Science: A History of Secret Programs, Medical Research, and Human Experimentation* (New York: St. Martin's Press, 2003), 117–80; Eileen Welsome, *The Plutonium Files: America's Secret Medical Experiments in the Cold War* (New York: Delta, 1999), 189–236, 255–382; BBC Radio 4, "Hidden history of US germ testing," http://news.bbc.co.uk/2/hi/programmes/file_on_4/4701196.stm (accessed June 4, 2007).

18. Ulf Schmidt, *Justice at Nuremberg: Leo Alexander and the Nazi Doctors' Trial* (New York: Palgrave Macmillan, 2004), 275–81; Moreno, *Undue Risk,* 250–51, 258–59; Hunt, *Secret Agenda,* 166–67, 172–73.

19. *New York Times,* August 2, 1977, 1.

20. "Les victimes canadiennes d'un programme de la CIA veulent poursuivre Ottawa," *Le Devoir,* January 8, 2007, http://www.ledevoir.com/2007/01/08/126752.html (accessed June 3, 2007); Canadian Press, "Montreal woman tries to launch suit over brainwashing," January 10, 2007, http://www.cbc.ca/canada/montreal/story/2007/01/10/qc-cia20070110.html (accessed June 3, 2007).

21. "Private Institutions Used in C.I.A. Effort to Control Behavior," *New York Times,* August 2, 1977, 1.

22. Central Intelligence Agency, Subject: Special Interrogation Program, March 19, 1951, CIA Behavior Control Experiments Collection (John Marks Donation), National Security Archive, Washington, DC (Copy provided by Egmont Koch, producer, ARD-TV).

23. *Opinion of George Cooper, Q.C., Regarding Canadian Government Funding of the Allan Memorial Institute in the 1950's and 1960's* (Ottawa: Minister of Supply and Services Canada, Cat. No. J2–63,1986), 32–33; Meeting at Ritz Carleton Hotel, June 1, 1951; Handwritten Note titled "PA 2–1–[illegible]–38, Appendix 21.

24. David Zimmerman, *Top Secret Exchange: The Tizard Mission and the Scientific War* (Montreal: McGill-Queen's University Press, 1996), 3–5, 7, 19–20, 29, 49–50, 96–129, 147–48, 154–66, 190–204; Ronald W. Clark, *Tizard* (London: Methuen, 1965), 386–402; R.V. Jones, "Tizard's Task in the 'War Years' 1935–1952," *Biographical Memoirs of the Fellows of the Royal Society,* vol. 7 (London: The Royal Society, 1961), 338–41.

25. Maxine F. Singer, "Foreward," in, James D. Ebert, ed., *This Our Golden Age: Selected Annual Essays of Caryl P. Haskins, President, Carnegie Institution of Washington 1956–1971* (Washington, DC: Carnegie Institution of Washington, 1996), ix–x.

26. *Opinion of George Cooper, Q.C.,* Meeting at Ritz Carleton Hotel, June 1, 1951, Appendix 21.

27. Ibid.

28. *Opinion of George Cooper, Q.C.,* 31–32; Marks, *Search for the "Manchurian Candidate,"* 29–31. Central Intelligence Agency, Minutes of Meeting, June 6, 1951, File: Artichoke Docs. 59–155, Box 5; Central Intelligence Agency, Memorandum For: Assistant Director, SI, Subject: Progress on BLUEBIRD, July 9, 1951, File: Artichoke Docs. 59–155, Box 5, CIA Behavior Control Experiments Collection (John Marks Donation), National Security Archive, Washington, DC.

29. Central Intelligence Agency, Proposed Study on Special Interrogation Methods, February 14, 1952, CIA Behavior Control Experiments Collection (John Marks Donation), National Security Archive, Washington, DC.

30. *New York Times,* August 2, 1977, 1

31. Harvey M. Weinstein, *Psychiatry and the CIA: Victims of Mind Control* (Washington, DC: American Psychiatric Press, 1990), 274; James Meek, "Nobody Is Talking," *The Guardian,* February 18, 2005; Marks, *Search for the "Manchurian Candidate,"* 32–33; Ignatieff, "What Did the C.I.A. Do to His Father?" 60.

32. *Opinion of George Cooper, Q.C.,* D.O. Hebb, W. Heron, and W.H. Bexton, "Annual Report, Contract DRB-X38, Experimental Studies of Attitude," 1952, Appendix 22.

33. *Opinion of George Cooper, Q.C.,* letter from Dr. D.O. Hebb to N.W. Morton, December 15, 1952, Appendix 23.

34. *Opinion of George Cooper, Q.C.,* letter from Dr. D.O. Hebb to N.W. Morton, November 2, 1953, Appendix 23; letter from Frederic Grunberg to George Cooper, QC, December 1985.

35. *Opinion of George Cooper, Q.C.,* "Proceedings of Fourth Symposium 1952 was distributed (Secret)," Memorandum from Ruth Hoyt, Human Resources Section, Defence Research Board, May 7, 1956, Appendix 22.

36. *Opinion of George Cooper, Q.C.,* letter from D.O. Hebb to N.W. Morton, January 11, 1954; letter from O.M. Solandt to the Minister, January 25, 1954, Appendix 23.

37. Arthur Blakely, "Life in a Cubicle I," *Gazette* (Montreal), April 25, 1956, 6; *Opinion of George Cooper, Q.C.,* letter from D.M. Watters to Dr. O.M. Solandt, July 26, 1954, Appendix 23; Memorandum To: OMS 17/9, Answer: OMS 17/19, Appendix 23.

38. *Opinion of George Cooper, Q.C.,* letter from Dr. O.M. Solandt to D.M. Watters, August 3, 1954, Appendix 24.

39. Central Intelligence Agency, Office Memorandum, To: Chief, Technical Branch, From: [Blacked out], Subject: National Meetings of the American Psychological Association, September 30, 1954; Fillmore N. Sanford, "Summary Report of the 1954 Annual Meeting," *American Psychologist* 9, no. 11 (1954): 708. At this same APA meeting, the presidential address for the "Division of Experimental Psychology," on September 6, was by D.O. Hebb ("Drives and the C.N.S. [Central Nervous System]"). See American Psychological Association, "Program of the Sixty-Second Annual Meeting of the American Psychological Association," 295, 500, 501. This presidential address, evidently somewhat revised, was published a year later as, D.O Hebb, "Drives and the C.N.S. (Conceptual Nervous System)," *Psychological Review* 62, no. 4 (1955): 243–54.

40. Letter from Peter N. Milner to the Editor, *McGill Tribune,* November 10, 1992 (copy provided by Mary Ellen Hebb).

41. "Tank Test Linked to Brainwashing," *New York Times,* April 15, 1956, 18; Brian Cahill, "'Isolation' Tests at McGill Hold Brain-Washing Clues," *Gazette* (Montreal), April 17, 1956; "'Brainwashing' Defence Found," *Gazette* (Montreal), April 26, 1956, 1.

42. "Psychiatrist Aids 'Germ' Confessor," *New York Times,* March 10, 1954, 3; "Eisenhower Gives Views on Schwable," *New York Times,* March 11, 1954, 15. Edgar H. Schein, "Patterns of Reactions to Severe Chronic Stress in American Army Prisoners of War of the Chinese," 253–69, and Louis J. West, "United States Air Force Prisoners of the Chinese Communists," 270–84, in *Symposium No. 4. Methods of Forceful Indoctrination: Observations and Interviews* (New York: Group of the Advancement of Psychiatry, 1957). Indicating the rise in defensive research in 1955–56, well after Hebb's DRB contract was over, a bibliography of 16 contemporary publications on the Korean brainwashing in West's essay lists two with no dates, two for 1954, three for 1955, and nine for 1956. (See, West, "United States Air Force Prisoners of the Chinese Communists," 270–71.)

43. Joseph Marguilies, *Guantanamo and the Abuse of Presidential Power* (New York: Simon & Schuster, 2006), 120–25; "Officers to Study Brainwash Issue," *New York Times,* August 23, 1954, 5; "Red Tactics Spur Code for P.O.W.s," *New York Times,* August 14, 1955, 1; "New Code Orders P.O.W.'s to Resist Brainwashing," *New York Times,* August 18, 1955, 1.

44. "Training Is Ordered on New P.O.W. Code," *New York Times,* August 20, 1955, 21; "'Brainwash' Course Backed by Marines," *New York Times,* September 15, 1955, 17; "U.S. Orders Review of 'Torture School,'" *New York Times,* September 17, 1955, 9; "The Air Force Suspends Its 'Brainwash' Course," *New York Times,* December 14, 1955, 42.

45. *Opinion of George Cooper, Q.C.,* statement by Dr. G.S. Field, Acting Chairman of the Defence Research Board, n.d., Appendix 23.

46. Peter Dale Scott, *Listening to the Candle: A Poem on Impulse* (Toronto: McClelland & Stewart, 1992), 6–7; Peter Dale Scott, personal communication, Melbourne, Australia, August 10, 2006.

47. Personal communications, retired medical doctors and McGill medical school graduates, March 13, 2006, September 30, 2007, October 1, 2007.

48. *Opinion of George Cooper, Q.C.,* 35–36.

49. D.O. Hebb, "This Is How It Was," Canadian Psychological Association, ca. 1980 (copy provided by Mary Ellen Hebb).

50. D.O. Hebb, *The Organization of Behavior: A Neuropsychological Theory* (New York: John Wiley & Sons, 1949); Hebb, "This Is How It Was."

51. Philip Solomon et al., eds., *Sensory Deprivation: A Symposium Held at Harvard Medical School* (Cambridge, MA: Harvard University Press, 1961), 239–57; Stephen E. Glickman, "Hebb, Donald Olding," in *Encyclopedia of Psychology,* ed. Alan E. Kazdin (New York: Oxford University Press, 2000), 105–6; D.O. Hebb, *Essay on Mind* (Hillsdale, NJ: Lawrence Erlbaum Associates, 1980), 96–97.

52. Woodburn Heron and D.O. Hebb, "Cognitive and Physiological Effect of Perceptual Isolation," in *Sensory Deprivation: A Symposium Held at Harvard Medical*

School, ed. Philip Solomon et al. (Cambridge, MA: Harvard University Press, 1961), v–xvi, 1–2, 6–33, 239–57; Solomon, *Sensory Deprivation,* v–xvi, 1–2, 239–57.

53. Marks, *Search for the "Manchurian Candidate,"* 23–25, 32–33, 106, 137–38, 201–2; Richard E. Brown, "Alfred McCoy, Hebb, the CIA and Torture," *Journal of the History of the Behavioral Sciences* 43, no. 2 (2007): 209.

54. Donald Wexler, Jack Mendelson, Herbert Leiderman, and Philip Solomon, "Sensory Deprivation: A Technique for Studying Psychiatric Aspects of Stress," *A.M.A. Archives of Neurology and Psychiatry* 79, no. 1 (1958): 225–33.

55. Lawrence E. Hinkle Jr., "A Consideration of the Circumstances under Which Men May Be Interrogated, and the Effects That These May Have upon the Function of the Brain" (n.d., ca. 1958), 1, 5, 6, 11–14, 18, File: Hinkle, Box 7, CIA Behavior Control Experiments Collection (John Marks Donation), National Security Archive, Washington, DC.

56. "KUBARK Counterintelligence Interrogation" (July 1963), File: Kubark, Box 1: CIA Training Manuals, National Security Archive, Washington, DC, 87–90.

57. *Times* (London), March 3, 1972; Lord Parker of Waddington, *Report of the Committee of Privy Counsellors Appointed to Consider Authorised Procedures for the Interrogation of Persons Suspected of Terrorism* (London: Stationery Office, Cmnd. 4901, 1972), Majority Report, 2, 4–5, 16–17.

58. "Ireland v. The United Kingdom," No. 5310/17, European Court of Human Rights, January 18, 1978, Separate Opinion of Judge Evrigenis, http://www.worldlii.org/eu/cases/ECHR/1978/1.html (accessed June 6, 2004).

59. Levine, "Collective Unconscionable."

60. Elizabeth Nickson, "My Mother, the CIA and LSD," *Observer* (London), October 16, 1994, 48–52; Weinstein, *Psychiatry and the CIA,* 110–20, 140–41; Gordon Thomas, *Journey Into Madness: Medical Torture and the Mind Controllers* (London: Bantam Press, 1988), 114, 166–70, 176–77; Marks, *Search for the "Manchurian Candidate,"* 132–41; D. Ewan Cameron et al., "The Depatterning Treatment of Schizophrenia," *Comprehensive Psychiatry* 3, no. 3 (1962): 65–76.

61. *Opinion of George Cooper, Q.C.,* 2–5, 41–44, 85–86, 96, 103–112, 117–22, 125–27; David Vienneau, "Ottawa Knew of Brain-washing: Ex-civil Servant," *Toronto Star,* April 16, 1986, A2; Joseph L. Rauh, Jr. and James C. Turner, "Anatomy of a Public Interest Case Against the CIA," *Hamline Journal of Public Law and Policy* 11, no. 2 (1990): 316, 325–30, 352–54; Weinstein, *Psychiatry and the CIA,* 278–81.

62. Rauh and Turner, "Anatomy of a Public Interest Case Against the CIA," 335.

63. David Vienneau, "No Secrets Hidden from CIA, Former Official Says," *Toronto Star,* April 14, 1986, A10.

64. *Opinion of George Cooper, Q.C.,* 97–99; David Vienneau, "No Secrets Hidden from CIA, Former Official Says," *Toronto Star,* April 14, 1986, A10.

65. David Vienneau, "Colleague Says McGill Doctor Probably Unaware of CIA Role," *Toronto Star,* April 17, 1986, A8; letter from Peter N. Milner to the Editor, *McGill Tribune,* November 10, 1992 (copy provided by Mary Ellen Hebb).

66. Rauh and Turner, "Anatomy of a Public Interest Case Against the CIA," 335 (footnote 33), 336–37; Vienneau, "Ottawa Knew of Brain-washing," A2.

67. Rauh and Turner, "Anatomy of a Public Interest Case Against the CIA," 307, 352–53.

68. *Opinion of George Cooper, Q.C.*, 70, 96, 104–12.

69. Rauh and Turner, "Anatomy of a Public Interest Case Against the CIA," 360–62.

70. Ibid., 333.

71. Weinstein, *Psychiatry and the CIA,* 92–95; Thomas, *Journey Into Madness,* 102–3, 152–63.

72. *Opinion of George Cooper, Q.C.*, 110–11.

73. *Opinion of George Cooper, Q.C.*, 35–36.

74. Alfred W. McCoy, *A Question of Torture, CIA Interrogation from the Cold War to the War on Terror* (New York: Metropolitan Books, 2006), 33.

75. Marks, *Search for the "Manchurian Candidate,"* 147–63; Weinstein, *Psychiatry and the CIA,* 133–35; Thomas, *Journey Into Madness,* 168; Lawrence E. Hinkle Jr. and Harold G. Wolff, "Communist Interrogation and Indoctrination of 'Enemies of the States': Analysis of Methods Used by the Communist State Police (A Special Report)," *Archives of Neurology and Psychiatry* 76 (1956): 116–17, 128–30, 134–35.

76. Thomas Blass, *The Man Who Shocked the World: The Life and Legacy of Stanley Milgram* (New York: Basic Books, 2004), 65–72, 235–42; Vienneau, "Ottawa Knew of Brain-washing," A2.

77. Stanley Milgram, *Obedience to Authority: An Experimental View* (New York: Harper & Row, 1974), 1–43; Blass, *The Man Who Shocked the World,* 76, 114–16; Stanley Milgram, "Group Pressure and Action Against a Person," *Journal of Abnormal and Social Psychology* 9, no. 2 (1964): 137–43.

78. "The Nuremberg Code," in Annas and Grodin, *The Nazi Doctors and the Nuremberg Code,* 2.

79. Philip Zimbardo, "When Good People Do Evil," *Yale Alumni Magazine* 70, no. 3 (January–February 2007): 42; Christopher R. Browning, *Ordinary Men: Reserve Police Battalion 101 and the Final Solution in Poland* (New York: HarperCollins, 1998), 159–89; Arthur G. Miller, *The Obedience Experiments: A Case Study of Controversy in Social Science* (New York: Praeger, 1986), 179–220.

80. "The Nuremberg Code," in Annas and Grodin, *The Nazi Doctors and the Nuremberg Code,* 2.

81. Stanley Milgram, "Group Pressure and Action Against a Person," *Journal of Abnormal and Social Psychology* 9, no. 2 (1964): 137–43.

82. In an interview with ARD-TV on March 3, 2007, the archivist at the Dachau KZ Memorial, Albert Knoll, "confirmed that the only papers from the medical experiments, which survived a burning action of the SS a couple of days before the U.S. Army freed the camp, had been seized, sent to the U.S. and analyzed by Beecher and his fellow experts." Hence, it is a facsimile of Dr. Beecher's copy of this Gestapo research report that today is on display at Dachau. (Emails from Egmont Koch, producer, ARD-TV, Hamburg, Germany, March 13, 2007, May 29, 2007.) Marks, *Search for the Manchurian Candidate,* 4–6; Technical Report no. 3331–45, "German aviation medical research at the Dachau concentration camp," October 1945, U.S. Naval Technical Mission to Europe, H MS c64, Box 11, f75, Harvard Medical Library; letter from Arthur M. Turner, MD, to Dr. Henry K. Beecher, February 7, 1947, Box 6, CIA Behavior

Control Experiments Collection (John Marks Donation), National Security Archive, Washington, DC.

83. Letter from Arthur M. Turner to Dr. Henry K. Beecher, March 24, 1947, Box 6, CIA Behavior Control Experiments Collection (John Marks Donation), National Security Archive, Washington, DC; letter from Henry K. Beecher to Colonel William S. Stone, August 29, 1950, Box 6, CIA Behavior Control Experiments Collection (John Marks Donation), National Security Archive, Washington, DC.

84. Letter from Henry K. Beecher to Colonel William S. Stone, June 15, 1950, Box 6, CIA Behavior Control Experiments Collection (John Marks Donation), National Security Archive, Washington, DC.

85. Letter from Henry K. Beecher to the Surgeon General, Department of the Army, October 21, 1951, Box 16, RG 319, NARA (copy provided by Egmont Koch, producer, ARD-TV).

86. Beecher to the Surgeon General, October 21, 1951.

87. Ibid.

88. Ibid.

89. Arnold M. Silver, "Questions, Questions, Questions: Memories of Oberursel," *Intelligence and National Security* 8, no. 2 (1993): 199–213; Randy Pruitt, "Camp King: A Casern with a Past," *Stars and Stripes,* January 18, 1993, 18–19; Egmont R. Koch and Michael Wech, *Deckname Artischocke* (Munich: Random House, 2003), 50, 89–121, 269; Bower, *The Paperclip Conspiracy,* 254–56.

90. Beecher to the Surgeon General, October 21, 1951.

91. Bower, *The Paperclip Conspiracy,* 255–58; U.S. Army, "SCHREIBER, Dr. Walter P., December 15, 1949, in Koch and Wech, *Deckname Artischocke,* 94; "Nuremberg Trial To End This Week," *New York Times,* August 28, 1946, 4; "German General Flees East Zone," *New York Times,* October 27, 1948, 7; "Accused Physician Demands an Inquiry," *New York Times,* February 13, 1952, 24.

92. Beecher to the Surgeon General, October 21, 1951.

93. Letter from Major Arthur R. Lund to whom it may concern, May 26, 1951; Project Title: Neuropsychiatry and Stress, 31 December 1954, Box 6, CIA Behavior Control Experiments Collection (John Marks Donation), National Security Archive, Washington, DC.

94. From: Prof. Ernst Rothlin, Chief Pharmacologist, Sandoz Co., Basel, Switzerland, "d-Lysergic Acid Diethylamide (LSD 25)," n.d., Box 6, CIA Behavior Control Experiments Collection (John Marks Donation), National Security Archive, Washington, DC.

95. Letter from Henry K. Beecher to Dr. E. Rothlin, August 4, 1952; letter from Henry K. Beecher to Colonel William S. Stone, August 29, 1950, Box 6, CIA Behavior Control Experiments Collection (John Marks Donation), National Security Archive, Washington, DC.

96. From Henry K. Beecher, MD, Consultant, Subject: Information from Europe Related to the Ego-Depressants, 6 August to 29 August 1952, September 4, 1952, CIA Behavior Control Experiments Collection (John Marks Donation), National Security Archive, Washington, DC (Copy provided by Egmont Koch, producer, ARD-TV).

97. Henry K. Beecher, "Experimental Pharmacology and Measurement of the Subjective Response," *Science* 116, no. 3007 (August 15, 1952): 157–58; letter from Henry K. Beecher to *Science,* 117, no. 3033 (February 13, 1953): 166–67.

98. Project Title: Neuropsychiatry and Stress, Addendum. Beecher (MD 92). Final Report, Response of Normal Men to Lysergic Acid Derivatives (Di- and Monoethylamide). Correlation of Personality and Drug Reactions, December 31, 1954, Box 6, CIA Behavior Control Experiments Collection (John Marks Donation), National Security Archive, Washington, DC.

99. Henry K. Beecher, *Measurement of Subjective Responses: Quantitative Effects of Drugs* (New York: Oxford University Press, 1959), 287, 309–11; J.M. von Felsinger, L. Lasagna, and H.K. Beecher, "Drug-Induced Mood Changes in Man: 2. Personality and Reactions to Drugs," *Journal of the American Medical Association* 157, no. 13 (March 26, 1955): 1113–19; von Felsinger, Lasagna, and Beecher, "The Response of Normal Men to lysergic acid derivatives (di- and mono-ethyl amides)," *Journal of Clinical and Experimental Psychopathology and Quarterly Review of Psychiatry and Neurology* 17, no. 4 (1956): 414–28; letter from Henry K. Beecher to Colonel William S. Stone, May 31, 1950; letter from Henry K. Beecher to Chauncey D. Leake, June 13, 1955; letter from Chauncey D. Leake to Henry K. Beecher, June 7, 1955, Box 6, CIA Behavior Control Experiments Collection (John Marks Donation), National Security Archive, Washington, DC.

100. Henry K. Beecher, "Experimentation in Man," *Journal of the American Medical Association* 169, no. 5 (January 31, 1959): 110, 120–22.

101. Moreno, *Undue Risk,* 243–45.

102. Goliszek, *In the Name of Science,* 179–80.

103. Moreno, *Undue Risk,* 241–42.

104. Henry K. Beecher, "Ethics and Clinical Research," *New England Journal of Medicine* 274, no. 24 (June 16, 1966): 1354–60.

105. Henry K. Beecher, "Response to the Ingersoll Lecture by a Physician," *Harvard Theological Review* 62, no. 1 (1969): 21–26; Lee and Shlain, *Acid Dreams,* 74–76.

106. "Faculty and Staff—Dr. Henry Knowles Beecher, 1904–1976," Countway Medical Library, Harvard University, https://www.countway.harvard.edu/archives/iotm/iotm_2002-01.shtm (accessed February 16, 2007).

107. Jay Katz, "'Ethics and Clinical Research' Revisited: A Tribute to Henry K. Beecher," *Hastings Center Report* 23, no. 5 (1993): 31–39.

108. Jon Harkness, Susan E. Lederer, and Daniel Wikler, "Laying Ethical Foundations for Clinical Research," *Bulletin of the World Health Organization* 79, no. 4 (2001): 365–66.

109. Harkness, Lederer, and Wikler, "Laying Ethical Foundations for Clinical Research," 365; Daniel J. Rothman, *Strangers at the Bedside: A History of How Law and Bioethics Transformed Medical Decision Making* (New York: Basic Books, 1991), 2–3, 70–84, 251; Moreno, *Undue Risk,* 239–42; Marks, *Search for the "Manchurian Candidate,"* 67n, 72n; Martin A. Lee and Bruce Shlain, *Acid Dreams: The Complete Social History of LSD: The CIA, the Sixties, and Beyond* (New York: Grove Press, 1985), 86.

CHAPTER 4

PSYCHOLOGISTS, DETAINEE INTERROGATIONS, AND TORTURE: VARYING PERSPECTIVES ON NONPARTICIPATION

Stephen Soldz and Brad Olson

Over the last several years, citizens throughout the world have been aghast at the American regime of abusive treatment of detainees in the so-called Global War on Terror. Moslems have been picked up, often on the most tenuous evidence, and thrown into American detention centers throughout the world, the most infamous of which are Guantánamo, the CIA's secret "black sites," and the former Abu Ghraib detention center. In these facilities, the detained are kept for weeks, months, years, or potentially their whole lives. They essentially have no rights, no legal mechanisms to win their release, and are subject to the harshest treatment, treatment that, more often than not, fits into the legal category of torture. When that treatment does not fit the legal definition of torture, it often constitutes "cruel, inhuman or degrading treatment" or those outrages upon personal dignity" that the world community pledged to forego with the signing of the Third Geneva Convention.[1] The treatment in U.S. detention centers has been condemned as illegal and immoral by Amnesty International (2004; Amnesty International, 2005, 2007), by the United Nations (United Nations Commission on Human Rights, 2006; United Nations Committee against Torture, 2006), by the Council of Europe (Council of Europe Committee on Legal Affairs and Human Rights, 2007), by countless newspapers and NGOs (Human Rights Watch, 2005a, 2005b, 2005c, 2006a, 2006b; Physicians for Human Rights, 2005; Physicians for Human Rights & Human Rights First,

2007), and, unforgettably, by numerous retired American admirals, generals, and diplomats.

Since reports surfaced in 2004 and 2005 that psychologists and other mental health professionals were consulting to interrogations (Bloche & Marks, 2005; Lewis, 2004) of so-called "enemy combatants" in Guantánamo and other U.S. detention centers, there has been considerable discussion among psychologists as to the ethics and advisability of participation in these interrogations. The American Psychological Association (APA) has consistently taken a pro-participation stance (American Psychological Association, 2005a, 2005b, 2007a; Brehm, 2007; Koocher, 2006; Levant, 2007), while numerous critics argued that participation violates guiding ethical principles of psychology. Moreover, these critics argued that psychologist participation constitutes collaboration with abusive interrogations.

Perhaps the best way to understand the differences between the APA and that of other organizations of health professionals is to contrast the statements made by the respective leaders of the APA and the American Psychiatric Association after their joint trip to Guantánamo in the fall of 2005. Psychiatric association President Sharfstein discussed the visit during his 2006 presidential address:

> If you were ever wondering what makes us different from psychologists, here it is. This is a paramount challenge to our ethics and our Hippocratic training. Judging from the record of the actual treatment of detainees, it is the thinnest of thin lines that separates such consultation from involvement in facilitating deception and cruel and degrading treatment. Innocent people being released from Guantanamo—people who never were our enemies and had no useful information in the War on Terror—are returning to their homes and families bearing terrible internal scars. Our profession is lost if we play any role in inflicting these wounds. (Sharfstein, 2006)

In contrast, APA President Levant, who was on the same trip, returned and issued this statement: "I accepted this offer to visit Guantanamo because I saw the invitation as an important opportunity to continue to provide our expertise and guidance for how psychologists can play an appropriate and ethical role in national security investigations. Our goals are to ensure that psychologists add value and safeguards to such investigations and that they are done in an ethical and effective manner that protects the safety of all involved" (American Psychological Association, 2005a).

Two years later, APA President Levant wrote a detailed account of his visit (Levant, 2007). He again took the military's claims at face value, virtually ignoring the repeated assertions by numerous reporters that psychologists played a critical role in making the abuse "tantamount to torture" as the Red Cross reported around the time of Levant's visit (Lewis, 2004).

After an extended period of discussion and debate, on May 22, 2006, the American Psychiatric Association endorsed a policy statement that unambiguously held that under no circumstances should psychiatrists take part in interrogations. Soon after, the American Medical Association adopted a similar policy.

The American Psychological Association, in contrast, has adamantly refused to endorse any such statement, saying only that psychologists should behave ethically. Initially, the organization did what organizations often do when embroiled in unwanted controversy—they appointed a task force, the Task Force on Psychological Ethics and National Security (PENS). The Task Force, appointed by President Levant, was given a broad mandate that shifted the focus from the interrogation abuses, channeling the task force to abstract principles that strongly endorsed participation of psychologists.

Unlike most task forces, the PENS report did not list the participants. The Task Force's membership was released only to the APA Council of Representatives and not to the membership at large. Only a year later, when the membership was published in *Salon* (Benjamin, 2006) did the broader APA membership learn that the Task Force contained six of nine voting members who were directly connected to military or intelligence agencies. Most of these six had been involved in interrogations at Guantánamo, or in Iraq, Afghanistan, or the CIA's secret "black sites." Also participating in PENS deliberations, as Task Force member Jean Maria Arrigo reported (Arrigo & Goodman, 2007), were several "observers," APA officials, and others with high-level Defense Department, intelligence agency, and White House connections.

Information about the task force's deliberations was also kept private. PENS members were not to discuss either the report or the process outside the Task Force.[2] In June 2005, a few days after its solo meeting concluded, the PENS Task Force issued its final report (American Psychological Association, 2005b). In a highly unusual procedure, the Association's Board of Directors immediately adopted the report without the usual discussion and approval by the broader-based Council of Representatives. In fact, apparently in violation of APA bylaws, the report has never been ratified by the Council. Not surprisingly, given its composition, the PENS report explicitly stated that it is ethical for psychologists to engage in national security interrogations: "It is consistent with the APA Ethics Code for psychologists to serve in consultative roles to interrogation and information-gathering processes for national security-related purposes" (American Psychological Association, 2005b).

While the PENS report reiterated that psychologists should not be involved in any way in "torture or other cruel, inhuman, or degrading treatment," the Task Force stated that it was not charged to conduct any type of investigation, and thus avoided confronting the question of whether interrogation abuses had occurred and whether psychologists played any role in abuses.[3]

Therefore, while the origin of the task force was due to controversy about psychologists' participation in abuses (sometimes amounting to torture), the report makes no mention of any specific facility or any actual evidence regarding detention and interrogation practices. In fact, discussion of alleged abuses was discouraged throughout the PENS process.

A year after the PENS report, in response to membership dissent, the APA passed a resolution at its 2006 convention condemning torture and cruel, inhuman, and degrading treatment or punishment. This resolution again made no explicit mention of the role of psychologists in the development of U.S. abuse nor of the interrogations controversy at all. Because of its abstract character—condemning torture and abuse in all circumstances but not in any particular setting—and because it was developed as a consensus compromise, the 2006 resolution had little impact on APA policy or on the participation of psychologists in U.S. interrogations.

The controversy and battles continued through the August 2007 Convention when the APA passed a resolution (American Psychological Association, 2007b) banning participation in 19 specific torture techniques. The APA Council simultaneously rejected overwhelmingly an amendment (the "moratorium" amendment) stating that psychologists should serve only as health providers in detention centers where human rights are violated. The 2007 APA resolution sparked further controversy. While the banning of specific techniques was a considerable improvement, the 2007 resolution remained riddled with significant problems. It was developed with such fine word parsing that, in places, it resembles the so-called "torture memos" by which the Bush administration redefined "torture" so that they could claim that the United States does not torture (Danner, 2004; Greenberg & Dratel, 2005).

Even in the hours prior to the vote, the resolution was modified with insertions that provided clear loopholes that may allow continued participation in abuse. Most significantly, a number of techniques are banned only when "used in a manner that represents significant pain or suffering or in a manner that a reasonable person would judge to cause lasting harm" (American Psychological Association, 2007b). A day prior to the vote, the word "severe" had been mysteriously entered in the language, thus raising the harm threshold, although "significant" was later accepted as a compromise. These reservations curiously echoed those used by the Bush administration to justify the CIA's "enhanced techniques" as being distinct from torture (Benjamin, 2007b).

While some techniques were declared unethical in all detention contexts by the resolution, other techniques—including forced nudity, isolation, and sleep and sensory deprivation—were declared unethical only when used for extracting information (interrogation). This limitation potentially avoids banning participation in common situations where psychologists are used in the "softening-up" process that could be defined as separate from interrogation. Even if one argues that "softening up" is part of the process of interrogation, a psychologist participating in the use of these techniques could make a reasonable argument that this was not the intention.

THE VARIED ARGUMENTS OF DISSENT

After several years of APA resolutions, the debate continues, largely due to critics of APA policy who have tended to become more cohesive over time. Despite this cohesion, there are different perspectives among these critics. This diversity of views has the strength of making various arguments, each appealing to distinct constituencies. Simultaneously, critics have encountered communication difficulties. We attempt to distinguish and clarify these argument lines and investigate their underlying meanings and potential implications of these arguments for policy and social action.

VIOLATION OF HUMAN RIGHTS

Perhaps the most widely used argument against psychologist participation is that psychologists should not participate in interrogations in settings where fundamental human rights are being systematically violated. To participate in such settings, proponents of this position argue, is to lend legitimacy to these rights violations. The human rights position was recently put forth by proponents of a moratorium on psychologist participation in interrogations at U.S. detention centers (Altman, 2007). This effort was defeated at the August 2007 APA Convention. Neil Altman, the resolution author, used this argument to justify it: "This moratorium is necessary as detainees may be currently denied protections outlined under the Geneva Conventions and interrogations techniques in violation of the 2006 APA Resolution Against Torture and Other Cruel, Inhuman, or Degrading Treatment or Punishment may be considered acceptable practice according to the Military Commissions Bill of 2006" (Altman, 2006).

Similarly, Division 48 argues that U.S. detention centers are in violation of international law, including the "UN Universal Declaration of Human Rights, the UN Basic Principles for the Treatment of Prisoners, and the UN International Covenant on Civil and Political Rights by denying due process of law to prisoners" (Society for the Study of Peace, 2007). They assert that the indefinite detention without trial and lack of legal representation characteristic of U.S. national security detentions violates the United States Reservations, Declarations and Understandings to the United Nations Convention Against Torture and the Geneva Conventions. These habeas corpus violations automatically make detention in those settings "cruel, inhuman, or degrading treatment or punishment" and thereby illegal under U.S. law.

Lott takes this argument further, stating that psychologists should not be present in any capacity in these centers. As she states:

> Can our ethics say it is okay to work in situations where this is not the case, in secrecy, in places in which violations of human rights systematically occur as a matter of institutional policy? Where prisoners are detained for indefinite periods

and not charged with any crimes? Where they are not protected by international human rights protocols or provisions of the U.S. Constitution? Would we have condoned psychologists working (in any role) in Nazi concentration camps? Should psychologists work in any setting where processes are not subject to open review by courts, community, and oversight groups? I believe the correct and ethical response must be NO. (Lott, 2006, p. 6)

Whether psychologists should be engaging in torture, abuse, and interrogations are not necessary for Lott's basic argument: Psychologists simply should not be in these settings in the present situation regardless of what they do there.

One corollary of this human rights–based position, if held separate from the other positions discussed here, is that, upon restoration of detainee rights (usually envisaged as being accomplished by a Democratic Congress in a future Democratic administration), the prohibition on psychologists' participation would end. From a strict human rights perspective, nonparticipation in interrogations is viewed as a temporary expedient, a response to the crisis facing the United States as human rights are systematically eviscerated under the Bush administration.

In the weeks prior to the 2007 Convention, the APA Board of Directors proposed a rival Substitute Motion 2 to the moratorium banning psychologist participation in a number of especially abusive techniques. Due to the parliamentary procedures in effect, the likely adoption of the Board motion would have automatically prevented a vote on the moratorium. As a result, moratorium supporters proposed amendments to the Board motion, and through negotiations, Substitute Motion 2 became a revised Substitute Motion 3, described earlier as the 2007 resolution.

Left separate as a solo amendment, a compromised variant of the moratorium resolution embodied a variation of the human rights perspective: "BE IT RESOLVED...[that] the roles of psychologists in settings in which detainees are deprived of adequate protection of their human rights, should be limited as health personnel to the provision of psychological treatment." As stated, this amendment was defeated by approximately 85 percent of APA Council members.

HISTORICAL AND OPERATIONAL RECORD OF PSYCHOLOGISTS AND ABUSE

A second line of critique of APA policy focuses upon the role of psychologists in developing, and disseminating a variety of abusive interrogation techniques, eventually institutionalizing those techniques as standard operating procedures. Psychologists have, to a large degree, been integrated into the interrogations at Guantánamo and the CIA's secret "black sites," as well as in Iraq and Afghanistan. Psychologists may have been selected over other professional for this role because of their historical experience with abusive techniques, perhaps most evident in the military's Survival, Evasion, Resistance, Escape (SERE) program, designed to train military personnel to resist brainwashing if captured and tortured (Doran, Hoyt, & Morgan, 2006; Otterman, 2007). Moreover, there is a long historical record of psychologists in abusive interrogations, including Cold War experiences investigating Communist "brainwashing" techniques for the CIA and the U.S. military, resulting in the development of a paradigm of psychological torture (Marks, 1991; McCoy, 2006).

This line of argument points to the historical record, now confirmed by the Defense Department's own Office of the Inspector General (OIG: Office of the Inspector General of the Department of Defense, 2006) that psychologists have been integral to the development of modern-day American torture and interrogation abuse. Awareness of physician and psychologist involvement in this abuse began with the 2004 leaking of reports conducted by the International Committee of the Red Cross Guantanamo to the *Washington Post* (Slevin & Stephens, 2004) and *New York Times* (Lewis, 2004). This awareness increased in 2005, including articles in the *New England Journal of Medicine* (Bloche & Marks, 2005) and other journals (Rubenstein, Pross, Davidoff, & Iacopino, 2005). Jane Mayer (2005) brought this involvement to mass consciousness in her 2005 *New Yorker* article "The Experiment," focusing on mental health professionals, psychiatrists, and psychologists at Guantánamo.

Reports in 2007 expanded knowledge of activities of former SERE psychologist and CIA contractors James Mitchell and Bruce Jessen (Benjamin, 2007a; Eban, 2007, Mayer, 2007) in torturing Abu Zubaydah and others in the CIA's secret prisons, and of how other U.S. interrogators and psychologists eagerly emulated the approach. The OIG Report (Office of the Inspector General, 2006) documented how SERE psychologists willingly provided the necessary training, while psychologists, including SERE and BSCT psychologists (members of Behavioral Science Consultation Teams at Guantánamo and elsewhere), helped transform SERE-based techniques into standard operating procedures.

In August 2007, Mayer (2005) added significant details regarding the activities of the CIA-contracted firm Mitchell, Jessen & Associates, and a Spokane, Washington, paper reported that a former APA president, Joseph Matarazzo, is one of five voting principals of this firm (Morlin, 2007).[4]

Mayer's (2005) recent article and an accompanying interview on *Democracy Now!* provides an important clue as to why it was critical to have psychologists involved in interrogations. During this interview, Mayer stated:

> [I]f you take a look at the so-called torture memos, the forty pages or so of memos that were written...right after 9/11...they're busy looking at the Convention Against Torture, basically, it seems, trying to figure a way around it. One of the things they argued, these lawyers from the Justice Department, is that if you don't intend to torture someone, if your intention is not just to inflict terrible pain on them but to get information, then you really can't be necessarily convicted of torture.

So how do you prove that your intent is pure? Well, one of the things they suggest is if you consult with experts who will say that what you're doing is just interrogation, then that might also be a good legal defense. And so, one of the roles that these SERE psychologists played was a legal role. They were the experts who were consulted in order to argue that the program was not a program of torture. They are to say, "We've got PhDs, and this is standard psychology, and this is a legitimate way to question people." (Mayer & Goodman, 2007)

Thus, according to Mayer, the prestige of psychology was central to the administration's attempts to parse words so as to evade criminal liability for their actions.

This historical and operational critique argues that the record of psychologists' participation in interrogations is sobering and that something must be done to recognize and address the fact that psychologists participating in interrogations in situations where abuse is occurring have often enough been willing participants and are always vulnerable to becoming contributors to and facilitators of abuse.

Those countering this argument have agreed that some psychologists may have behaved badly but contended that others, such as Michael Gelles, worked to stop abuse (Dedman, 2006a, 2006b; Mayer, 2006; Savage, 2005). It should be noted, however, that Jane Mayer's (2006) *New Yorker* article "The Memo," describing the efforts to stop the abuses flowing from Gelles's reports, is subtitled "How an internal effort to ban the abuse and torture of detainees was thwarted." In other words, it is an account of a failure to stop abuse, not of a success. It also should be noted that, unlike BSCT and SERE psychologists, Gelles was supported by his chain of command in his reservations regarding some of the tactics in use at Guantánamo (Dedman, 2006b; Mayer, 2006). We are aware of no instance in which a psychologist has successfully stopped abuse in opposition to his or her chain of command. If those instances do exist, they are rare in relation to the number of psychologists engaged in these activities.

In order to clarify the circumstances surrounding Gelles's actions, Uwe Jacobs, the Executive Director of Survivors International, an organization in San Francisco that treats torture survivors, wrote, on March 23, 2007, an open letter to Mike Gelles. Jacobs commended Gelles for honorably reporting human rights abuses, but also put forth that we, as psychologists and as citizens, need reliable and detailed information on exactly what did and did not happen in the various detention centers, and what roles psychologists played in known abusive events. Vague claims by partisans that psychologists, even particular psychologists, prevented abuse are not evidence. This need for concrete evidence is particularly true if we are to soundly assess the so-far largely unsubstantiated claim that psychologists, more often than not, play a role in stopping abuse as opposed to perpetuating it.

The argument from the historical record suggests that psychologists should be extremely leery of involvement in interrogation situations not subject to stringent oversight. This record further suggests that psychologists may, in fact, be more willing than other health professionals to engage in ethically dubious activities, perhaps as a way of demonstrating their "value" to the military and intelligence institutions they serve (Lewis, 2006). The historical record also suggests that ethical platitudes to not engage in torture often are insufficient to keep psychologists from engaging in or otherwise assisting unethical activities.

SITUATIONAL CONTEXT IN MILITARY AND IN DETENTION CENTERS

Another common argument used by APA critics can be called the "situational context" position. This argument is that there are specific factors in the armed forces and intelligence agencies, as well as in the U.S. detention centers, that militate against autonomous ethical decision making. In other words, there are more powerful and dangerous social influences at work than is presumed by APA ethics statements on this issue. Zimbardo, for example, has clearly articulated this position, consistent with his overall situationist orientation emphasizing the influence of social situations on individual behavior (Zimbardo, 2006, 2007). Social influence–related factors affecting psychologists aiding detainee interrogations include military discipline and the chain of command; norms of brotherhood and allegiance; secrecy; the fact that individuals are often unaware of the whole context of their actions as they are given only a small fraction of total information; pressures to conform and "not to blow the whistle on ethically questionable activities" (Zimbardo, 2007); the absence of easy access to independent colleagues for discussion of problematic or ethically questionable situations; and the intense pressure on interrogators to "get results." A careful reading of the voluminous literature on detention centers shows these situational and institutional factors to have played a role in each of these closed and isolated settings; they are systemic.

The recent historical record illustrates the danger of going against the grain. In fact, many military officers and civilians have been severely punished simply for conscientiously doing their job. One has only to think of the punishment of the "bad apple" National Guard MPs and the National Guard General Karpinski for Abu Ghraib abuses, while the military systematically, through 10 investigations, blocked any look at the culpability of top military and civilian leadership.

A consistent feature of this administration, and of the contemporary U.S. military, is the negative consequences often faced by those expressing reservations with official policy. Just ask Lt. Commander Charles Swift, "recently named one of the 100 most influential lawyers in the country by the *National Law Journal*" (Shukovsky, 2006). Commander Swift received notice that his 23-year military career was ended two weeks after winning the historic Hamdan Supreme court case obtaining legal rights for detainees. Others, including Major Michael Mori (Allard, 2007), Lt. Cmdr. Matthew, Diaz (Golden, 2007), General Antonio Taguba, (Hersh, 2007), and Jesselyn Radack (McCollam, 2003) were denigrated, sidelined, and ultimately forced out of the military for performing their duties honorably in ways that put them in conflict with administration policy.

Zimbardo argues that the APA's PENS (Presidential Taskforce on Ethics and National Security):

> utilized the wrong model for its ethical deliberations about psychologists as consultants to military interrogations. The model featured in this task force report is that of a psychologist working for the military as an independent contractor, making rational moral decisions within a transparent setting, with full power to confront, challenge, and expose unethical practices. It is left up to that individual to be alert, informed, perceptive, wise, and ready to act on principle when ethical dilemmas arise. (Zimbardo, 2007, p. 5)

Costanzo, Gerrity, and Lykes (2006) elaborate on the situational perspective by detailing social psychological research illustrating pressures that interrogators face. Those tasked as interrogators are supposed to obtain information from detainees who may, or may not, be telling the truth or possess any truth to tell, bias can thus enter the process. Since psychological professionals, as Costanzo et al. point out, can detect deception at rates at best only slightly better than chance, they are in a near-impossible situation. The dilemma is this: Should the interrogator accept a detainee's claims of ignorance? Or should that interrogator press ever harder to make certain the detainee is not, in fact, insulting him or her (i.e., the interrogator) through deception? One can only imagine the pressures on military and intelligence psychologists whose professional advancement requires them to lead others to believe they possess a special expertise in detecting dissimulation. The reality is that the science behind their abilities has little more established validity than the notorious field of phrenology or any other of the misguided ideas littering psychology's history.

The same overconfidence and its subsequent danger is evident in the illusion that psychologists often prevent "behavioral drift" to keep "interrogations safe and ethical" (Brehm, 2007). The training and experience of most psychologists provides little expertise in this area. Moreover, the interrogation psychologist is asked to play numerous and conflicting roles in this supposed "safety officer" position: as the interrogator's therapist (to calm him or her down if they get out of hand); as an attorney, to keep interrogations safe, legal, and ethical, as numerous military and APA sources have claimed (American Psychological Association, 2005b; Levant, 2007; Office of the Army Surgeon General, 2005); and, simultaneously, to play the interrogator's accomplice in the interrogation process, as consultant strategist. It is beyond the ability of most psychologists, and of most human beings, to simultaneously carry out such varied and conflicting roles.[5]

Based on this situational analysis, Zimbardo argues that psychologists involved in interrogations need the guidance of a detailed casebook from the APA that would discuss ethical decision making according to the complex situations faced. Costanzo et al. argue for greater ethical guidance for psychologist interrogation consultants. However, it is far from clear how a casebook or other ethical guidance, however detailed, would counter the numerous and often conflicting situational pressures encountered. It seems unlikely that a casebook would counter conformity pressures or any of the negative social sanctions for disrupting military norms of allegiance. Legal ethics to vigorously defend one's client did not prevent Lt. Commander Charles Swift from being forced out of the Navy after he won a landmark Supreme Court case (Brenner, 2007). Why, then, would one expect sequestered interrogating psychologists to be subject to less pressure? More consistent with the situational analysis is that psychologists not participate at all in these national security interrogations.

PSYCHOLOGY AS HELPING/HEALTH PROFESSION

The final perspective we have encountered concerns the nature of psychology as a helping or health care profession—in other words, one dedicated to "strive to benefit those with whom they work and take care to do no harm. In their professional actions, psychologists seek to safeguard the welfare and rights of those with whom they interact professionally and other affected persons," as our Ethics Code states so beautifully in its Principle A (American Psychological Association, 2002). This perspective is to be contrasted with the opposing position of throwing this beneficence principle overboard and becoming a profession that tolerates the use of psychological knowledge and expertise to manipulate people in any direction desired by those at the top of the organizational hierarchies, be they members of the military, CIA, or, for that matter, in domestic prisons or corporations.

One focus of concern has been the 2003 change in ethics code clause 1.02 (known as 1.03 in the 1992 code). Prior to 2003, the ethics code required psychologists to adhere to the code, despite conflicting laws or orders: "If the demands of an organization with which psychologists are affiliated or for whom they are working conflict with this Ethics Code, psychologists clarify the nature of the conflict, make known their commitment to the Ethics Code, and to the extent feasible, resolve the conflict *in a way that permits adherence to the Ethics Code*" (italics added) (American Psychological Association, 1992). The 2003 revision eliminated this requirement to adhere to the code: "If psychologists' ethical responsibilities conflict with law, regulations, or other governing legal authority, psychologists make known their commitment to the Ethics Code and take steps to resolve the conflict. If the conflict is unresolvable via such means, *psychologists may adhere to the requirements of the law, regulations, or other governing legal authority*" (italics added) (American Psychological Association, 2002).

This change has been of great concern to APA critics, as it could lead military or intelligence psychologists to participate in abusive interrogations if so ordered. Furthermore, it subjected the "ethical" guidance for these psychologists to the Bush administration's legally and ethically dubious reinterpretations of torture (Greenberg & Dratel, 2005).

As long as 1.02 was in effect, no pious words about torture or other cruel, inhuman, or degrading treatment could be effective. One major contribution of the resolution passed at the 2007 APA convention is that it explicitly overrides clause 1.02: "Be it resolved that the American Psychological Association affirms that there are no exceptional circumstances whatsoever, whether induced by a state of war or threat of war, internal political instability or any other public emergency, that may be invoked as a justification for torture or cruel, inhuman, or degrading treatment or punishment, including the invocation of laws, regulations, or orders" (American Psychological Association, 2007b).

From the helping profession perspective, the issue here goes beyond these ethics code issues. What is at stake is whether psychologists are to take those noble words "strive to benefit those with whom they work and take care to do no harm" seriously. In the present culture, it is impossible for psychologist participation to meet this beneficence criterion. There is no sense in which manipulating imprisoned people to get them to say what they do not wish to say or do not know will benefit them. Additionally, revealing information could lead to the irreparable harm of lifetime incarceration or even execution. Defenders of the current APA policy of psychologist participation have chosen to demean the beneficence criterion by raising silly counterexamples (e.g., scolding children). In any serious discussion, we would suggest that alleged counterexamples deserve more intense ethical scrutiny before being taken seriously, because many psychologists do not see Principle A as "quaint" (Olson, 2006). Surely a claim that psychologists engage in many questionable activities is not an argument for even more questionable actions that clearly violate both the letter and the spirit of Principle A.

When a psychological researcher proposes to manipulate or deceive college research participants for the purpose of an experiment, there are detailed guidelines for what is allowed. Informed consent and IRB-approval procedures are required. Similar steps must be taken before obtaining any information via interview or questionnaire from college students, who are told explicitly that they are always capable of walking out the door, without suffering any negative consequences. These procedures exist because psychologists as a profession have unequivocally decided that the ability to use our knowledge and expertise to manipulate and deceive is a dangerous power and should be exercised only with extreme caution and under diligent independent scrutiny.

Why, then, is it ethical for a psychologist to use these powerful tools to manipulate some of the most powerless individuals on the face of the earth? Why is it ethical to manipulate those locked away in American detention centers where they are deprived of all rights, even the right to know the evidence that leads to their detention? Or to challenge that detention or the tactics used in interrogating or incarcerating them in impartial court? Surely, those caught in these detention centers, whether innocent or guilty, should be at the center of our ethical concern, just as we place other vulnerable populations, such as domestic prisoners, at the center of our concern in regard to research ethics.

From a perspective of fostering well-being, there is another issue that too often gets lost in the discussion. There is a distinction between those techniques and procedures that it might be ethical for interrogators to use, and what ought to be ethical for psychologists to use. Interrogation, by its nature, often involves manipulation of human minds. In the opinion of many, interrogators may use virtually any approach or technique that is not specifically proscribed as torture or cruel, inhuman, or degrading treatment. This is not the place to debate distinctions between what is ethical for a psychological professional versus for what is ethical for other interrogators. Yet, simply because an act is acceptable for a professional interrogator does not make it ethical or appropriate for psychologists, members of a profession dedicated to beneficence and the avoidance of harm.

We have a primary responsibility to our own discipline. Unfortunately, underlying APA positions and resolutions is a merging of what is legal (and what is effective) with what is ethical behavior for psychologists. Thus, both the 2006 and 2007 APA resolutions against torture ban participation only in activities judged to be violations of treaties to which the United States is signatory, activities which are already illegal. The implication is that no higher standard holds for psychologists than for professional interrogators. From that perspective, any interrogation activity outside of torture or of cruel, inhuman, or degrading treatment is, by default, ethical for a psychologist.

The American Psychiatric Association and American Medical Association have developed policies based on the position that members of a healing profession should not be engaged in interrogation activities harmful to those acted upon. Both professional health organizations have adopted the clear position that their members should not directly participate in interrogations, whether domestic or national security interrogations of "enemy combatants." Thus, the American Psychiatric Association position states: "No psychiatrist should participate directly in the interrogation of person [sic] held in custody by military or civilian investigative or law enforcement authorities, whether in the United States or elsewhere. Direct participation includes being present in the interrogation room, asking or suggesting questions, or advising authorities on the use of specific techniques of interrogation with particular detainees" (American Psychiatric Association, 2006).

Similarly, the American Medical Association stated: "Physicians must not conduct, directly participate in, or monitor an interrogation with an intent to intervene, because this undermines the physician's role as healer. Because it is justifiable for physicians to serve in roles that serve the public interest, the AMA policy permits physicians to develop general interrogation strategies that are not coercive, but are humane and respect the rights of individuals" (American Medical Association, 2006).

Defenders of the APA position state that psychologists are engaged in a wider variety of professional activities than are psychiatrists or other physicians. Yet medical doctors similarly participate in a variety of occupational roles in society. Consistent with the advancement of well-being, the AMA policy makes clear that there is a fundamental commitment to furthering the welfare of individuals as well as that of society that is superordinate over all other roles. In our opinion, psychology should hold itself to similar standards. Otherwise, it stands to sacrifice the status and protections afforded those whose mission is helping others.

Among psychologists, there has been little discussion of whether direct participation in domestic interrogations are ethical or desirable. Those who oppose stricter APA policies have stated that one risk to broadening the ethical stand on national security interrogations is that it would lead to other questions about the ethicality of psychologist practices and perhaps raise the hackles of forensic psychologists. This "slippery slope" argument has been one of the major forces impeding change in the APA's interrogation policy. The idea is that any APA statement prohibiting psychologists from working in a particular setting, no matter how abusive, is a great risk. It is always disconcerting to discover so much fear surrounding restrictions of unethical behavior. The profession must address this fear that has already done much to prevent it from addressing important issues.

Martha Davis, a psychologist and police consultant, in a talk at the 2007 APA convention, identified two additional concerns that militate against psychologist participation in national security interrogations (Davis, 2007). She presented a case from Guantánamo where the relationship between a therapeutic psychologist and a BSCT psychologist led to the destruction of trust necessary for treatment; the patient stopped speaking to the provider and experienced extreme, subsequent deterioration of mental and physical health. This case illustrates one of the dangers posed to therapeutic actions by the participation of psychologists in potentially abusive interrogations. Even domestic clients may wonder what a particular psychologist was doing when torture and abuse were government policy.

Davis also argues that BSCT psychologists (the same argument would apply to other intelligence psychologists, in the CIA, for example) are not psychologists in the sense usually meant by the term. They are, rather, intelligence officers with responsibilities to those in the intelligence chain of command. The military may require state licensure, but these "psychologists" are not actually subject to the disciplinary procedures of licensing boards, due to the secrecy with which they conduct their intelligence work. Geographical considerations may play a role as well. When Major John Leso's role in the abusive interrogation of Mohammed al-Qahtani became public, a psychologist filed an ethics complaint with the New York State licensing board. The complaint was soon rejected, as the board claimed no authority for actions occurring outside the state.

CONCLUSION

As discussed here, critics of current APA policy draw upon varied arguments in opposing psychologist participation in interrogations. In our view, each of these arguments has merit. Psychologists do not belong in facilities where massive violations of human rights are the norm. Psychologists have a special responsibility to oppose abusive interrogations in U.S. detention facilities. Our colleagues have played a central role in the development of these techniques, turning them into standard operating procedures in high-profile U.S. interrogations. Moreover, the prestige of psychology has been used as justification for the adoption of abusive techniques and as protection from potential legal accountability for those involved in and for those who authorized abuses. Most fundamentally, we believe that the surrender of the principle of beneficence and a dedication to the promotion of well-being will cause the profession and the broader society irreparable harm.

There are two contrasting aspects of the diversity of arguments used by opponents of psychologist participation in national security interrogations. The first is that these varied lines of reasoning have led to some degree of miscommunication among the community of critics attempting to change APA policy. There have been many stakeholders making cogent arguments for change, but they have not always come together effectively for collective action. There have also been a multitude of communications channels that have at times posed impediments to coordinated action.

Another way to interpret this multiplicity of arguments and channels is that they constitute major strengths of the change efforts and the movement as a whole. The arguments call attention to diverse logical and contextual aspects of this issue that will define the psychology profession for years to come. Distinct arguments often speak to different individuals (from different professions and subdisciplines within the psychological field). Many of those mobilized are primarily concerned with making a statement against the human rights violations, while others are most incensed with the idea that their profession may be contributing to the Bush administration's torture regime (Benjamin, 2007b; Levine, 2007; Soldz, 2006b, 2006c). Yet others are uneasy about the future of a profession that refuses to definitively proclaim that certain roles and activities are simply inappropriate for psychologist practitioners.

In a previous paper (Olson & Soldz, 2007), we argued that the correct conclusion from empirical and ethical arguments was that psychologists should not participate in any direct way in interrogations within U.S. detention centers. We still agree with that position. A profession that has minimal safeguards and less concern for its members' actions under severe detention conditions than for what its members do to American undergraduates truly marks a profession that has lost its way. In no uncertain terms, it reflects a profession in danger of losing its soul. Fortunately, diverse voices are trying to define psychology as a profession devoted to promoting individual and social welfare, one that abhors the idea of contributing in any way to "breaking them [the detainees] down" (Physicians for Human Rights, 2005).

The variety of arguments against psychologist participation and the weak arguments in defense of current APA policies (Soldz, 2006a, 2006b, 2006c, 2007) confirm the fragility of the APA base. When reasoned arguments are met with silence or obfuscation, it suggests the policy may be based upon a structural weakness in the organization as a whole. When psychologists do not rise up and change the system, it reflects a more permanent moral fracture. Fortunately, there has been many strong, consistent, and diverse voices attempting to set psychology securely on a consistent ethical basis. At the APA Annual Convention in 2007, many of these voices came together for the first time, contributing to a rich dialog, a vibrant voice, and an evident portent of positive change. The forces in support of the status quo are strong, however; the ultimate resolution of this conflict is far from certain. The APA leadership may well run out the clock until the end of the Bush administration, hoping, no doubt, that pressure for change will dissipate with a change in Washington. If no change is forthcoming, however, future generations will likely look back upon American psychology in the early twenty-first century with horror. Truly, the future of psychology as a profession working to improve human well-being is at stake.

NOTES

1. We frequently use the term "abuse" in this chapter to include all types of abusive or coercive interrogation tactics, whether legally classifiable as "torture" or as "cruel, inhuman, or degrading treatment or punishment" (Office of the United Nations High Commissioner for Human Rights, 1984).

2. The report does, however, indicate several issues where agreement within the group could not be reached.

3. It has since become evident that several PENS members were in chains of command that had been involved in implementing, teaching, and creating standard operating procedures for abusive interrogations (Eban, 2007; Office of the Inspector General of the Department of Defense, 2006; Soldz, Reisner, & Olson, 2007).

4. Just to be clear, we are aware of no evidence as to whether Dr. Matarazzo had knowledge of these activities of the firm. He has flatly stated that he is against torture.

5. See the PENS task force report's prohibition against "mixed-roles" (American Psychological Association, 2005b) and the APA ethics code regarding conflicts of interest and dual loyalty for further descriptions of this problem (American Psychological Association, 2002).

REFERENCES

Allard, T. (2007, March 5). Hicks trial at risk if Mori taken off case. Retrieved October 12, 2007, from http://www.theage.com.au/news/national/hicks-trial-at-risk-if-mori-taken-off-case/2007/03/04/1172943276209.html.

Altman, N. (2006). Resolution for a moratorium on psychologist participation in interrogations at US detention centers holding foreign detainees, so-called "enemy combatants": Summary and overview. Retrieved August 24, 2007, from http://www.apa.org/ethics/pdfs/2006moratoriumresolutionsummaryandoverview.pdf.

Altman, N. (2007, February). A moratorium on psychologist involvement in interrogations at US detention centers for foreign detainees. Retrieved August 24, 2007, from http://www.apa.org/ethics/pdfs/resolution22307.pdf.

American Medical Association. (2006, June 12). New AMA ethical policy opposes direct physician participation in interrogation. Retrieved August 21, 2006, from http://www.ama-assn.org/ama/pub/category/16446.html.

American Psychiatric Association. (2006, May 22). APA passes position statement barring psychiatric participation in interrogation of detainees. Retrieved June 12, 2006, from http://www.psych.org/news_room/press_releases/06-36PositionStatementonInterrogation.pdf.

American Psychological Association. (1992, 2002). Ethical principles of psychologists and code of conduct. Retrieved October 10, 2007, from http://www.apa.org/ethics/code1992.html.

American Psychological Association. (2002). Ethical principles of psychologists and code of conduct. Retrieved February 27, 2007, from http://www.apa.org/ethics/code2002.html.

American Psychological Association. (2005a, October 23). APA President Ronald F. Levant Visits Naval Station at Guantanamo Bay. Retrieved June 12, 2006, from http://www.apa.org/releases/gitmo1023.html.

American Psychological Association. (2005b, June). Report of the American Psychological Association Presidential Task Force on Psychological Ethics and National Security. Retrieved June 12, 2006, from http://www.apa.org/releases/PENSTaskForceReportFinal.pdf.

American Psychological Association. (2007a, September). Frequently asked questions regarding APA's policies and positions on the use of torture or cruel, inhuman or degrading treatment during interrogations. Retrieved October 9, 2007, from http://www.apa.org/releases/faqinterrogation.html.

American Psychological Association. (2007b, August 19). Reaffirmation of the American Psychological Association position against torture and other cruel, inhuman, or degrading treatment or punishment and its application to individuals defined in the United States code as "enemy combatants." Retrieved August 24, 2007, from http://www.apa.org/governance/resolutions/councilres0807.html.

Amnesty International. (2004, October 27). Human dignity denied: torture and accountability in the "war on terror." Retrieved October 9, 2007, from http://www.amnestyusa.org/document.php?lang=e&id=9DEF4263FC2E35CA80256FE7004FE4C0.

Amnesty International. (2005, April 28). One year after Abu Ghraib, torture continues. Retrieved April 28, 2005, from http://web.amnesty.org/web/web.nsf/print/2B050D9CE255EF8580256FF1003656EB.

Amnesty International. (2007). Close Guantánamo. Retrieved October 10, 2007, from http://www.amnestyusa.org/War_on_Terror/Close_Guantanamo/page.do?id=1031039&n1=3&n2=821&n3=1074.

Arrigo, J.M., & Goodman, A. (2007, August 20). APA interrogation task force member Dr. Jean Maria Arrigo exposes group's ties to military. Retrieved September 9, 2007, from http://www.democracynow.org/article.pl?sid=07/08/20/1628234.

Benjamin, M. (2006, July 26). Psychological warfare. Retrieved August 21, 2006, from http://www.salon.com/news/feature/2006/07/26/interrogation/print.html.

Benjamin, M. (2007a, June 21). The CIA's torture teachers. Retrieved September 5, 2007, from http://www.salon.com/news/feature/2007/06/21/cia_sere/print.html.

Benjamin, M. (2007b, August 21). Will psychologists still abet torture? Retrieved September 5, 2007, from http://www.salon.com/news/feature/2007/08/21/psychologists/index.html?source=rss&aim=yahoo-salon.

Bloche, M.G., & Marks, J.H. (2005, June 22). Doctors and interrogators at Guantanamo Bay. *New England Journal of Medicine.* Retrieved June 28, 2005, from http://content.nejm.org/cgi/reprint/NEJMp058145v1.pdf.

Brehm, S.S. (2007, January 9). Letter to the *Washington Monthly.* Retrieved January 18, 2007, from http://www.apa.org/releases/washingtonmonthly.pdf.

Brenner, M. (2007, March). Taking on Guantánamo. Retrieved April 14, 2007, from http://www.vanityfair.com/politics/features/2007/03/guantanamo200703.

Costanzo, M., Gerrity, E., & Lykes, M.B. (2006). The use of torture and other cruel, inhumane, or degrading treatment as interrogation devices [Electronic Version]. *Analyses of Social Issues and Public Policy, 6,* 1–14. Retrieved June 21, 2006, from http://www.spssi.org/SPSSI_Statement_on_torture.pdf#search=%22apa%20zimbardo%20guantanamo%20%22.

Council of Europe Committee on Legal Affairs and Human Rights. (2007, June 7). Secret detentions and illegal transfers of detainees involving Council of Europe member states: Second report. Retrieved October 10, 2007, from http://news.bbc.co.uk/2/shared/bsp/hi/pdfs/marty_08_06_07.pdf.

Danner, M. (2004). *Torture and truth: America, Abu Ghraib, and the war on terror.* New York: New York Review of Books.

Davis, M. (2007). *Psychologists Betrayed.* Paper presented at the American Psychological Association annual convention.

Dedman, B. (2006a, October 24). Can the "20th hijacker" of Sept. 11 stand trial? Aggressive interrogation at Guantanamo may prevent his prosecution. Retrieved October 24, 2006, from http://www.msnbc.msn.com/id/15361462/.

Dedman, B. (2006b, October 24). Gitmo interrogations spark battle over tactics: The inside story of criminal investigators who tried to stop abuse. Retrieved October 24, 2006, from http://www.msnbc.msn.com/id/15361458/from/ET/.

Doran, A. P., Hoyt, G., & Morgan, C. A. III (2006). Survival, Evasion, Resistance, and Escape (SERE): Preparing military members for the demans of captivity. In C. H. Kennedy & E. A. Zillmer (Eds.), *Military psychology: Clinical and operational applications* (pp. 241–261). New York: Guilford.

Eban, K. (2007, July 17). Rorschach and awe. Retrieved September 5, 2007, from http://www.vanityfair.com/politics/features/2007/07/torture200707?printable=true&currentPage=all.

Golden, T. (2007, October 21). Naming names at Gitmo. Retrieved October 23, 2007, from http://www.nytimes.com/2007/10/21/magazine/21Diaz-t.html?_r=2&oref=slogin&adxnnlx=1193061770-z/G5TYJwWHSLDHwQFoyRzg&pagewanted=print.

Greenberg, K. J., & Dratel, J. L. (Eds.). (2005). *The torture papers: The road to Abu Ghraib.* New York: Cambridge University Press.

Hersh, S. (2007, June 25). The General's Report. Retrieved June 16, 2007, from http://www.newyorker.com/reporting/2007/06/25/070625fa_fact_hersh?printable=true.

Human Rights Watch. (2005a, April 27). Abu Ghraib only the "tip of the iceberg." Retrieved April 27, 2005, from http://hrw.org/english/docs/2005/04/27/usint10545_txt.htm.

Human Rights Watch. (2005b, April). Getting away with torture? Command responsibility for the U.S. abuse of detainees. Retrieved April 24, 2005, from http://www.hrw.org/reports/2005/us0405/.

Human Rights Watch. (2005c, September 24). New accounts of torture by U.S. troops: Soldiers say failures by command led to abuse. Retrieved September 25, 2005, from http://www.hrw.org/english/docs/2005/09/25/usint11776.htm.

Human Rights Watch. (2006a). Guantanamo: Detainee accounts. Retrieved January 29, 2007, from http://hrw.org/backgrounder/usa/gitmo1004/gitmo1004.pdf.

Human Rights Watch. (2006b, July). "No blood, no foul": Soldiers' accounts of detainee abuse in Iraq. Retrieved January 18, 2007, from http://hrw.org/reports/2006/us0706/.

Jacobs, U. (2007, March 25). Uwe Jacobs of Survivors International asks questions of Michael Gelles. Retrieved March 26, 2007, from http://psychoanalystsopposewar.org/blog/2007/03/25/uwe-jacobs-of-survivors-international-asks-questions-of-michael-gelles/.

Koocher, G. (2006, February). Speaking against torture. Retrieved June 14, 2006, from http://www.apa.org/monitor/feb06/pc.html.

Levant, R. F. (2007). Visit to the U.S. Joint Task Force Station at Guantanamo Bay: A first-person account. *Military Psychology, 19*(1), 1–7.

Levine, A. (2007, January 8). Collective Unconscionable: How psychologists, the most liberal of professionals, abetted Bush's torture policy. Retrieved January 8, 2007, from http://www.washingtonmonthly.com/features/2007/0701.levine.html.

Lewis, N. A. (2004, November 30). Red Cross finds detainee abuse in Guantánamo. Retrieved November 30, 2004, from http://www.nytimes.com/2004/11/30/politics/30gitmo.html?oref=login&adxnnl=1&oref=login&adxnnlx=1101831750-FbT+0bYfbchtnBvKJVZOBw&pagewanted=print&position=.

Lewis, N. A. (2006, June 7). Military alters the makeup of interrogation advisers. Retrieved June 8, 2006, from http://www.nytimes.com/2006/06/07/washington/07detain.html.

Lott, B. (2006). APA and the participation of psychologists in situations in which human rights are violated: Comment on "Psychologists and the use of torture in interrogations" [Electronic Version]. *Analyses of Social Issues and Public Policy, 7*, 1–9. Retrieved June 19, 2007, from http://www.asap-spssi.org/pdf/0701Lott.pdf.

Marks, J.D. (1991). *The search for the "Manchurian candidate."* New York: Norton.

Mayer, J. (2005, July 11). The experiment: Is the military devising new methods of interrogation at Guantánamo? *New Yorker.*

Mayer, J. (2006, February 20). The memo. Retrieved August 24, 2006, from http://www.newyorker.com/printables/fact/060227fa_fact.

Mayer, J. (2007, August 13). The black sites. Retrieved September 5, 2007, from http://www.newyorker.com/reporting/2007/08/13/070813fa_fact_mayer?printable=true.

Mayer, J., & Goodman, A. (2007, August 8). The black sites: A rare look Inside the C.I.A.'s secret interrogation program. Retrieved September 5, 2007, from http://www.democracynow.org/article.pl?sid=07/08/08/1338248.

McCollam, D. (2003). The trials of Jesselyn Radack. Retrieved October 15, 2007, from http://www.law.com/jsp/article.jsp?id=1056139907383.

McCoy, A.W. (2006). *A question of torture: CIA interrogation, from the Cold War to the War on Terror* (1st ed.). New York: Metropolitan Books/Henry Holt and Co.

Morlin, B. (2007, August 12). Expert has stake in cryptic local firm. Retrieved September 5, 2007, from http://www.spokesmanreview.com/tools/story_pf.asp?ID=204358.

Office of the Army Surgeon General. (2005, April 13). Final report: Assessment of detainee medical operations for OEF, GTMO, and OIF. Retrieved September 10, 2006, from http://www.armymedicine.army.mil/news/detmedopsrprt/detmedopsrpt.cfm.

Office of the Inspector General of the Department of Defense. (2006, August 25). Review of DoD-directed investigations of detainee abuse. Retrieved June 1, 2007, from http://www.fas.org/irp/agency/dod/abuse.pdf.

Office of the United Nations High Commissioner for Human Rights. (1984). Convention against torture and other cruel, inhuman or degrading treatment or punishment. Retrieved August 23, 2006, from http://www.unhchr.ch/html/menu3/b/h_cat39.htm.

Olson, B. (2006). Human rights and the ethics of psychologist-involved interrogations. *Community Psychologist, 39*(4), 55–57.

Olson, B., & Soldz, S. (2007). Positive illusions and the necessity of a bright line forbidding psychologist involvement in detainee interrogations [Electronic Version]. *Analyses of Social Issues and Public Policy, 7*, 1–10. Blackwell Publishing. Reprinted with permission. Retrieved June 28, 2007, from http://www.asap-spssi.org/default.htm.

Otterman, M. (2007). *American torture: From the Cold War to Abu Ghraib and beyond.* Ann Arbor, MI: Pluto Press.

Physicians for Human Rights. (2005, May). Break them down: Systematic use of psychological torture by U.S. forces. Retrieved June 12, 2006, from http://physiciansfor humanrights.org/library/report-2005-may.html.

Physicians for Human Rights, & Human Rights First. (2007, August). Leave no marks: Enhanced interrogation techniques and the risk of criminality. Retrieved October 9,

2007, from http://physiciansforhumanrights.org/library/documents/reports/leave-no-marks.pdf.

Rubenstein, L., Pross, C., Davidoff, F., & Iacopino, V. (2005). Coercive US interrogation policies: A challenge to medical ethics. *Journal of the American Medical Association, 294* (12), 1544–1549.

Savage, C. (2005). Split seen on interrogation techniques: Navy official says many back stance against coercion. Retrieved March 12, 2007, from http://www.boston.com/news/world/latinamerica/articles/2005/03/31/split_seen_on_interrogation_techniques?mode=PF.

Sharfstein, S. (2006). Presidential Address: Advocacy as Leadership. Retrieved March 7, 2007, from http://www.factnet.org/?p=14.

Shukovsky, P. (2006, July 1). Gitmo win likely cost Navy lawyer his career. Retrieved March 7, 2007, from http://seattlepi.nwsource.com/national/276109_swift01.html.

Slevin, P., & Stephens, J. (2004, June 10). Detainees' medical files shared: Guantanamo interrogators' access criticized. Retrieved September 20, 2007, from http://www.washingtonpost.com/ac2/wp-dyn/A29649–2004Jun9?language=printer.

Society for the Study of Peace, Conflict, and Violence: Peace Psychology Division 48 (2007, April). Call for an APA moratorium resolution. Retrieved August 24, 2007, from http://www.webster.edu/peacepsychology/2007Moratorium/MoratoriumStatement07.html.

Soldz, S. (2006a, December 14). Abusive interrogations: A defining difference between psychiatrists and psychologists. Retrieved September 20, 2007, from http://www.dissidentvoice.org/Dec06/Soldz14.htm.

Soldz, S. (2006b). Protecting the torturers: Bad faith and distortions from the American Psychological Association. Retrieved January 19, 2007, from http://www.counterpunch.org/soldz09062006.html.

Soldz, S. (2006c, August 1). Psychologists, Guantanamo and torture: A profession struggles to save its soul. Retrieved January 19, 2007, from http://www.counterpunch.org/soldz08012006.html.

Soldz, S. (2007, April 13). Aid and comfort for torturers: Psychology and coercive interrogations in historical perspective. Retrieved April 20, 2007, from http://www.counterpunch.org/soldz04132007.html.

Soldz, S., Reisner, S., & Olson, B. (2007, June 7). A Q&A on psychologists and torture: The Pentagon's IG report contradicts what the APA has said about the involvement of psychologists in abusive interrogations. Retrieved June 10, 2007, from http://www.counterpunch.org/soldz06072007.html.

United Nations Commission on Human Rights. (2006, February 15). Situation of detainees at Guantánamo Bay. Retrieved June 14, 2006, from http://www.ohchr.org/english/bodies/chr/docs/62chr/E.CN.4.2006.120_.pdf.

United Nations Committee against Torture. (2006, May 19). Consideration of reports submitted by state parties under Article 19 of the convention: Conclusions and recommendations of the Committee against Torture: United States. Retrieved June 14, 2006, from http://www.ohchr.org/english/bodies/cat/docs/AdvanceVersions/CAT.C.USA.CO.2.pdf.

Zimbardo, P.G. (2006, July 19). Commentary on the report of the American Psychological Association's Presidential Task Force on Psychological Ethics and National Security (PENS). Retrieved December 31, 2006, from http://www.zimbardo.com/downloads/ZimPENSReport.pdf.

Zimbardo, P.G. (2007). Thoughts on psychologists, ethics, and the use of torture in interrogations: Don't ignore varying roles and complexities [Electronic Version]. *Analyses of Social Issues and Public Policy, 7,* 1–9. Retrieved August 27, 2007, from http://www.asap-spssi.org/pdf/0701Zimbardo.pdf.

CHAPTER 5

DOCTORS AS PAWNS? LAW AND MEDICAL ETHICS AT GUANTÁNAMO BAY

Jonathan H. Marks

INTRODUCTION

At a recent symposium, I was asked to address the question: "Guantánamo Bay: How should we respond?" When I thought about this question, it occurred to me that we talk about "responding" in a number of ways. We respond in games, such as chess or bridge. But the detention policy of the Bush Administration (the Administration) is not a game—certainly not from the perspectives of those who are being (or have been) detained at Guantánamo Bay for prolonged periods since the "global war on terror" began. We also respond in conversation. However, we should not permit rhetoric to distract from action on the ground. Statements of interrogation and detention policy are one thing (especially when prepared for public consumption or in response to public criticism); interrogation and detention practices may be quite another. We respond in negotiation. That model, too, makes me uncomfortable. My intuition and my legal training tell me that some things should simply not be negotiable, among them certain absolute commitments to fundamental human rights: freedom from cruel, inhuman, and degrading (CID) treatment, as well as freedom from torture. This is, after all, the position adopted in two core human rights treaties: the International Covenant on Civil and Political Rights (ICCPR),[1] and the Convention against Torture and Other Cruel, Inhuman or Degrading Treatment or Punishment (Torture Convention).[2] Finally, and perhaps most charitably, our "response" may be viewed as part of the political process—as deliberative democracy taking its natural course. But the political process seems to be taking far too long.

This chapter is reprinted from Marks, Jonathan H. "Doctors as Pawns? Law and Medical Ethics at Guantánamo Bay." *Seton Hall Law Review* Vol. 37, pp. 711–731, 2007. Reprinted with permission.

There are detainees at Guantánamo who have been in United States custody for five years, and every additional day of detention deepens the profound psychological impact on them.[3] Three of the Guantánamo detainees have already taken their own lives.[4*] Additionally, at least twenty-five detainees have failed in their suicide attempts (in some cases, multiple attempts),[5] while many more are clinically depressed.[6]

As I contemplated my own response to the Administration's counterterrorism policy for the symposium, I became preoccupied with three major concerns. First, despite my comments above, the treatment of detainees at Guantánamo and elsewhere does appear to have evolved into a kind of multi-party, multi-dimensional game of chess. The familiar array of players includes the three branches of government and the Fourth Estate—at times critical, but often stenographic[7]—as well as lawyers, academics, and members of human rights and civil liberties groups. However, health professionals at Guantánamo Bay—whether nominally serving in a care-giving capacity or as adjuncts to the interrogation mission—are also involved, as are their professional organizations.[8] A related concern, which I articulate further below, is that health professionals—whether physicians, psychologists, nurses, medics, or others—who have served or now serve at Guantánamo Bay, have become pawns in the mistreatment of detainees and in the debate over their treatment.

Second, a substantial part of the "game" of politico-legal move and counter-move has involved the re-interpretation of the scope, meaning, and application of legal norms—particularly international legal norms. Three of the most conspicuous casualties in this process have been the definition of torture, the prohibition of cruel, inhuman, and degrading treatment and punishment, and the basic protections in Common Article Three of the Geneva Conventions.[9] When legal protections for detainees are being undermined, it is all the more important that professional ethics (in particular, medical ethics) speak clearly and that codes of ethics do not become subordinate to, or dependent upon, unilateral reinterpretations of legal doctrine. The ethics of health professionals should embrace fundamental standards of human rights and the laws of war, as recognized and interpreted by the international legal order in whose formation the United States played such a pivotal role.[10] However, if health professionals are to retain our trust, and if they are to maintain the social and cultural status engendered by their perceived humanitarian ethos, their codes of ethics should do more than simply reflect the most fundamental legal prohibitions.

Third, the focus on Guantánamo Bay conveniently distracts attention from other detention centers, such as Bagram in Afghanistan and numerous

---

*Shortly after this article was published, there was a fourth suicide at Guantánamo Bay. See White, J. (2007). Death of Guantanamo Detainee Is Apparent Suicide, Military Says. *Washington Post*, May 31, A8, available at http://www.washingtonpost.com/wp-dyn/content/article/2007/05/30/AR20070 53002580_pf.html.

unidentified "black sites" operated by the Central Intelligence Agency (CIA) across the globe[11]—where interrogation practices and the role of health professionals have come under far less public scrutiny. There is a danger that Guantánamo Bay has or will become a staged detention center, while more egregious treatment of detainees is conducted elsewhere. Following the first newspaper reports about the existence of these "black sites" operated by the CIA, one experienced U.S. interrogator observed:

> Its [sic] so nice to be secret. No trouble over human rights. So secret that most of the military or government have no idea where they are. No rights, human or otherwise have to be dealt with. Let a few inaccessible places be released through controlled media informants and then AI [Amnesty International] and all the rest will be concentrating on those places while we continue to work in the real centers.[12]

Since details of these detention centers remain undisclosed and classified, it is difficult to say much about the role of medical professionals at those sites. Although we can speak with some degree of confidence about their role at Guantánamo Bay, we should keep in mind that we are only talking about one piece of the interrogation picture.

HEALTH PROFESSIONALS AND INTERROGATION AT GUANTÁNAMO

It is possible to describe in some detail the roles that health professionals played in the design and implementation of interrogation strategies at Guantánamo Bay thanks to the tens of thousands of documents obtained by the American Civil Liberties Union (ACLU) under the Freedom of Information Act (FOIA), not to mention several other documents that have been leaked to the press. Since these roles have been described in considerable detail elsewhere,[13] I review them only briefly here.

Psychiatrists and psychologists were brought into the interrogation process not as gatekeepers or health care advocates for detainees, but as adjuncts to the interrogation mission. Although some of them clearly had no professional background or training relevant to interrogation,[14] they were considered "behavioral science consultants"[15]—assigned to teams known colloquially as "Biscuits"[16]— and their input was deemed "essential" in both the design of interrogation strategies and the interpretation of intelligence at Guantánamo Bay.[17] They advised interrogators how to ramp up interrogation stressors in order to overcome the apparent resistance of detainees to questioning.[18] The kinds of stressors used at Guantánamo Bay are now common knowledge, having been the subject of numerous newspaper reports and internal U.S. Army (Army) investigations.[19] They include sleep deprivation and manipulation, exposure to loud noise and temperature extremes, and the use of stress positions.[20] Some reports indicate that behavioral science personnel used information derived from detainees' medical records as the basis for their advice.[21] In one instance, for example, they advised interrogators to exploit a detainee's fear of the dark.[22] Army documents also record that behavioral scientists were "on hand" to monitor interrogations, and that they were supposedly given the power to intervene if interrogations got out of hand.[23]

Although there is evidence that Biscuit personnel monitored interrogations both inside and outside the interrogation room[24]—in the latter case through one-way mirrors—there is little evidence that they intervened to prevent interrogations from going too far. On the contrary, Army documents suggest that behavioral science personnel (as well as some caregivers) stood by while detainees were abused. Mohammed Al Qahtani, the so-called "20th hijacker,"[25] was exposed to an aggressive interrogation regime at Guantánamo Bay for up to twenty hours per day for forty-eight days over a fifty-four day period at the end of 2002 and beginning of 2003.[26] The interrogation log—obtained by *Time Magazine*—records the presence of a psychologist during parts of the interrogation.[27] However, the process still spiraled out of control, putting Al Qahtani's health in grave danger. On one occasion, Al Qahtani's pulse dropped to thirty-five beats per minute, and on two occasions his temperature dropped to ninety-five degrees.[28] To add insult to injury, when Al Qahtani was re-hydrated with three bags of intravenous fluids, interrogators refused to let him take a bathroom break, and he had no option but to wet himself.[29]

This is not the only example of medical treatment or its sequelae being deployed for strategic purposes. Force-feeding of hunger strikers at Guantánamo Bay is being conducted with the assistance of medical personnel who are caregivers, not adjuncts to the interrogation mission.[30] After some U.S. Navy physicians refused to force-feed detainees, the Department of Defense began screening doctors assigned to Guantánamo Bay to ensure they would be willing to participate.[31] The practice of force-feeding has been defended by the Pentagon as being necessary to protect the health of detainees.[32] However, there are a number of reasons to doubt this claim. First, reports indicate that, in contrast with its use in federal prisons, force-feeding is being administered long before the health of detainees is seriously threatened by their hunger strike.[33] Second, detainees have reportedly been forced to sit in their own urine and feces while strapped into a chair for "postfeed observation."[34] Third, the Pentagon regards hunger strikes and suicide attempts as acts of "asymmetric warfare,"[35] rather than signs of desperation on the part of those being detained for an indefinite period on grounds that are often still unclear.[36] This view undermines the claim by the Assistant Secretary of Defense for Health Affairs, William Winkenwerder, Jr., M.D., that the Pentagon's "intentions are good" and that they are "seeking to preserve life."[37] How can the policy of force-feeding be *both* ethically responsible medical treatment and a response tactic in asymmetric warfare?

THE EVOLUTION (OR REVOLUTION) OF LEGAL DOCTRINE

In order to pave the way for the use of more aggressive interrogation techniques against so-called "high-value detainees" such as Al Qahtani, the Administration recognized that a number of legal hurdles needed to be addressed. As a result, they embarked on what I have described elsewhere as a series of exercises in legal exceptionalism, in which legal protections and prohibitions were dispensed with on the grounds that they were geographically limited (*spatial exceptionalism*), that they did not apply to a particular group (*collective exceptionalism*), or that their true meaning had been hitherto misunderstood (*interpretive exceptionalism*).[38] For present purposes, I will focus on just three examples, but there are many more.

First and foremost, the Administration wanted to make sure that interrogators deploying these techniques would not incur criminal responsibility for torture. This objective led to the August 2002 memorandum from then-Assistant Attorney General Jay Bybee to then-White House Counsel Alberto Gonzalez, entitled *Re: Standards of Conduct for Interrogation under 18 U.S.C. 2340–2340A*.[39] The document narrowly defined physical torture to require pain "equivalent in intensity to the pain accompanying serious physical injury, such as organ failure, the permanent impairment of a significant bodily function, or even death."[40] For pain or suffering to rise to the level of mental torture, the memo added, "it must result in significant psychological harm of significant duration, e.g. lasting for months or even years."[41] Even if these thresholds are crossed and the interrogator *knows* they are being crossed, the memo contends that the interrogator would not be guilty of torture under U.S. criminal law "if causing such harm is not his objective."[42] Nor would he have committed torture, according to the memo, if he "could show that he acted in good faith by taking steps such as surveying professional literature, *consulting with experts,* or reviewing evidence gained from past experience."[43] On the view set out in this memo—which was not revoked and replaced by the Department of Justice until after photographs of detainee abuse at Abu Ghraib had been published[44]—the advice of behavioral science experts would be critical, at the very least, in order to insulate interrogators from domestic criminal liability.[45]

Having tried to narrow the definition of torture, the Administration continued to emphasize that the United States does not torture.[46] However, that still left the prohibition on CID treatment or punishment as a potential impediment to more aggressive interrogation strategies. As a party to both the ICCPR[47] and the Torture Convention,[48] the United States has committed itself to the prohibition against CID treatment, as well as torture. The ICCPR clearly states that this is an obligation to which no exception is permitted,[49] and the Torture Convention imposes an obligation on parties to review interrogation rules to ensure that they do not result in CID treatment.[50] When the United States ratified both treaties, it made reservations defining CID to mean cruel and unusual treatment or punishment prohibited by the Fifth, Eighth, and Fourteenth Amendments to the United States Constitution.[51] The Bush Administration took the view that these reservations served not only to redefine the type of conduct that would be considered CID, but also operated to limit the geographic scope of the Unites States' international obligations so that they did not apply to aliens detained outside the United States.[52] This view created, in effect, a "legal black hole" into which Guantánamo Bay, nominally leased by the United States from Cuba, conveniently appeared to fall.[53] This was the position which Senator John McCain sought to address in the so-called "McCain Amendment," now section 1003 of the Detainee Treatment Act of 2005.[54] Its provisions were intended to make clear that the prohibition of CID treatment applies irrespective of the nationality and geographic location of the detainee.[55] But when President Bush signed the Detainee Treatment Act into law, he issued a presidential signing statement declaring that the Administration would interpret the detainee provisions "in a manner consistent with the constitutional authority of the President to supervise the unitary executive branch and as Commander in Chief and consistent with the constitutional limitations on judicial power."[56] This firm assertion of presidential power naturally raised serious doubts about the practical impact of the legislation on the Administration's detention and interrogation policy.[57]

Another important doctrinal reformulation—or exercise in legal exceptionalism—concerns the Geneva Conventions. Common Article Three of the Geneva Conventions provides protections that have long been understood as the low watermark for treatment of detainees, irrespective of their status.[58] Although so-called unlawful combatants are not entitled to the full array of protections applicable to prisoners of war, they are to be protected from cruel, humiliating, or degrading treatment *and* from outrages on personal dignity.[59] They are also to be treated humanely.[60] The formal position of the Administration, determined in February 2002, was that the Geneva Conventions did not apply to detainees who are members of Al Qaeda, because Al Qaeda is neither a state nor a party to the Conventions.[61] However, that position was unequivocally rejected by the Supreme Court of the United States in *Hamdan v. Rumsfeld* in June 2006.[62] The Department of Defense responded to this decision with a memorandum calling for a review of directives and policies to ensure compliance with Common Article Three.[63] But just a few weeks later, in September 2006, the President publicly criticized the provisions of Common Article Three for being too vague.[64] Congress addressed the President's concerns later that month, passing the Military Commissions Act of 2006 (MCA).[65] The MCA purports to confer on the President the authority to "interpret the meaning and application of the Geneva Conventions."[66] It remains to be seen how the President will respond to this provision. But there is a real danger that the Executive will view it as providing *carte blanche* to define Article Three's protections narrowly.

Although the MCA states that "[n]othing in this section shall be construed to affect the constitutional functions and responsibilities of...the judicial branch of the United States,"[67] this provides little comfort given the MCA's attempts to strip the federal courts of habeas corpus jurisdiction over detainees,[68] and to prevent them from invoking the Geneva Conventions "as a source of rights" in domestic litigation.[69] If the President does narrowly redefine the scope of protections in the Geneva Conventions, it is therefore likely to be some time before a federal court will be given the opportunity to correct this. That delay will be too long, not just for detainees at Guantánamo Bay and elsewhere, but also for health professionals with whom they have contact.

Whatever the Administration's interpretation of the Geneva Conventions, health professionals would be well-advised to remember that international legal norms—as commonly understood by other nations and, in the case of the Geneva Conventions, as authoritatively interpreted by the International Committee of the Red Cross (ICRC)[70]—will be violated by more aggressive interrogation strategies long before the mental and physical health or well-being of detainees are implicated. For example, the prohibition of outrages on personal dignity in Common Article Three was clearly breached by soldiers who placed underwear on the heads of detainees or forced them to assemble naked in pyramid formation.[71] Second, medical personnel may be complicit in the commission of grave breaches of the Geneva Conventions—also known as war crimes—if they advise on or monitor the use of interrogation tactics that qualify as torture or inhuman treatment or that "willfully cause great suffering."[72] War crimes attract universal jurisdiction.[73] So even if health professionals were not concerned about potential prosecution in the United States,[74] they would be ill-advised to ignore the possibility of being arrested and tried while visiting another country.

LAW AND MEDICAL ETHICS

In the face of the Administration's efforts to circumvent international legal protections for detainees in the war on terror, the voice of professional ethics is especially important. Professional ethics should not be an entirely autonomous enterprise. In particular, ethical codes for physicians, psychologists, and other health professionals should incorporate basic standards that reflect fundamental protections found in international human rights law and the laws of war.[75] The Report of the American Psychological Association's Task Force on Psychological Ethics and National Security in July 2005 notably failed to do this. Proscriptions against psychologists' participation in abusive interrogation were not defined by reference to international law. They were merely tied to "applicable" U.S. rules and regulations as "developed and refined" since 9/11.[76] When one recalls the administration's efforts to "refine" legal norms, the dangers inherent in this approach are manifest. The report also fails to recognize that since the vast majority of detainees in the war on terror are foreign nationals, the propriety of their treatment is far more likely to be judged by international standards than by domestic ones, particularly if the latter are more lax.

It is possible simply to tie ethical constraints on health professionals to international legal prohibitions—an approach taken in the United Nations Principles of Medical Ethics.[77] For example, physicians are prohibited from using their knowledge and skills to assist in an interrogation that adversely affects the health or condition of a detainee *and* is "not in accordance with the relevant international instruments."[78] These instruments would obviously include the Geneva Conventions, the ICCPR, and the Torture Convention. But giving legal norms the last word on the limits of professional conduct leaves psychiatrists and psychologists without clear guidance in the face of disagreements between lawyers and policymakers about the application of those norms. The efforts to redefine the scope and meaning of the Geneva Conventions and the prohibition of CID treatment in core human rights treaties—discussed above—provide two powerful illustrations of this point.[79]

Some codes of professional ethics impose firm constraints on health professionals, irrespective of the applicable legal norms. For example, the World Medical Association's Regulations in Times of Armed Conflict state that it is unethical for physicians to "[w]eaken the physical or mental strength of a human being without therapeutic justification" or to "[e]mploy scientific knowledge to imperil health."[80] It is difficult to understand how a physician with these prohibitions in mind would have felt able to participate in the kinds of aggressive interrogation stressors deployed at Guantánamo Bay. At the very least, the express purpose of coercive counter-resistance tactics such as prolonged isolation and sleep deprivation was to weaken the mental and physical strength of detainees.[81] In light of this, the American Medical Association (AMA) might have been expected to respond clearly and speedily to revelations of the involvement of American physicians in aggressive interrogations.

However, the AMA did not formally take a position on the role of physicians in interrogation until the summer of 2006.[82] The new ethical guidelines provide that "[p]hysicians must neither conduct nor directly participate in, or monitor an interrogation, because a role as physician-interrogator undermines the physician's role as healer."[83] However, physicians are permitted to participate in "developing effective interrogation strategies for general training purposes," provided those strategies are humane and respectful of individuals' rights, and do not "threaten or cause physical injury or mental suffering."[84] The American Psychiatric Association adopted a similar position in May 2006, prohibiting psychiatrists from "direct participation" in interrogation, defined to include "being present in the interrogation room, asking or suggesting questions, or advising authorities on the use of specific techniques of interrogation with particular detainees."[85] The psychiatrists' association also permits its members to provide training to interrogators on "recognizing and responding to persons with mental illnesses, on the possible medical and psychological effects of particular techniques and conditions of interrogation, and on other areas within their professional expertise."[86]

Although the guidelines of both the AMA and the American Psychiatric Association therefore leave open the possibility of giving general advice and training to military and civilian personnel in either law enforcement or intelligence branches, they make clear that physicians should stay out of the interrogation room—and, for that matter, any adjoining observation room—and that they should not give advice on specific interrogation techniques for specific detainees. By contrast, the August 2006 resolution of the American Psychological Association cleared the way for continued participation of psychologists in individual interrogations at Guantánamo Bay.

That resolution admittedly improves on the organization's 2005 task force report by providing that "psychologists shall work in accordance with international human rights instruments relevant to their roles."[87] However, the remainder of the document simply ties the prohibitions on psychologists' conduct to the basic legal prohibitions on torture and CID treatment. Thus, psychologists must not "knowingly engage in, tolerate, direct, support, advise, or offer training" in such treatment.[88] Nor shall they "provide knowingly any research, instruments, or knowledge that facilitates" such treatment.[89] Nor shall they "knowingly participate in any procedure in which [such treatment] is used or threatened."[90] And should they be present when torture or CID treatment occurs, they should try to stop the abuse and "failing that, exit the procedure."[91] In essence, these regulations require psychologists to obey the laws that bind us all. Beyond that, psychologists have only their consciences as a guide.[**]

The egregious abuse of detainees at Guantánamo Bay (and elsewhere) raises real concerns about the role of psychologists in military interrogations, and emphasizes the need for firmer guidance. Dr. Koocher, President of the American Psychological Association in 2006, claims that psychologists are best placed to detect and prevent "behavioral drift" on the part of interrogators—that is, the slide into unprofessional and ultimately illegal behavior.[92] But he fails to

---

[**]After this article was first published, the American Psychological Association adopted a further resolution entitled "Reaffirmation of the American Psychological Association Position Against Torture and Other Cruel, Inhuman, or Degrading Treatment or Punishment and Its Application to Individuals Defined in the United States Code as 'Enemy Combatants'" (August 19, 2007; available at http://www.apa.org/gover nance/resolutions/councilres0807.html). That resolution contains an absolute prohibition on the direct or indirect participation of psychologists in a number of interrogation tactics such as water-boarding, stress positions and exposure to temperature extremes. However, the resolution appears to suggest that isolation, sensory deprivation, over-stimulation and sleep deprivation are only problematic when "used in a manner that represents significant pain or suffering or in a manner that a reasonable person would judge to cause lasting harm." On this view, these tactics could still be used as instruments of distress during interrogation pursuant to the advice of a psychologist.

recognize that there are powerful social and institutional pressures on health professionals associated with the intelligence mission, including military psychologists, that weigh heavily against intervening—pressures that may well have been responsible for the Biscuit psychologist's failure to intervene in the aggressive interrogation of Al Qahtani.[93]

Put simply, interrogators are not the only people subject to "behavioral drift"—it may equally affect the psychologists charged with identifying and preventing it.[94] Furthermore, the American Psychological Association's new guidelines create the additional problem of what I call *definitional drift*. By tying the principal constraints on psychologists' conduct to the prohibition on torture and CID treatment, the American Psychological Association's summer 2006 resolution leaves psychologists vulnerable to drifting definitions, in particular the Administration's efforts to redefine those norms. This vulnerability is particularly important in light of the Administration's emerging preference for staffing Biscuits with psychologists rather than psychiatrists[95]—a preference that predates, but has been reinforced by, the new professional guidelines for physicians in general, and psychiatrists in particular.[96]

CONCLUSION

The involvement of health professionals in interrogation is hardly new. To give just one example, congressional testimony describes the role of an American physician in a form of torture known as the "water cure" in the war in the Philippines more than a hundred years ago.[97] There too, the victims of aggressive interrogation and torture were considered undeserving of the protections of the laws of war—a precedent for current exceptionalism expressly justified on grounds that enemy "insurgents" were "not civilized."[98] However, the systematic involvement of mental health professionals in U.S. Army interrogation practice was a significant development. Writing some months before this development occurred, M. Gregg Bloche—who trained as both a lawyer and a physician—observed that the "unreflective willingness of most Western physicians to employ clinical skills for myriad state purposes suggests that their ethical sensitivity to the problem of extra-clinical consequences does not greatly exceed that of their colleagues in countries where gross human rights abuse is endemic."[99] Bearing this in mind, he emphasized the need for the training of health professionals in both ethics and international human rights norms, for institutional mechanisms to nurture professional autonomy, and for international support from (among others) professional bodies.[100]

The importance of these recommendations is highlighted not only by revelations of health professionals' complicity in detainee abuse, but also by recent statements of an experienced U.S. interrogator in the war on terror. He notes that, in addition to the predictable pressure to support the military objectives of their colleagues, some health professionals may have financial anxieties too. In the interrogator's words:

> Most of the PAs [physician assistants] or doctors that we use have been through medical school due to military scholarships. They owe the military big bucks. If they refused to aid us then they might be brought up on charges in an internal trial and would be forced to repay the military.[101]

I do not intend to suggest that military health professionals are venal. On the contrary, the vast majority pursue careers in the military—despite the call of more lucrative private practice—for noble and altruistic reasons. However, it would be foolish to pretend either that those financial pressures do not exist or that they cannot have an impact—even subconsciously—on an individual's moral calculus. Furthermore, if social and financial pressures are not sufficient to bring on board health professionals despite their ethical qualms, interrogators may use other means to procure their cooperation and compliance with the interrogation mission.

We already know that military personnel at Guantánamo Bay were manipulated. They were told that the detainees were "the worst of the worst."[102] According to Department of Defense documents, the vast majority had been handed over to U.S. forces by Pakistan or the Northern Alliance in exchange for large bounties—and most of them were not alleged to have committed any hostile acts against either the United States or its allies.[103] Health professionals, in particular, are not in a position to verify the provenance of a detainee. Nor do they have the knowledge or expertise to assess the security threat posed by a particular detainee.[104] So health professionals are in a position of ignorance and uncertainty that may be exploited. The interrogator quoted above has also indicated that intelligence personnel may lie to health professionals:

> If the people are worried about doctors and psychologists aiding their own military in time of war, we can just have those who do work with us say we are not harming anyone. If they worry about our methods then we say that all plans of interrogation have approved the tactics as non "stressful." *As you can lie to a terrorist to get information then you can lie to any group that interferes with the job of making the people safe.*[105]

The interrogator also noted that if the use of doctors or physician assistants becomes problematic (or "too much," in his words), interrogators "would then make use of our ParaRescue or Combat Medics for medical expertise in interrogations."[106] This is important since much of the discussion to date has been about the role of psychiatrists and psychologists in interrogation. Now that the AMA and the American Psychiatric Association have issued guidelines that seek to keep doctors out of the interrogation room—and empower them both legally and practically to refuse to participate[107]—the spotlight has focused on psychologists.[108] But we would do well to remember that other types of health professionals may also be implicated.

The recent proliferation of Department of Defense manuals and directives—most notably, the new Army interrogation manual prohibiting the use of "waterboarding," hooding, and military dogs in interrogation[109]—is presumably intended to suggest that the Administration is trying to redress the errors of the past. But it is not clear how these policy documents will play out on the ground. Arguably, they may be of little relevance at the present time since detainees who have been held for years at Guantánamo Bay can no longer have actionable intelligence (even if they once did so), and there would be little point in interrogating them. However, fundamental questions remain about detainees held by the CIA, whatever their location.*** The CIA is contesting the ACLU's FOIA applications, so its practices are still shrouded in secrecy, and detainees in its custody will not benefit from the provisions of the new Army field manual.[110] Furthermore, in a recent radio interview, Vice President Cheney was asked: "Would you agree a dunk in water is a no-brainer if it can save lives?"[111] Mr. Cheney replied: "It's a no-brainer for me."[112] In the same interview, he agreed that the debate over interrogation techniques was "a little silly."[113] These comments reveal a failure at the highest levels of government to internalize the most fundamental norms of human rights law and the laws of war. In such an environment, health professionals should still be considered "at risk"—that is, in danger of becoming accomplices to the perpetration of war crimes in the counterterrorism mission. Looking forward, one of the most important questions is:

How will *they* respond?

NOTES

The author would like to thank Jean Maria Arrigo for providing access to the indispensable archive materials referred to in the body of this article, and M. Gregg Bloche for generous collaboration and support without which this article could not have been written.

***In July 2007, after this article was published, the President issued an executive order addressing the CIA's detention and interrogation operations: *see* http://www.whitehouse.gov/news/releases/2007/07/20070720-4.html (July 20, 2007). The order only prohibits "willful and outrageous acts of personal abuse done for the purpose of humiliating or degrading the individual in a manner so serious that any reasonable person, *considering the circumstances,* would deem the acts to be beyond the bounds of human decency" (emphasis added). The circumstances envisaged are that the detainee is "likely to be in possession of information that: (1) could assist in detecting, mitigating, or preventing terrorist attacks...or (2) could assist in locating the senior leadership of al Qaeda, the Taliban, or associated forces." The order does not specify which interrogation tactics are approved. However, it requires that "interrogation practices are determined by the Director of the CIA, *based upon professional advice,* to be safe for use with each detainee with whom they are used" (emphasis added). So the order clearly envisages the continued participation of health professionals in the design of individual CIA interrogation plans. *See also* De Young, K. (2007). Bush Approves New CIA Methods: Interrogation of Detainees to Resume. *Washington Post,* July 21, A1, available at http://www.washingtonpost.com/wp-dyn/content/article/2007/07/20/AR2007072001264.html.

1. G.A. Res. 2200A (XXI), 21 U.N. GAOR, Supp. No. 16, at 52, U.N. Doc. A/ 6316 (Dec. 16, 1966), *available at* http://www.unhchr.ch/html/menu3/b/a_ccpr.htm (stating in Article 4 that there can be no derogation from the prohibitions on either torture or cruel, inhuman, or degrading treatment even "[i]n time of public emergency which threatens the life of the nation").

2. G.A. Res. 39/46, annex, 39 U.N. GAOR, Supp. No. 51, at 197, U.N. Doc. A/39/ 51 (Dec. 10, 1984) (stating in Article 2(2) that "[n]o exceptional circumstances whatsoever, whether a state of war or a threat of war, internal political instability or any other public emergency, may be invoked as a justification of torture").

3. *See generally* PHYSICIANS FOR HUMAN RIGHTS, BREAK THEM DOWN: SYSTEMATIC USE OF PSYCHOLOGICAL TORTURE BY US FORCES 48–71 (2005), *available at* http:// www.physiciansforhumanrights.org/library/documents/reports/break-them-down-the.pdf (explaining the long-term psychological impact of prolonged isolation and aggressive interrogation procedures).

4. Josh White, *Three Detainees Commit Suicide at Guantánamo,* WASH. POST, June 11, 2006, at A01.

5. *Id.*

6. It has been reported that one-fifth of Guantánamo detainees are on antidepressants. *See, e.g.* Editorial, *Inside Guantánamo: How We Survived Jail Hell,* OBSERVER (London), Mar. 14, 2004, *available at* http://observer.guardian.co.uk/uk_news/story/ 0,6903,1168937,00.html.

7. *See* Jonathan H. Marks, *Apology or Apologia: The Fourth Estate and the Case for War in Iraq, in* THE AGE OF APOLOGY: THE WEST FACES ITS OWN PAST (Gibney et al. eds., 2007).

8. The role of professional organizations will be discussed in Part IV, *infra.*

9. *See, e.g.,* Geneva Convention Relative to the Treatment of Prisoners of War, art. 3, Aug. 12, 1949, 6 U.S.T. 3316, 75 U.N.T.S. 135 ("Third Geneva Convention").

10. *See* Jonathan H. Marks, *Uphold International Law,* RALEIGH NEWS & OBSERVER, Feb. 16, 2003, at A29 (noting the irony of the United States' efforts to undermine the international legal order that the United States worked so hard to establish).

11. The President admitted the existence of these sites in September 2006. *See* Dan Eggen & Dafna Linzer, *Secret World of Detainees Grows More Public,* WASH. POST, Sept. 7, 2006, at A18 (noting that details of the sites remain classified).

12. Correspondence between a U.S. Counterintelligence Liaison Officer and Jean Maria (2002–2005) (on file at the Project on Ethics and Art in Testimony, Irvine, CA) [hereinafter Arrigo Papers]. An additional copy is archived at *Intelligence Ethics Collection,* Hoover Institution Archives, Stanford University, Stanford, CA (restricted until January 1, 2010). This is, of course, just one interrogator's view of human rights. The correspondence also indicates that there have been deliberate efforts to distract and mislead the press during the war on terror. Another communication states: "[E]mbedded reporters are now being put in one vehicle and taken to staged events while the rest of the unit goes to do its job.... The use of names of the prisoners will be replaced by codes so nobody can try to trace them." *Id.*

13. *See, e.g.,* M. Gregg Bloche & Jonathan H. Marks, *When Doctors Go To War,* 352 NEW ENG. J. MED. 3, 3–6 (2005); M. Gregg Bloche & Jonathan H. Marks, *Doctors and*

Interrogators at Guantánamo Bay, 353 NEW ENG. J. MED. 6, 6–8 (2005); STEVE H. MILES, OATH BETRAYED: TORTURE, MEDICAL COMPLICITY AND THE WAR ON TERROR 43–67 (2006).

14. *See, e.g.,* Bloche & Marks, *Doctors and Interrogators at Guantánamo Bay, supra* note 13. However, some mental health professionals were sent to Survival, Evasion, Resistance, and Escape ("SERE") school where U.S. soldiers are trained to resist interrogation at the hands of enemy captors. *See* M. Gregg Bloche & Jonathan H. Marks, *Doing Unto Others as They Did Unto Us,* N.Y. TIMES, Nov. 14, 2005, at 21; *see also* Jonathan H. Marks, *Doctors of Interrogation,* 35 HASTINGS CTR. REPORT 17, 18 (2005) (discussing whether health professionals were employed for their professional expertise or in order to add an imprimatur of decency to the process).

15. Bloche & Marks, *Doing Unto Others as They Did Unto Us, supra* note 14.

16. Marks, *supra* 14, at 17 (discussing whether health professionals were employed for their professional expertise or in order to add an imprimatur of decency to the process).

17. *Id.*

18. *Id.*

19. *Id.* at 17–22.

20. *See, e.g.,* PHYSICIANS FOR HUMAN RIGHTS, BREAK THEM DOWN: SYSTEMATIC USE OF PSYCHOLOGICAL TORTURE BY US FORCES (2005), *available at* http://www.physiciansforhumanrights.org/library/documents/reports/break-them-down-the.pdf.

21. Neil Lewis, *Interrogators Cite Doctors' Aid at Guantánamo Prison Camp,* N.Y. TIMES, June 24, 2005, *available at* http://www.nytimes.com/2005/06/24/politics/24gitmo.html?ex=1277265600&en=b1960558c2ad9fa4&ei=5088&partner=rssnyt&emc=rss.

22. *Id.*

23. Marks, *Doctors of Interrogation, supra* note 14, at 18.

24. *Id.* at 17.

25. He was not, of course, the only Al Qaeda suspect to be branded "the 20th hijacker." *See, e.g.,* Seymour M. Hersh, *The Twentieth Man: Has the Justice Department Mishandled the Case against Zacarias Moussaoui?,* NEW YORKER, Sept. 30, 2002, *available at* http://www.newyorker.com/fact/content/articles/020930fa_fact.

26. ARMY REG. 15–6: FINAL REPORT, INVESTIGATION INTO FBI ALLEGATIONS OF DETAINEE ABUSE AT GUANTÁNAMO BAY, CUBA DETENTION FACILITY (*as amended* June 9, 2005), 13–21, *available at* http://www.defenselink.mil/news/Jul2005/d20050714report.pdf.

See Adam Zagorin & Michael Duffy, *Inside the Interrogation of Detainee 063,* TIME, June 12, 2005, *available at* http://www.time.com/time/magazine/printout/0,8816,1071284,00.html; *see also* Interrogation Log Detainee 063, Nov. 23, 2002, http://www.time.com/time/2006/log/log.pdf (presenting a partially-redacted copy of the interrogation log); *see also* Steve Miles, *Medical Ethics and the Interrogation of Detainee 063,* 7 Am. J. Bioethics 3, *available at* http://www.bioethics.net/journal/j_articles.php?aid=1140 (discussing this interrogation from a medical ethics perspective).

28. *See* Zagorin & Duffy, *supra* note 27.

29. *Id.*

30. Susan Okie, *Glimpses of Guantánamo-Medical Ethics and the War on Terror,* 353 NEW ENG. J. MED. 2529, 2530 (2006).

31. *Id.*

32. Luke Mitchell, *God Mode,* HARPER'S MAGAZINE, July 2006, *available at* http://www.harpers.org/GodMode.html (Aug. 24, 2006).

33. George Annas, *Hunger Strikes at Guantánamo—Medical Ethics and Human Rights in a "Legal Black Hole,"* 355 NEW ENG. J. MED. 1377, 1379–80 (2006).

34. *Id.* at 1377; Nancy Sherman, *Holding Doctors Responsible at Guantánamo,* 16 KENNEDY INST. OF ETHICS J. 199, 201 (2006).

35. BBC News, *Guantánamo Suicides "Acts of War",* June 11, 2006, http://news.bbc.co.uk/2/hi/americas/5068606.stm.

36. Mark Denbeaux et al., *No-Hearing Hearings—CSRT: The Modern Habeas Corpus? An Analysis of the Proceedings of the Government's Combatant Status Review Tribunals at Guantánamo,* Nov. 2005, http://law.shu.edu/news/final_no_hearing_hearings_ report.pdf (finding Department of Defense documents indicate that "[t]he Government did not produce any witnesses in any [Combatant Status Review Tribunal] hearing and did not present any documentary evidence to the detainee prior to the hearing in 96% of the cases").

37. Mitchell, *supra* note 32.

38. *See* Jonathan H. Marks, *9/11 + 3/11 + 7/7 = ? What Counts in Counterterrorism?,* 37 COLUM. HUM. RTS. L. REV. 559, 578–83 (2006).

39. Memorandum from Jay S. Bybee, Assistant Att'y Gen., U.S. Dep't of Justice, to Alberto R. Gonzales, White House Counsel, Re: Standards of Conduct for Interrogation under 18 U.S.C. §§ 2340–2340A (Aug. 1, 2002), *available at* http://www.washington post.com/wp-srv/nation/documents/dojinterrogation memo20020801.pdf [hereinafter Bybee Memo]. Sections 2340–2340A, which define the criminal offense of torture in the United States, were enacted in order to comply with the United States' obligations under the Convention Against Torture and Other Cruel, Inhuman or Degrading Treatment or Punishment (1984). See H.R. Rep. No. 103-482, at 229 (1994)(Conf. Rep.). The drafters of the Bybee memo drew on (and were admittedly facilitated by) understandings made by the United States when it ratified the Convention in 1994. *See* Sanford Levinson, *"Precommitment" and "Postcommitment": The Ban on Torture in the Wake of September 11,* 81 TEX. L. REV. 2013,2036–38 (2003). The text of the ratification instrument is available at http://www.unhchr.ch/html/menu2/6/cat/treaties/convention-reserv.htm.

40. Bybee Memo, *supra* note 39, at 1.

41. *Id.*

42. *Id.* at 4.

43. *Id.* at 8 (emphasis added).

44. Although the document was revoked in June 2004, it was not formally replaced until December 2004, just days before the confirmation hearings of Attorney General Alberto Gonzales. *See* Memorandum from Daniel Levin, Acting Assistant Attorney General to James B. Comey, Deputy Attorney General, Re: Legal Standards Applicable under 18 U.S.C. §§ 2340–2340A (Dec. 30, 2004), *available at* http://www.usdoj.gov/olc/dagmemo.pdf.

45. *See* Bybee Memo, *supra* note 39, at 8.

46. *See, e.g.,* Statement by the President on United Nations International Day in Support of Victims of Torture, http://www.whitehouse.gov/news/releases/2003/06/20030626-3.html (June 23, 2003) (stating that the "United States is committed to the world-wide elimination of torture and we are leading this fight by example").

47. ICCPR, *supra* note 1.

48. Torture Convention, *supra* note 2.

49. For an authoritative interpretation of the ICCPR on this point, see Human Rights Committee, General Comment No. 20 (1992), ¶ 3, *available at* http://www.unhchr.ch/tbs/doc.nsf/(Symbol)/6924291970754969c12563ed004c8ae5?Opendocument (last visited Feb. 5, 2007).

50. Torture Convention, *supra* 2, arts. 11 & 16.

51. For the text of the United States' ratification of the Torture Convention, *see* 36 CONG. REC. S10091 (1990), *available at* http://www.unhchr.ch/html/menu2/6/cat/treaties/convention-reserv.htm. For the text of the United States' ratification of the ICCPR, see http://www.unhchr.ch/html/menu3/b/treaty5_asp.htm (last visited Nov. 25, 2006).

52. *See* Gonzales Nomination Transcript, *available at* http://www.humanrightsfirst.com/us_law/etn/gonzales/statements/gonz_testimony_010604.htm (last visited Mar. 30, 2006).

53. *See* Johan Steyn, *Guantánamo Bay: The Legal Black Hole,* 53 INT'L & COMP. L.Q. 1–15 (2004).

54. *See* Detainee Treatment Act of 2005, Pub. L. No. 109–48, § 1003, 119 Stat. 2680, 2739–2744 (2005).

55. *See id.*

56. Statement of President George W. Bush Upon Signing of H.R. 2863, Dec. 30, 2005, *available at*http://www.whitehouse.gov/releaseas/2005/12/10551230-8.html; *see also* T.J. Halstead, Cong. Res. Serv., *Presidential Signing Statements: Constitutional and Institutional Implications,* Sept. 20, 2006, *available at* http://www.fas.org/sgp/crs/natsec/RL33667.pdf (analyzing the impact of signing statements).

57. It should be noted that a provision similar to the McCain Amendment also appears in the Military Commissions Act of 2006, Pub. L. No. 109-366, 120 Stat. 2600. However, the Military Commissions Act is problematic for several other reasons, some of which are discussed below. *See* notes 65–69 and accompanying text; *see also* Human Rights Watch, Q and A: Military Commissions Act of 2006, *available at* http://hrw.org/backgrounder/usa/qna1006/usqna1006web.pdf (briefly analyzing and critiquing the Military Commissions Act) [hereinafter Human Rights Watch].

58. *See, e.g.,* International Committee for the Red Cross, *Commentary on Geneva Convention III, Article 3,*http://www.icrc.org/ihl.nsf/COM/375-590006?OpenDocument (last visited Mar. 14, 2007); Michael John Garcia, Cong. Res. Serv., *The War Crimes Act: Current Issues,* Oct. 2, 2006, *available at* http://www.fas.org/sgp/crs/intel/RL33662.pdf; *see also* Ruth Wedgwood & R. James Woolsey, *Law and Torture,* WALL ST. J., June 28, 2004, at A10.

59. Third Geneva Convention, *supra* note 9, art. 3.

60. *Id.* A similar obligation is found in Article 10 of the ICCPR, which provides that "[a]ll persons deprived of their liberty shall be treated with humanity and with respect for the inherent dignity of the human person." ICCPR, *supra* note 1, art. 10.

61. Office of the White House Press Secretary, Fact Sheet: Status of the Detainees at Guantánamo, Feb. 7, 2002, *available at* http://www.whitehouse.gov/news/releases/2002/02/20020207-13.html.

62. Hamdan v. Rumsfeld, 126 S. Ct. 2749, 2794–95 (2006).

63. Memorandum from Gordon England, Deputy Secretary of Defense to the Secretaries of the Military Departments et al., Application of Common Article 3 of the Geneva Conventions to the Treatment of Detainees in the Department of Defense (July 7, 2006), *available at* http://www.defenselink.mil/news/Aug2006/d20060814comm3.pdf.

64. The President acknowledged that the "Supreme Court's ruling [in Hamdan] . . . said that we must conduct ourselves under the Common Article 3 of the Geneva Convention." He added: "And that Common Article 3 says that there will be no outrages upon human dignity. It's very vague. What does that mean, 'outrages upon human dignity?' That's a statement that is wide open to interpretation." Transcript of Sept. 15, 2006, Press Conference of the President, *available at* http://www.whitehouse.gov/news/releases/2006/09/20060915-2.html.

65. Military Commissions Act of 2006, Pub. L. No. 109-366, 120 Stat. 2600.

66. *Id.* § 6(a)(3)(A).

67. *Id.*

68. *Id.* § 7. *See also* Gerald L. Neuman, *The Military Commissions Act and the Detainee Debacle: A Response,* 48 Harv. Int'l L.J. Online 33 (2007), http://www.harvardilj.org/online/105 (arguing that Congress did not have the power to permanently abrogate the writ of habeas corpus) and Robert M. Chesney, *Judicial Review, Combatant Status Determinations, and the Possible Consequences of* Boumediene, 48 Harv. Int'l L.J. Online 62 (2007), http://www.harvardilj.org/online/110 (observing that the "slowly grinding process of developing and stabilizing our detainee laws and policies unfortunately is not yet near its conclusion").

69. *Id.* at § 5. In particular, this section seeks to prevent the Geneva Conventions from being invoked as a source of rights in habeas corpus or other civil proceedings against the United States, and any of its current or former officers, employees, or agents. *Id.*

70. Int'l Comm. of the Red Cross, International Humanitarian Law—Treaties of Documents 1 (2005), http://www.icrc.org/ihl.nsf/CONVPRES?OpenView (ICRC's authoritative commentary on the Geneva Conventions).

71. BG Furlow & Lt. Gen. Schmidt, Investigation into FBI Allegations of Detainee Abuse at Guantánamo Bay, Cuba Detention Facility 19 (June 9, 2005) (indicating that Guantánamo Bay detainee, Al Qahtani, "was forced to wear a woman's bra and had a thong placed on his head during interrogation"). For the infamous image of a human pyramid at Abu Ghraib, which has become emblematic of detainee abuse in the war on terror, see *New Yorker,* at http://www.newyorker.com/online/slideshows/slideshows/040510onslpo_prison_02 (last visited Feb. 10, 2007).

72. *See* Third Geneva Convention, *supra* note 9, art. 130, *available at* http://www.unhchr.ch/html/menu3/ b/91.htm; for a discussion of the War Crimes Act in the United States, *see also* Garcia, *supra* note 58.

73. For a more detailed discussion of universal jurisdiction and its theoretical foundations, see Jonathan H. Marks, *Mending the Web: Universal Jurisdiction, Humanitarian Intervention and the Abrogation of Immunity by the Security Council,* 42 Colum. J. Transnat'l L. 445 (2004).

74. The Military Commissions Act also amends the War Crimes Act. Military Commissions Act of 2006, Pub. L. No. 109-366, 120 Stat. 2600. For a brief summary of the material revisions, see Human Rights Watch, *supra* note 57.

75. *See* Leslie London et al., *Dual Loyalty Among Military Health Professionals,* 15 CAMBRIDGE Q. OF HEALTHCARE ETHICS 381, 385–86 (2006) (discussing the value of a human rights perspective). In the remainder of this section, I will argue that human rights should be the foundation of a health professional's ethical obligations, but not the limit of those obligations.

76. REPORT OF THE AMERICAN PSYCHOLOGICAL ASSOCIATION PRESIDENTIAL TASK FORCE ON PSYCHOLOGICAL ETHICS AND NATIONAL SECURITY (2005), *available at* http://www.apa.org/ releases/PENSTaskForceReportFinal.pdf [hereinafter Presidential Task Force]; *see also* Tara McKelvey, *First Do Some Harm,* AMERICAN PROSPECT, Sept. 1 2005, http:// www.prospect.org/web/printfriendly-view.ww?id=10110 (critiquing the task force, many of whose members had military or national security affiliations); Michael Benjamin, *Psychological Warfare,* SALON.COM, July 26, 2006, available at http://www.salon.com/ news/feature/2006/07/26/interrogation/index.html; Mark Benjamin, *Psychologists' Group Still Rocked by Torture Debate,* SALON.COM, Aug. 4, 2006, http://www.salon.com/news/ feature/2006/08/04/apa/.

77. Principles of Medical Ethics Relevant to the Role of Health Personnel, Particularly Physicians, in the Protection of Prisoners and Detainees Against Torture and Other Cruel, Inhuman or Degrading Treatment or Punishment, G.A. Res. 37/194, Annex, U.N. Doc. A/RES/37/194 (Dec. 18, 1982), *available at* http://www.un.org/documents/ ga/res/37/a37r194.htm.

78. *Id.* at princ. 4.

79. *See supra* Part III.

80. WORLD MEDICAL ASSOCIATION, REGULATIONS IN TIMES OF ARMED CONFLICT ¶ 2 (2006),*available at* http://www.wma.net/e/policy/a20.htm[hereinafter REGULATION IN TIMES OF ARMED CONFLICT]. These provisions were in effect in 2002 when the aggressive interrogation strategies were introduced at Guantánamo Bay. *See* Amnesty International, Ethics Codes and Declarations Relevant to the Health Professions, ACT 75/05/00, at 18 (4th ed., 2000). Following the revelations of physician participation in interrogation in the war on terror, two more instances of unethical behavior were added to the list in May 2006. The regulations now state that it is also unethical for a physician to "[e]mploy personal health information to facilitate interrogation[,]" or to "[c]ondone, facilitate or participate in the practice of torture or any form of cruel, inhuman or degrading treatment." REGULATION IN TIMES OF ARMED CONFLICT, *supra,* at ¶2(d) and (e). The latter, in particular, should already have been obvious.

81. *See* Bloche & Marks, *Doing Unto Others as They Did Unto Us, supra* note 14 (discussing the source of the aggressive interrogation strategies deployed at Guantánamo Bay).

82. *See* Jonathan H. Marks, *The Silence of the Doctors,* THE NATION, Dec. 26, 2005, *available at* http://www.thenation.com/docprem.mhtml?i=20051226&5=marks (critiquing the AMA's failure to speak out sooner).

83. AM. MED. ASS'N, OPINION OF THE COUNCIL ON ETHICAL AND JUDICIAL AFFAIRS: PHYSICIAN PARTICIPATION IN INTERROGATION (2006), *available at* http://www.ama-assn.org/ama1/ pub/upload/mm/475/cejo4i06.doc. This followed the revision to the World Medical Association's Declaration of Tokyo (Guidelines for Physicians Concerning Torture and other Cruel, Inhuman or Degrading Treatment or Punishment in Relation to Detention and Imprisonment) in May 2006 to provide that "[t]he physician shall not use nor allow to

be used, as far as he or she can, medical knowledge or skills, or health information specific to individuals, to facilitate or otherwise aid any interrogation, legal or illegal, of those individuals." The revised Declaration is available at http://www.wma.net/e/policy/c18.htm.

84. AM. MED. ASS'N, *supra* note 83. In a press release, the Chair of the AMA's Council on Ethical and Judicial Affairs, Priscilla Ray, M.D., stated that because "it is justifiable for physicians to serve in roles that serve the public interest," the "AMA policy permits physicians to develop general interrogation strategies that are not coercive, but are humane and respect the rights of individuals." *See* Press Release, AMA, New AMA Ethical Policy Opposes Direct Physician Participation in Interrogation (Jun. 12, 2006), http://www.ama-assn.org/ama/pub/category/16446.html. Neither the policy statement nor the press release addresses the question of whether physicians would ordinarily possess the expertise to advise on what interrogation techniques might generally be effective. For a discussion of potential rationales for seeking medical advice on interrogation, see Marks, *Doctors of Interrogation, supra* note 14.

85. Am. Psychiatric Ass'n, Psychiatric Participation in Interrogation of Detainees: Position Statement (2006), *available at* http://www.psych.org/edu/other_res/lib_arch ives/archives/200601.pdf.

86. *Id.*

87. *Compare* Am. Psychol. Ass'n, Resolution Against Torture and Cruel, Inhuman, and Degrading Treatment or Punishment (Aug. 9, 2006), *available at* http://www.apa.org/governance/resolutions/notortureres.html [hereinafter Resolution Against Torture], *with* PRESIDENTIAL TASK FORCE, *supra* note 76 (the former incorporating human rights standards in the manner described in the text accompanying this note, the latter stating that the Task Force "did not reach consensus on . . . [t]he role of human rights standards in an ethics code").

88. Resolution Against Torture, *supra* note 87.

89. *Id.*

90. *Id.*

91. *Id.*

92. Gerald P. Koocher, *Varied and Valued Roles,* MONITOR ON PSYCHOL. July–Aug. 2006, at 5, *available at* http://www.apa.org/monitor/julaug06/pc.html. The same claim was made by the Director of the American Psychological Association's Ethics Office in Stephen Behnke, *Ethics and Interrogations: Comparing and Contrasting the American Psychological, American Medical and American Psychiatric Association Positions,* MONITOR ON PSYCHOL., July–Aug. 2006, at 66, *available at* http://www.apa.org/monitor/julaug06/interrogations.html.

93. The psychologist referred to here is discussed in the text accompanying note 27 above. See also Marks, *Doctors of Interrogation, supra* note 14.

94. Ironically, one of the members of the APA's PRESIDENTIAL TASK FORCE has argued that its report (*see* note 76, *supra*) was itself the result of behavioral drift. Telephone interview with Jean Maria Arrigo, Ph.D, Founder, Project on Ethics and Art in Testimony, in Irvine, Cal. (Dec. 1, 2006).

95. DEP'T OF DEFENSE INSTRUCTION NO. 2310.08E, MEDICAL PROGRAM SUPPORT FOR DETAINEE OPERATIONS (2006), *available at* http://www.fas.org/irp/doddir/dod/i2310_08.pdf. "[P]hysicians are not ordinarily assigned duties as [behavioral science

consultants], but may be so assigned, with the approval of [the Assistant Secretary of Defense for Health Affairs], in circumstances when qualified psychologists are unable or unavailable to meet critical mission needs." *Id.* at E2.2. This follows the recommendation of Maj. Gen. Martinez-Lopez in April 2005 that physicians should not be assigned to Biscuits. *See* Office of the Surgeon General, Army, Final Report, Assessment of Detainee Medical Operations for OEF, GTMO, and OIF (2005), *available at* http://www.globalsecurity.org/military/library/report/2005/detmedopsrpt_13apr2005.pdf.

96. *See* Ken Hausman, *Military Looks to Psychologists for Advice on Interrogation,* Psychiatr. News, July 7, 2006, at 4, *available at* http://pn.psychiatryonline.org/cgi/content/full/41/13/4 (discussing a statement made by the Assistant Secretary of Defense for Health Affairs, William Winkenwerder, Jr., to the effect that the different stances adopted by the psychologists' and psychiatrists' professional associations "contributed" to the Pentagon's preference for staffing Biscuits with psychologists).

97. S. Comm. Rec. on the Philippines, at 1527–32 (1899–1921) (testimony of Charles S. Riley), *reprinted in* Henry F. Graff, American Imperialism and the Philippine Insurrection (1969) 72–80 and *discussed in* Marks, *The Silence of the Doctors,supra* note 82, at 26.

98. S. Comm. Rec. on the Philippines, at 558–64 (1899–1921) (testimony of Gen. Hughes) *reprinted in* Henry F. Graff, *supra* note 97, 64–72; *see also* Marks, *What Counts, supra* note 38, at 579.

99. M. Gregg Bloche, *Caretakers and Collaborators,* 10 Cambridge Q. Healthcare Ethics 275, 278 (2001).

100. *Id.* at 283.

101. The Arrigo Papers, *supra* note 12.

102. Erik Saar and Viveca Novak, Inside the Wire: A Military Intelligence Soldier's Eyewitness Account of Life at Guantánamo 193 (2005).

103. Mark Denbeaux et al., Report on Guantánamo Detainees: A Profile of 517 Detainees through Analysis of Department of Defense Data 2–3 (2006), *available at* http://law.shu.edu/news/Guantánamo_report_final_2_08_06.pdf. In addition, among the detainees were both children and the senescent. *See* Oliver Burkeman, *Children Held at Guantánamo,* Guardian, Apr. 24, 2003, *available at* http://www.guardian.co.uk/afghanistan/story/0,1284,942347,00.html; Times Wire Reports, *Oldest Guantánamo Detainee Returns Home,* L.A. Times, Aug. 29, 2006, A8 (reporting that Haji Nasrat Khan, an Afghan detainee, who was "at least 71" and uses a walker, has been sent home).

104. *See* London, *supra* note 75, at 386.

105. The Arrigo Papers, *supra* note 12 (emphasis added).

106. *Id.*

107. International humanitarian law prohibits states from requiring medical professionals to act contrary to their codes of ethics. *See* Bloche & Marks, *Doctors and Interrogators at Guantánamo Bay, supra* note 14; Marks, *What Counts, supra* note 38 at 582.

108. *See, e.g.,* Michael Benjamin, *Psychological Warfare,* Salon.com, July 26, 2006, http://www.salon.com/news/feature/2006/07/26/interrogation/index.html; Mark Benjamin, *Psychologists' Group Still Rocked by Torture Debate,* Salon.com, Aug. 4, 2006, http://www.salon.com/news/feature/2006/08/04/apa/.

109. *See* FM 2-22.3 (FM 34-52), Human Intelligence Collector Operations ¶ 5-75 (2006), *available at* http://www.fas.org/irp/doddir/army/fm2-22-3.pdf.

110. Although current CIA interrogation guidelines are classified, previous CIA manuals have been made public. *See, e.g.,* KUBARK Counterintelligence Interrogation (1963), *available at* http://www.gwu.edu/~nsarchiv/NSAEBB/NSAEBB27/01-01.htm.

111. *See* Demetri Sevastopulo, *Cheney Endorses Simulated Drowning: Says Use of Water Boarding to Get Terrorist Intelligence is "no brainer",* Fin. Times (London), Oct. 26, 2006, *available at* http://www.msnbc.msn.com/id/15433467/; *see also* Dan Eggen, *Cheney Defends "Dunk in the Water" Remark Addressing Alarm Over the Comment, Vice President Says He Was Not Referring to Waterboarding,* Wash. Post, Oct. 28, 2006, at A02, *available at* http://www.washingtonpost.com/wp-dyn/content/article/2006/10/27/AR2006102700560.html.

112. *See* Sevastopulo, *supra* note 111.

113. *Id.*

CHAPTER 6

NEUROPSYCHIATRIC EFFECTS OF SOLITARY CONFINEMENT

Stuart Grassian

My observations and conclusions regarding the psychiatric effects of solitary confinement have been cited in a number of federal court decisions, for example: *Davenport v. DeRobertis,* 844 F.2d 1310, and *Madrid v. Gomez,* 889 F.Supp. 1146. From time to time I have been consulted by attorneys regarding a number of detainees at Guantánamo, and a number of other individuals accused of terrorist activities.

In the course of this work, I prepared a lengthy report entitled "The Psychiatric Effects of Solitary Confinement." This work has subsequently been published in the *Washington University Journal of Law and Policy* 2006, vol. 22, pp. 325–383. It describes the extensive body of literature, including clinical and experimental literature, regarding the effects of decreased environmental and social stimulation; as well as, specifically, observations concerning the effects of solitary confinement on prisoners. That article provides a fairly extensive bibliography of the medical literature on this subject.

I offer here a general overview of the issue, and a discussion of observations of Jose Padilla,[1] one individual who has been incarcerated in the United States as a result of accusations of al Qaeda affiliation.

GENERAL OVERVIEW OF THE PSYCHIATRIC EFFECTS OF SOLITARY CONFINEMENT

Solitary confinement—that is, confinement of a prisoner alone in a cell for all or nearly all of the day, with minimal environmental stimulation and minimal opportunity for social interaction—can cause severe psychiatric harm.[2] It has indeed long been known that severe restriction of environmental and social stimulation has a profoundly deleterious effect on mental functioning; this issue has, for example, been a major concern for many groups of patients,[3] including, for example, patients in intensive care units, spinal patients immobilized by the need for prolonged traction, and patients with impairment of their sensory apparatus (such as eye-patched or hearing-impaired patients). This issue has also been a very significant concern in military situations and in exploration[4]—polar and submarine expeditions, and in preparations for space travel.

In regard to solitary confinement, the United States was actually the world leader in introducing prolonged incarceration—and solitary confinement—as a means of dealing with criminal behavior; the "penitentiary system"[5] began in the United States in the early nineteenth century, a product of a spirit of great social optimism about the possibility of rehabilitation of individuals with socially deviant behavior. This system, originally embodied as the "Philadelphia System," involved almost an exclusive reliance upon solitary confinement as a means of incarceration, and also became the predominant mode of incarceration—both for post conviction and also for pretrial detainees—in the several European prison systems which emulated the American model.

The results were catastrophic. The incidence of mental disturbances among prisoners so detained, and the severity of such disturbances, was so great that the system fell into disfavor and was ultimately abandoned. During this process, a major body of clinical literature developed that documented the psychiatric disturbances created by such stringent conditions of confinement.[6] The paradigmatic disturbance was an agitated confusional state that, in more severe cases, had the characteristics of a florid delirium, characterized by severe confusional, paranoid and hallucinatory features, and also by intense agitation and random, impulsive violence—often self-directed.

The psychiatric harm caused by solitary confinement became exceedingly apparent. Indeed by 1890, in *In re Medley,* 10 S.Ct. 384, the U.S. Supreme Court explicitly recognized the massive psychiatric harm caused by solitary confinement: "This matter of solitary confinement is not...a mere unimportant regulation as to the safe-keeping of the prisoner...[E]xperience [with the penitentiary system of solitary confinement] demonstrated that there were serious objections to it. A considerable number of the prisoners fell, after even a short confinement, into a semi-fatuous condition, from which it was next to impossible to arouse them, and others became violently insane; others still, committed suicide; while those who stood the ordeal better were not generally reformed, and in most cases did not recover sufficient mental activity to be of any subsequent service to the community" (10 S.Ct. at 386).

The consequences of the Supreme Court's holding were quite dramatic for Mr. Medley. Mr. Medley had been convicted of having murdered his wife. Under the Colorado statute in force at the time of the murder, he would have been executed after about one additional month of incarceration in the county jail. But in the interim between Mr. Medley's crime and his trial, the Colorado legislature had passed a new statute that called for the convicted murderer to be, instead, incarcerated in solitary confinement in the State Prison during the month prior to his execution. Unhappily, simultaneously with the passage of the new law, the legislature rescinded the older law, without allowing for a bridging clause which would have allowed for Mr. Medley's sentencing under the older statute.

Mr. Medley appealed his sentencing under the new statute, arguing that punishment under this new law was so substantially more burdensome than punishment under the old law, as to render its application to him *ex post facto*. The Supreme Court agreed with him, even though it simultaneously recognized that if Mr. Medley was not sentenced under the new law, he could not be sentenced at all. Despite this, the Court held that this additional punishment of one month of solitary confinement was simply too egregious to ignore; the Court declared Mr. Medley a free man, and ordered his release from prison.

Dramatic concerns about the profound psychiatric effects of solitary confinement have continued into the twentieth century, both in the medical literature, and in the news. The alarm raised about the "brainwashing" of political prisoners of the Soviet Union and of Communist China—and especially of American prisoners of war during the Korean War—gave rise to a major body of medical and scientific literature concerning the effects of sensory deprivation and social isolation, including a substantial body of experimental research.[7]

This literature, as well as my own observations, has demonstrated that, deprived of a sufficient level of environmental and social stimulation, individuals will soon become incapable of maintaining an adequate state of alertness and attention to the environment. Indeed, even a few days of solitary confinement will predictably shift the electroencephalogram (EEG) pattern towards an abnormal pattern characteristic of stupor and delirium.[8]

This fact is, indeed, not surprising. Most individuals have, at one time or another, experienced, at least briefly, the effects of intense monotony and inadequate environmental stimulation. After even a relatively brief period of time in such a situation, an individual is likely to descend into a mental torpor—a "fog"—in which alertness, attention, and concentration all become impaired. In such a state, after a time, the individual becomes increasingly incapable of processing external stimuli, and often becomes "hyperresponsive" to such stimulation; for example, a sudden noise or the flashing of a light jars the individual from his stupor, and becomes intensely unpleasant. Over time, the very absence of stimulation causes whatever stimulation *is* available to become noxious and irritating; individuals in such a stupor tend to avoid any stimulation, and progressively to withdraw into themselves and their own mental fog.

An adequate state of responsiveness to the environment requires both the ability to achieve and maintain an attentional set—to *focus* attention—and the ability to *shift* attention. The impairment of alertness and concentration in solitary confinement leads to two related abnormalities.

The inability to *focus,* to achieve and maintain attention, is experienced as a kind of dissociative stupor—a mental "fog" in which the individual cannot focus attention, cannot, for example, grasp or recall when he attempts to read or to think.

The inability to *shift* attention results in a kind of "tunnel vision" in which the individual's attention becomes *stuck*—almost always on something intensely unpleasant—and in which he cannot *stop* thinking about that matter; instead, he becomes obsessively fixated upon it. These obsessional preoccupations are especially troubling. Individuals in solitary easily become preoccupied with some thought, some perceived slight or irritation, some sound or smell coming from a neighboring cell, or—perhaps most commonly, by some bodily sensation— tortured by it, unable to stop dwelling on it. I have examined countless individuals in solitary confinement who have become obsessively preoccupied with some minor, almost imperceptible bodily sensation, a sensation which grows over time into a worry, and finally into an all-consuming, life-threatening illness.

In solitary confinement, ordinary stimuli become intensely unpleasant, and small irritations become maddening. Individuals in such confinement brood upon normally unimportant stimuli, and minor irritations become the focus of increasing agitation and paranoia.

Individuals experiencing such environmental restriction find it difficult to maintain a normal pattern of daytime alertness and nighttime sleep. They often find themselves during the day incapable of resisting their bed—incapable of resisting the paralyzing effect of their stupor—and yet incapable at night of any restful sleep. The lack of meaningful activity is far compounded by the effect of continual exposure to artificial light, and diminished opportunity to experience natural daylight. And the individuals' difficulty in maintaining a normal day-night sleep cycle is often far worsened by the constant intrusions on nighttime dark and quiet—steel doors slamming shut, flashlights shining in their face, and so forth.

There are, of course, substantial differences in the effects of solitary confinement upon different individuals. Those most severely affected are generally individuals with evidence of subtle neurological or attention deficit disorder, or with some other vulnerability; this includes, for example, individuals with psychopathic personality disorders, who appear to experience a chronic underarousal of their central nervous system, leading them to have a pathological need for external stimulation. When such particularly vulnerable individuals are exposed to conditions of solitary confinement, they are especially likely to descend into states of florid psychotic delirium, marked by severe hallucinatory confusion, disorientation, and even incoherence, and by intense agitation and paranoia; these psychotic disturbances often have a dissociative character, and individuals so affected often do not recall events that occurred during the course of the confusional psychosis. Other individuals—generally, individuals with more stable personalities and greater ability to modulate their emotional expression and behavior, and individuals with stronger cognitive functioning—are less severely affected. However, all of these individuals will still experience a degree of stupor, difficulties with thinking and concentration, obsessional thinking, agitation, irritability, and difficulty tolerating external stimuli (especially noxious stimuli).

Individuals with stronger cognitive capabilities will often struggle to ward off stupor by generating their own stimulation internally—that is, by their own intellectual processes—but such individuals will almost invariably struggle against the inexorable pull towards obsessional thinking. It is very common for an inmate who spends virtually his entire day alone and without meaningful environmental, social, or occupational stimulation to become obsessively fixated on particular—even minor—features of his environment, and to become increasingly incapable of tolerating any change or increased deprivation in that environment. The inmate has very little to distract his attention from some, even minor, noxious event or stimulus. Inmates in solitary not only experience a deprivation of stimulation, but also experience a sense of helplessness—of loss of control over their environment. They become intolerant of change, of uncertainty, of their own passivity and helplessness in the face of their environment.

As noted before, EEG studies have corroborated some of these findings, demonstrating that, even after a few days of solitary confinement, the EEG will characteristically shift in the direction of stupor and delirium. Moreover, one study[9] from the Balkan conflict demonstrated that even after release from solitary confinement, there are continuing EEG abnormalities; the EEG shows excessive spike reaction to environmental (in that case, visual) stimulation. In other words, the "hyperresponsivity to external stimuli," which is found clinically in individuals exposed to solitary confinement, is also seen in EEG recordings, and this disturbance continues for some unknown period of time after release from solitary.

Jose Padilla

The terms "segregated confinement," "SHU (Special Housing Unit) confinement," "solitary confinement," etc., all generally refer to confinement alone in a cell anywhere from about 56–90 square feet, with minimal opportunities for social interaction, conjoint recreation or religious services, minimal educational or occupational programming, and very limited environmental stimulation. In general in such settings, an inmate spends about 22–23 hours/day in his cell, with individual exercise and showering representing most of the time spent outside the cell. Administrative and environmental conditions can vary. Radio is often available, television sometimes; the opportunity for nonlegal phone calls varies; visitation, however, is almost invariably noncontact. Some cells have windows affording a view of the outside world, but in many, there either is no window to the outside, or the window is only translucent and affords virtually no opportunity to see the outside world.

Jose Padilla's attorneys attempted unsuccessfully to present evidence at trial that Mr. Padilla was subjected to intentionally brutal conditions of interrogation during his confinement in the Naval Brig. In any event, it is not disputed that Mr. Padilla was confined in solitary confinement in the Naval Brig in South Carolina from June 2002 until January 2006. While administrative procedures regarding his confinement varied over time, for the vast majority of this detention, he had virtually no human contact at all. Even when he was allowed out of his cell into a Day Room–type area, he was entirely alone, except for the guards with whom he had virtually no interaction. His cell was quite small, about 80 square feet, and contained only a sink, toilet, and steel-plate bed, which was attached to the concrete wall of the cell. It apparently lacked a table or a place to sit other than the bed. It is my understanding that he was not even provided a mattress for considerable portions of his confinement, and when a mattress was provided, it was a very thin mattress, only about three inches thick. There are allegations that the temperature in his cell was intentionally adjusted to leave him extremely cold for extended periods of time. His cell had a narrow window, but the glass was painted over in such a manner that it was completely opaque, preventing him not only from seeing out of the window, but even from ascertaining whether it was day or night. The cell was lit by a fluorescent light over which he had no control; it was on 24 hours/day, though it was dimmed in intensity during the hours of 10 PM to 5 AM. The cell had a hinged solid steel door which added to his isolation. No one other than himself was housed on his tier, and he could not hear even the conversations between the guards.

He was utterly isolated from other people. During the entire period of his incarceration, he received only two social phone calls from his mother, and had only one social visit from his mother. Although his attorneys were assigned to his case in 2002, the government did not allow them to meet with him until March 2004; afterwards, he received attorney visits approximately once a month. During the first months of his incarceration, Mr. Padilla was visited with some regularity by an imam, but then this was discontinued, and afterwards he had no contact with a Moslem clergyman. Other than his attorney visits, his only other contact was with representatives of the Red Cross, who periodically monitored his conditions of confinement.

He ate alone; for breakfast and lunch, food was passed through a food slot in his cell door, and he ate sitting on his bed, with the tray balanced on his knees. He was given no access at all to canteen, so he had no way of augmenting or varying the food provided by the prison. Towards the end of his confinement in the Brig, he was able to come out of his cell to the Day Room area for dinner, but even then he was utterly alone. Towards the latter part of his incarceration there, he was also allowed into an outdoor exercise yard for about two hours a day, but even then, he was again utterly alone; the exercise yard was enclosed on all four sides by a high concrete wall, and was covered by a heavy metal fencing. His ability to obtain books to occupy himself apparently varied considerably during his incarceration in the Brig. His conditions were apparently made especially stringent during the first year of his confinement there, especially during a several-month period of time when he was apparently being interrogated intensively. During the first approximately two years, he had no access to television; however, following a court order in 2005, he is able to watch broadcast TV in the Day Room a few hours per day.

His isolation was made even more disturbing because, even though he had no social interaction, he was constantly being observed; his cell was constantly monitored by video camera, and for the first year of his confinement in the Brig, the door to his tier was opened every few minutes for more direct observation; the constant banging of that heavy metal door made sleep very difficult for him.

While Mr. Padilla's conditions of confinement varied throughout the three years, eight months he was kept in the Naval Brig, his attorneys have developed evidence that there was one particularly harsh period of confinement. Apparently, beginning approximately in late November 2002 until early April 2003, Mr. Padilla was subjected to even more extreme isolation and perceptual deprivation. After his arrival at the Naval Brig on June 10, 2002, up until late November 2002, Mr. Padilla was given reading materials, including but not limited to a copy of the Qu'ran, fairly regular recreation time, and opportunity for showering. However, commencing in late November 2002, Mr. Padilla was apparently stripped of all reading materials, including the Qu'ran, and his opportunities for out-of-cell exercise and for showering were severely curtailed. During this period of time, it was not unusual for Mr. Padilla to go four, five, or six days without even brief (generally no more than a few minutes at most) rounding by Brig staff, who were, in any event, under instruction not to converse with him. And other than these intermittent, brief rounds, during this several-month period of time, Mr. Padilla went through long stretches (e.g. 34, 17, 15 days) without any human contact. And when he did have such contact, it was inevitably with a Naval interrogator.

The daily logs show that in this time period, Mr. Padilla was deprived of all reading material—the Qu'ran, magazines, newspapers—as well as of television and radio. During that time period, he was also allowed out-of-cell recreation very infrequently. In one stretch of time, he went 21 days straight without being offered any out-of-cell exercise, and there were other stretches of 15-, 13-, 7-, 6-, 5-, and 4-day intervals between offers of out-of-cell time. Moreover, what opportunities were afforded him were always in solitude, and often indoors in another, albeit somewhat larger, windowless cell, in which he could do little but walk around in circles.

During this 20-week period, Mr. Padilla had approximately 10 hours of recreation time in total; about 30 minutes per week, an average of less than

4 minutes a day, a deprivation that, in my experience, is unprecedented even in the harshest conditions of solitary confinement in state and federal penitentiaries in the United States.

And Mr. Padilla suffered other deprivations as well during this period. He was denied regular access to shower facilities, and commonly experienced periods of several—up to six—days without access to a shower in this time period. Again, in my experience, this level of deprivation is not seen even in the harshest conditions of prison confinement in the United States.

There is also evidence that Mr. Padilla suffered other forms of abuse during this period of intense deprivation and interrogation. These include apparently credible allegations of intentional sleep disruption, physical abuse, having to sleep on a metal slab in a cold cell with no blanket or insulation against the cold and hard metal and concrete surfaces. (Concerns are also raised about possible forced drugging, though there is apparently little confirmatory evidence of this.)

Mr. Padilla was transferred to the Miami Federal Detention Center in January 2006. He has been housed continually in the facility's Special Housing Unit (SHU), where inmates are kept in solitary confinement; it was in this setting that I met him in December 2006.

Since he is being housed there in response to the Special Administrative Measures (SAMS) governing his incarceration, he is housed in an especially isolated wing of the SHU; there are no inmates at all near his cell, and he cannot even hear other inmates' voices. As a prisoner subject to SAMS procedure, he suffers deprivations far beyond that of an ordinary inmate in the FDC-Miami SHU, much less that of an ordinary federal prisoner at the FDC.

For instance, Mr. Padilla's social visits and telephone contacts are extremely curtailed. His only authorized social visitor, his mother, must request a visit 14 days in advance of her anticipated visit, and these visits are constantly monitored. After Mr. Padilla arrived in FDC, his counsel finally managed to arrange a visit with his mother (noncontact, in separate rooms, able to see each other through a thick window, but requiring telephones to be able to speak with each other). Yet when Mr. Padilla's mother arrived at the facility, she was flanked by two FBI agents who explained that they would remain present during the entire visit; Mr. Padilla and his mother were informed that her visits would always be monitored in some such fashion. Her visits became so emotionally oppressive for her and for her son as well, that eventually she gave up visiting her son altogether. Even leaving his cell at all has become an oppressive ordeal for Mr. Padilla. Despite the massive security surrounding Mr. Padilla, each time he returns to his cell he must submit to a body cavity search.

Moreover, unlike other federal inmates, Mr. Padilla has essentially no phone privileges. Moreover, he does not get to purchase anything at all from the prison commissary, thus allowing him no opportunity, for example, to purchase anything to eat to vary from the prison diet. His reading material is restricted in volume—preventing him from having even the full documentary material provided by his attorneys.

He has told his attorney that he refuses his recreation time because it is in a dark, caged area in the SHU, on the 12th floor of the FDC. The place scares him, and going there is nowhere near worthwhile, especially in light of the body cavity search he would have to undergo afterwards. Moroever, Mr. Padilla has no television, extremely limited access to reading materials, and no contact with any human being other than his counsel and his guards. He was eventually given some access to a radio, but this access was severely limited in scope; the controls lie outside his cell, and he is allowed to listen to only three stations, which are clearly labelled on the radio, and even then, it is the guards, not Mr. Padilla, who determine when the radio will be on, what station will be tuned in, and at what volume.

Effects of Confinement

Mr. Padilla had no evidence of any mental illness prior to his arrest and incarceration in 2002. As a young child, he apparently was well behaved, a good student, and a caring son and oldest brother. As a teenager, he became entangled with peers in serious delinquent behavior and served some time in juvenile detention. During his incarceration, he was introduced into the Moslem religion, and eventually he converted to Islam. When he was 28 years old, he moved to Egypt, where he married and had a family. The U.S. government claims that he became involved in al Qaeda in Egypt, although this claim is vigorously disputed.

Mr. Padilla was arrested when he arrived at the Chicago airport in June 2002; he was then brought to MCC-Manhattan, where he was housed in solitary for about one month before being transferred to the Naval Brig in South Carolina. When seen then by his first defense counsel, he presented himself as an affable, cooperative, thoughtful person who took an active interest in his legal case. In addition, he recurrently spoke of his concern for his family and of his great desire to have contact with them. He maintained good eye contact, had no facial grimacing, and was easily engaged in conversation.

After Mr. Padilla was transferred to the Brig, he had no further contact with any family or attorney until almost two years later, when, as a result of a court order, he was allowed to have attorney visits. His attorney was struck by how different he was now. He was extremely quiet, and seemed to have a terribly difficult time maintaining eye contact. He kept repeating—often inappropriately and oddly—how well he was being treated by his captors. It was unusual, even somewhat eerie. When a subject was brought up even remotely close to his case or to his confinement, he would begin to twitch. When he was asked if something was wrong, he would quickly respond: "My back hurts; I'm getting help for it; I'm fine"—quickly shutting off any further discussion. By the time he was transferred to FDC-Miami, he appeared obviously anxious, jittery, and grimacing, and his eyes blinking. When anything of substance was raised, his face would begin grimacing grotesquely, and he would start blinking rapidly. He would keep looking behind him, tense and disconnected. He would almost compulsively say how well he had been treated, how much he trusted the government. He even expressed the idea that if there were trouble, his mother could write a letter to President Bush; he was sure he would help her out.

It was utterly irrational. After all, it was *Bush* who had *put* him in jail. And the irrationality did not stop there. He trusted the government (the people trying to convict him) but he distrusted his attorneys because he thought they were secretly trying to lock him away in a psychiatric hospital, from which he would never escape and his mother would never see him again. He kept telling her that he was "fine," while it was becoming increasingly apparent to her that he was not. Her son seemed so agitated, so odd, so irrational, that finally his mother could bear it no more; she blurted out: "Did they torture you?" He turned towards her, his face grimacing, his eyes blinking, and in panic and rage he demanded: "Don't you ever, ever, ask that question again."

But on one visit, he *did* say something about the Brig—not much, but something. He told his mother that it was very bad. They kept him totally isolated. They put him in a room with no light at all. They made him drink pills. Sometimes they made it so cold, and they would not give him a blanket to cover himself. His mother could not ask more details after that; he completely clammed up.

Mr. Padilla's attorneys have noted a great number of odd behaviors and statements that Mr. Padilla has made. For example, Mr. Padilla consistently has denied—even to his own attorneys—that he has any mental health problems. Yet he once claimed that he was administered the psychedelic drug LSD while in the Brig. It is, of course, a terribly important claim. *If* he were in fact administered this drug against his will, this would be an apparent major violation of his civil liberties. But if were *not* so drugged, why would he make this claim? Why would he choose to claim that the drug was a *psychedelic*? After all, arguably psychedelics are not at all the most obvious choice. But the claim would make perfect sense if, in fact, Mr. Padilla experienced a "psychedelic-like" experience in solitary at the Brig—that is, an acute, frightening, confusional state marked by mulitple perceptual distortions and hallucinatory phenomena. In short, his statement strongly suggests that he experienced the paradigmatic disturbance associated with solitary confinement—a brief confusional hallucinatory psychosis.

One of his attorneys described observations of Mr. Padilla that have caused him to have concern about his client's mental state:

- In 2005, Mr. Padilla apparently began having repetitive episodes of intense shortness of breath, chest tightness, and sudden fear—classic symptoms of panic attacks. These episodes had never occurred prior to his incarceration.

- Some of Mr. Padilla's attitudes and behavior suggest a growing paranoia. For example, he was provided by the prison with a facsimile of a letter from his mother, and became convinced that it was a forgery. His attorney then tried another approach; he had Mr. Padilla's mother write him a letter and mail it to the Attorney's office. Mr. Patel then himself brought the letter to Mr. Padilla so he could review it, and despite this strict chain of custody, Mr. Padilla still was convinced that the handwriting was not his mother's, and that the letter was a forgery.

- Similarly, when the prison administration tried to substitute another (non-Moslem) clergyman for the (apparently no longer available) imam visits, Mr. Padilla became suspicious that this man was not really a clergyman, but rather an agent of the government, trying to extract information from him.

The attorney also finds it puzzling and disturbing that Mr. Padilla never attempts to contact him, never even sending him correspondence. Similarly, Mr. Padilla refuses or declines to put any requests in writing. Indeed, a senior prison administrative official commented that Mr. Padilla is so quiet and immobile that he seems "like a piece of furniture." At times, Mr. Padilla seems confused, disoriented. Sometimes he loses track, not just of the day, but even of the year.

Another of his attorneys described his frustration that the utter void of communication from Mr. Padilla severely impaired the defense's efforts to help him. He tells them virtually nothing of his confinement in the Brig—not even the very limited information which he gave his mother. There is clearly exculpatory material that the defense has discovered—information that was obviously known by Mr. Padilla but was never revealed to his attorneys. As a result, the attorneys have spent days and weeks attempting to ferret out even the smallest scraps of information about Mr. Padilla's case, a frustrating, inefficient, and ineffective method or developing their case—so much so that it troubles their moral sense that they are not able to fulfill their ethical and professional responsibility to their client. And as noted by others, Mr. Padilla just keeps repeating irrational statements: He trusts the government and not them. He keeps repeating that he is "fine." When they try in the most gentle way to broach any subject about Egypt or about the Brig, his eyes blink fiercely, his mouth grimaces oddly, and in a half-smile, half-terror, he says he wants to go back to his cell now—that he is "tired." Then he tells them that they have gone over all this before (whereas in fact he has *never* told them about the subject). And then again he insists he is "tired" and insists that he be allowed to go back to his cell.

In summary, Mr. Padilla manifests severe effects of long-term solitary confinement. It should, however, first be noted that two psychologists who evaluated him both reached the conclusion that Mr. Padilla suffers from Posttraumatic Stress Disorder (PTSD) as a result of those conditions of confinement and of the interrogation he endured at the Naval Brig in Charleston. I concur with that conclusion. He manifests a number of symptoms of that disorder, altogether suggestive that he suffers profoundly from it. These include hypervigilance (constantly looking around over his shoulder while his attorney is talking with him), avoidance (being willing to speak with his attorneys about a number of subjects, but not about what happened to him in the Brig, and wanting to literally leave the room when the subject is brought up), physiological reactivity when reminded of the trauma (his eyes start blinking wildly, and he begins making odd, eerie facial grimaces), and a profound sense of helplessness (for example, repeatedly telling one of his attorneys that there was nothing he could do for Mr. Padilla in regard to those conditions and his interrogation, because the government was all-powerful). Moreover, his tendency to identify with his captors rather than his own attorneys (the so-called "Stockholm Syndrome") strongly suggests a profound fear and sense of helplessness.

But his symptomatic presentation suggests even more than this. He has become profoundly suspicious, apparently paranoid at times (e.g., his conviction that his mother's letter was a forgery). His grimacing and eye blinking, often accompanied by a strange, tense spreading of his lips as though in an attempt to smile, has an eerie, psychotic feel to it. He perseverates (repeating the same thought over and over again, even though the thought makes little sense in the first place). There is, indeed, a fundamental irrationality in his thinking about his case; he continually repeats that his attorneys already know everything, that "we have gone over all this before," when in fact he has virtually *never* been willing to talk about *any* of these issues with any of his attorneys.

In short, his presentation suggests not simply a reaction to fear and trauma, but really a *disorganizing, psychotic* reaction. It is very significant that one of his paranoid fears is that his attorneys are trying to put him away forever in a psychiatric hospital. Of course, they intend nothing of the sort. What they *did* want was only for him to be evaluated in a clinical setting, removed from the continuing stress of solitary confinement. They had no thought whatsoever that he should *remain* in any such facility. Why, then, would Mr. Padilla come to fear this? No one had even raised it as a possibility. Why would *he* think of it? Obviously, the fear must have come from inside of him—from some vague recognition that he had become very ill.

Among people with the most severe cases of PTSD, there *are* some for whom the trauma is so disorganizing that they become paranoid or psychotically disorganized when their attention is pointed to reminders of the trauma. This phenomenon is fairly rare, although not unheard of. Indeed, there is a long history to the use of isolation and perceptual deprivation by interrogators as a means of destroying an inmate's sense of identity and his will to resist. As described in my Washington University article, the U.S. intelligence services became acutely aware of this issue as a result of concern about "brainwashing" of American prisoners of war during the Korean War, as well as by the Soviet KGB.

Research funded by the U.S. government described the Soviet detention prisons of that era:

> Incarceration in these prisons is almost universally in solitary confinement, in a cell approximately ten feet by six feet in size....An almost invariable feature of the management of any important suspect under detention is a period of total isolation in a detention cell...The effects upon prisoners of the regimen...are striking...He becomes increasingly anxious and restless...As it continues, the prisoner becomes increasingly dejected and dependent. He gradually gives up all spontaneous activity within his cell...Finally, he sits and stares with a vacant expression, perhaps twisting a button on his coat. Ultimately he may reach a state of depression in which...he pays little attention to his surroundings. In this state the prisoner may have illusory experiences...Some prisoners may become delirious and have...hallucinations.[10]

There have been multiple reports that the United States has, at times, come to copy some of these same techniques in its own interrogation procedures. It is certainly clear that the U.S. Department of Defense is entirely aware of the potentially catastrophic effects of prolonged isolation. Thus, *if,* as Mr. Padilla's defense contends in its *Motion to Dismiss for Outrageous Government Conduct,* there was a systematic use of isolation and physical and emotional abuse as a means of forcing him to become psychologically dependent upon his captors, and to destroy will to resist interrogation, then his psychological deterioration and inability to assist in his own defense would have likely been inevitable. Yet even if those contentions were *not* entirely accurate, Mr. Padilla has still undergone a profound, tremendously prolonged psychological stress, involving extended periods of utter isolation and deprivation. His solitary confinement now spans over 57 months continuously, under the most stringent of conditions, conditions rarely or never found in even the harshest of civilian prisons.

I have evaluated many individuals who were so traumatized by their incarceration in solitary that they developed a PTSD as a result of that incarceration, a disorder that lingered well after their release from such confinement. Typically, their terrifying traumatic memory is of their own experience of psychological deterioration during the ordeal. Some such individuals cannot even talk about what happened, cannot focus their attention towards it at all. Doing so is unbearable, or perhaps more likely in Mr. Padilla's case, it is psychotically disorganizing.

NOTES

1. *United States of America vs. Jose Padilla,* U.S. Dist. Ct., SD Fla, 04-60001-CRCooke-Brown.

2. Grassian, S. (2006). "The Psychiatric Effects of Solitary Confinement," *Washington University Journal of Law and Policy* 22: 325–383. Grassian, S. (1983). "Psychopathological Effects of Solitary Confinement," *American Journal of Psychiatry* 140: 1450–1454.

3. See, for example, Downs, F. (1974). "Bed rest and sensory disturbances," *American Journal of Nursing* 74(3): 434–438. Ellis, R. (1972). "Unusual sensory and thought disturbances after cardiac surgery," *American Journal of Nursing* 72(11): 2021–2025. Jackson, C.W., Jr. (1969). "Clinical sensory deprivation. A review of hospitalized eye patients," In J.P. Zubek (Ed.), *Sensory deprivation: Fifteen years of research* New York: Appleton-Century-Crofts. Kornfeld, D.S., Zimberg, S., & Malm, J.R. (1965). "Psychiatric complications of open-heart surgery," *New England Journal of Medicine* 273(6): 287–292. Lazarus, H.R., & Hagens, J.H. (1968). "Prevention of psychosis following open-heart surgery," *American Journal of Psychiatry* 124(9): 1190–1195. Ziskind, E. (1958). "Isolation stress in medical and mental illness," *Journal of the American Medical Association* 168(11): 1427–1431. Ziskind, E., Jones, H., Filante, W., & Goldberg, J. (1960). "Observations on mental symptoms in eye patched patients: Hypnagogic symptoms in sensory deprivation," *American Journal of Psychiatry* 116: 893–900.

4. See for example Bennett, A.M.H. (1961). "Sensory Deprivation in Aviation," In Solomon, P., Kubzansky, P.E., Leiderman, P.H., Mendelson, J.H., Trumbull, R., & Wexler, D. (Eds.) *Sensory Deprivation* Cambridge, MA: Harvard University Press. Cochrane, J.J., & Freeman, S.J.J., (1989). "Working in Arctic and sub-arctic conditions: Mental health issues," *Canadian Journal of Psychiatry* 34: 884–890. Freedman, S. & Greenblatt, M. (1960). "Studies in Human Isolation IV: Hallucinations and Other Cognitive Findings," *U.S. Armed Forces Medical Journal* 11: 1479–1497. Gunderson, E.K. (1963). "Emotional symptoms in extremely isolated groups," *Archives of General Psychiatry* 9: 362–368. Gunderson, E.K., & Nelson, P.D. (1963). "Adaptation of small groups to extreme environments," *Aerospace Medicine* 34: 1111–1115.

5. Rothman, D. (1971). *The Discovery of the Asylum.* Boston: Little Brown & Company.

6. Nitsche, P., Wilmanns, K. (1912). *The History of the Prison Psychoses.* New York: Nervous and Mental Disease Publishing Company.

7. Meltzer, M. (1956). "Solitary Confinement." In GAP (Group for the Advancement of Psychiatry) Symposium #3: Factors Used to Increase the Susceptibility of Individual to Forceful Indoctrination. New York. Sutker, P., et al. (1991). "Cognitive Deficits and Psychopathology Among Former Prisoners of War and Combat Veterans of the Korean Conflict," *American Journal of Psychiatry* 148(1): 67–72.

8. See, for example Zubek, J. (1969). "Physiological and Biochemical Effects," In *Sensory Deprivation: Fifteen Years of Research.* New York: Appleton-Century Crofts.

9. Vrca, A., et al. (1996). "Visual Evoked Potentials in Relation to Factors of Imprisonment in Detention Camps," *International Journal of Legal Medicine* 109(3): 114–117.

10. Hinkle, L., & Wolf, H. (1956). "Communist Interrogation and Indoctrination of 'Enemies of the States': Analysis of Methods Used by the Communist State Police," *Archives of Neurology and Psychiatry* 1956: 115–174.

CHAPTER 7

PRISON AND THE DECIMATION OF PRO–SOCIAL LIFE SKILLS

Terry A. Kupers

The aim of torture is to destroy the individual's will, to break the individual down and obliterate a sense of autonomy and agency, thus turning that individual into a shell of a person who lacks the will to resist, or even to be human in the sense that being human requires personal agency. Following revelations about the abuses carried out by the U.S. military at Abu Ghraib, I was interviewed by journalists a number of times about parallels between the shocking abuses there and at Guantánamo and the everyday realities of American prisons. Of course, there are parallels—the stripping naked, the threats of great bodily harm, the purposeful humiliations, the central aim of invoking terror in captives and breaking their will to withhold information or to resist any command from their captors. For example, in 2002, I submitted a Declaration as a psychiatric expert witness about unconstitutional conditions on Death Row at Mississippi State Penitentiary in Parchman.[1] I included this description of the special punishment to which Mr. Willie Russell, the lead plaintiff, had been subjected for two years:

> Willie Russell describes his experience being housed in Cell 225 for two years, one of four "punishment" cells on Death Row with plexiglass doors (covering the standard door). I have seen this kind of double door in super-maximum security units in other states. Once one is locked inside such a cell, the temperature and humidity begin to rise within minutes because the plexiglass (or lexsan, an indestructible form of plastic) retains the heat and humidity within the cell. The temperature rises rapidly, and life in the cell becomes unbearable. In the summer heat at Parchman, this one aspect of the punishment cells would make them entirely unacceptable by any standard of human decency or of health and mental health minimum standards. But in addition to this cruel and entirely excessive and punitive measure that clearly

serves no legitimate penological objective, Mr. Russell reports that his cell is always filthy, the rain pours in through the walls onto his bed, the toilet floods the cell with backflow from other prisoners' toilets, there are bugs everywhere, the cell is filled with mosquitoes at night, he cannot sleep at night because the lights are on 24 hours per day, he is not permitted to have a fan, he is not permitted television or radio and there are no activities, and he is even more isolated than other prisoners on Death Row because the lexsan shield on his door makes it impossible for him to talk to anyone. For two years, he was permitted no mattress, no pillow and no sheets, and had only a blanket and the concrete for a bed. This kind of punitive deprivation and degradation is barbaric, and shocking to human sensibilities. It is the kind of cruel and unusual punishment that is well known to cause intense anxiety and rage, psychiatric breakdown, and in a large proportion of cases, suicide.

I feel very privileged to have served as an expert witness in dozens of class action lawsuits challenging unconstitutional prison conditions, the denial of adequate mental health services to prisoners with serious mental illness, and the sexual abuse of prisoners. The plaintiff prevailed in the Willie Russell class action, and conditions are much improved at Parchman today. But this work is ongoing. In fact, by looking for the concrete details of unconstitutional abuses, we risk missing the larger point. Modern prisons do not need grotesque techniques of torture to break people and destroy their autonomy and human agency. The breaking and destroying occur in countless subtle and imperceptible ways, and thus are not as prone to draw attention from human rights groups or courts concerned about Eighth Amendment (protection from cruel and unusual punishment) constitutional violations.

Do human rights abuses and Eighth Amendment constitutional violations in American prisons qualify as Psychological Torture (PT)? This is a complicated question. In a contribution to this volume, Dr. Almerindo Ojeda distinguishes between an "extensional definition" of PT—whereby a set of practices are delineated that constitute PT—and an "intensional definition" of PT, whereby the intentions of the perpetrators must be examined before the practices can be declared PT.[2] Dr. Ojeda proposes that the extensional definition is adequate, and the torturers' intentions do not need to reach specific criteria for PT to be in evidence. The practices Dr. Ojeda lists in the extensional definition include isolation, deprivation of food, water, sleep, spatial disorientation through confinement in small places with nonfunctional windows, temporal disorientation due to denial of natural light (and I would add a lack of clocks and watches), sensory deprivation or overstimulation, induced desperation through indefinite detention or random placement, and so forth. Just about every one of the practices Dr. Ojeda lists are present in supermaximum security units I have toured, though the entire list is not necessarily in evidence in each facility. For example, supermaximum security units are also called "control units" because of the total control staff have over even the smallest details of the prisoner's life, including how much toilet paper or how many sanitary napkins he or she will be permitted to have. Or, in supermaximum confinement units, many prisoners experience induced desperation, for example fearing that they will never be released because the severe isolation exacerbates their anger about what they consider unfair and excessive punishment, and they are very aware of the fact that their anger will lead them to get into arguments with officers that will result in additional disciplinary write-ups or "tickets," and therefore additional time in isolation. Many prisoners in such settings have confided that they are certain they will never get out of segregation alive. Of course, the express purpose of isolated confinement in American prisons is not to break the will of the prisoner so he or she will bow to intimidation and confess. Actually, it is unclear what, precisely, is the purpose of isolation in American prisons. Is it to punish, and if so, is the punishment reasonable, is it excessive, does it serve acceptable penological objectives? Is the purpose to "correct" unacceptable behavior, and if so, is the method of correction effective? Such questions are debated widely today, even as we learn that prison violence rates are not improved when supermaximum security units are built, and we learn that prisoners who have had long stints in supermaximum security units have a very difficult time adjusting to prison programs or life in the community after they are released from supermax confinement. But Dr. Ojeda's extensional definition does not require that we establish that the intention of isolated confinement is to break down prisoners so they will be incapable of functioning in society; the fact is that the practices themselves fulfill the extensional definition of PT, and there is much evidence that practices and conditions within American supermaximum security units do cause human breakdown.

In the big picture, destroying a prisoner's ability to cope in the free world is the worst thing prison does, and in the process, there are all the elements of torture even if there are no hoods, water-boarding or electric cords. Crowding, a lack of rehabilitation opportunities, excessive reliance on isolation as punishment, the restriction of visits and contacts with the outside world, the pervasiveness of sexual abuse, disrespect at every turn, the failure of prerelease planning—all these things add up to throwing the prisoner who completes a term out into the world broken, with no skills, and a very high risk of recidivism.

A HISTORIC WRONG TURN

Prison conditions matter quite a lot. Compare two prison environments. One is an effectively run prison in which a population cap guarantees each prisoner a cell of his own and an opportunity to hold a prison job and play basketball in the gymnasium at the end of a hard day's work. The other is an overcrowded prison in which there are not enough cells to go around, so three or four prisoners are stuffed into cells designed for one. The prisoner who is lowest in the dominance hierarchy has to sleep on a thin pad on the floor, while his two cellmates sleep in bunks, there being almost no floor space for any of the three to get to the toilet inside the cell without walking over the prisoner lying on the floor. In the over-crowded prison, there is no gymnasium, because the building that once was the site of basketball games is now filled with wall-to-wall bunks where 150 to 200 prisoners sleep. Add to this incredible social density the problem of noise—the more individuals there are in a space, the higher the noise level. And add to this depressing picture huge problems with hygiene. Where the prisoner in a single cell can pride himself on the cleanliness of his toilet and sink area, the impromptu toilets along the wall of the ex-gymnasium dormitory tend to remain always dirty and frequently flooded.

In crowded, noisy, unhygienic environments, human beings tend to treat each other terribly. Imagine sleeping in a converted gymnasium with 150 to 200 prisoners. There are constant lines to use the toilets and phones, and altercations erupt when one irritable prisoner thinks another has been on the phone too long. There are rows of bunks blocking the view, so beatings and rapes can go on in one part of the dorm while officers sit at their desks in another area. The noise level is so loud that muffled screams cannot be heard. Meanwhile the constant noise and unhygienic conditions cause irritability on everyone's part. Individuals who are vulnerable to attack and sexual assault—for example, smaller men, men suffering from serious mental illness, and gay or transgender persons—have no cell to retreat to when they feel endangered. Is it any wonder that research clearly links prison crowding with increased rates of violence, psychiatric breakdowns, rapes, and suicides.[3]

This kind of overcrowding did not always prevail in American prisons. In the 1970s, when I began serving as a psychiatric expert about the destructive effects of horrible prison conditions on the mental health of prisoners, crowding was just becoming a problem. Driven by the "War on Drugs" and calls for tougher sentencing, the prison population was beginning to grow geometrically and gymnasiums were being converted to dormitories at an alarming rate. (The prison population in the United States has by now multiplied by a factor of 10 since the early 1970s.) I testified about the way crowding, a lack of meaningful activities, and noise caused elevated rates of violence, suicide, and psychiatric breakdown. At the same time, in the context of a "tough on crime" sensibility, there were campaigns to lengthen prison sentences for every variety of crime, and make the time "harder." Legislators and administrators certainly did not want to be accused of "coddling" criminals, so they repeatedly slashed funding for prison rehabilitation programs.

A wrong turn was taken in American penology in the late 1980s, a tragic mis-step that has yet to be corrected and is causing irreparable harm. There was accelerating overcrowding while rehabilitation programs were being defunded, downsized, or closed. Prison educational programs were dismantled. Politicians would not even mention prison rehabilitation for fear of losing elections.

There was a slightly earlier moment, in the mid-1980s, when prison violence was totally out of control. This could have been a time when departments of corrections admitted they had made a big mistake crowding the prisons and dismantling rehabilitation programs. And then they could have reversed the crowding (which would require profound changes in sentencing) while reinstating rehabilitation and education programs. Many experienced wardens and penologists were arguing at the time that prisoners, if they are to cooperate with the program in prison and learn to be law-abiding citizens, need meaningful activities and need to have amenities and activities they would hate to lose. Ignoring that voice of experience, legislators and correctional administrators decided instead to "lock up" the prisoners they deemed troublemakers ("the worst of the worst"). They bowed to increasingly shrill demands for absolute control inside the prison walls. The supermaximum security prison was born. The SHU, or Security Housing Unit, at Pelican Bay State Prison in Northern California was the flagship, and the initials "SHU" became the generic term for supermaximum confinement.

My expert testimony in the 1970s focused mainly on the destructive effects of jail and prison crowding, plus other toxic conditions such as poor lighting, high noise levels and so forth. A decade later, there was still unconscionable crowding, but the new concern regarding human breakdown was excessive solitary confinement. A growing proportion of prisoners, especially prisoners suffering from mental illness, were being sent to what used to be called "the hole," but instead of spending 10 days or a month in a dark dungeon, they found themselves in a high tech, superclean, supermax cell where the lights would be kept on around the clock and the doors open and shut by remote control.

Human contact is limited to the scheduled arrivals of an officer at the prisoner's cell door to deliver or pick up a food tray. The prisoners have great difficulty sleeping because the steel and cinder block design of these units magnifies sound, and the banging of doors and hollering of prisoners with mental illness wakes them throughout the night. Deprived of sleep, lacking in human contact and entirely idle, many inhabitants of supermaximum security units suffer emotional breakdown of all kinds. In addition, a large and disproportionate number of prisoners suffering from serious mental illness tend to collect in supermaximum security units, where their psychiatric condition deteriorates on account of the idleness and isolation.[4]

A growing number of prisoners are actually spending years in punitive solitary confinement only to be set free with a few dollars and a bus ticket when their release date arrives. They have "maxed out of the SHU." They return to their community, having had no human contact for years, no preparation to help them "go straight," and full of rage about the brutal conditions they have been forced to endure. Is it any surprise this group of ex-prisoners are very prone to relapse into substance abuse and crime?

The advent of the supermaximum security prison culminated the wrong turn: crowding unprecedented numbers of prisoners into the prisons, dismantling or

downsizing rehabilitation and education programs, and then punishing the prisoners who respond to the resulting crowding and idleness with rule-breaking by
locking them in solitary segregation units. Elsewhere in this volume, Stuart
Grassian presents the evidence that supermaximum security units cause much
psychiatric damage.[5] In fact, incarceration itself causes psychiatric damage, and
then isolated confinement serves to exaggerate the general ill effects of prison.
But isolation is not the only culprit. There are other turnings in the way prisons
are run that cause unnecessary damage. I will turn to the bad example of harsh
visit restrictions.

VISIT RESTRICTIONS

One of the strongest predictors of post-release success is the quality of a
prisoner's ongoing contact with loved ones.[6] Yet prison policies are making it
increasingly difficult for family and friends to visit and remain in close touch
with prisoners. Visiting is only one of many ways family contact is discouraged.
For example, there are a growing number of restrictions and delays of prison
mail, the rationale being security, but the actual effect being reduction in contact
between the prisoner and the outside world. Likewise, there are rules limiting the
personal items, including pictures of loved ones, a prisoner can have in her cell,
and the kinds of packages families can send prisoners. Homemade cookies
cannot be mailed to prisoners in many states; instead, families are limited to
purchasing prepackaged commercial goodies from approved vendors.

Often, when visitors do manage to get to their loved one's prison, they
face long waits in line and increasingly intrusive searches. A few years ago, the
California Department of Corrections embarked on a policy of x-raying all
visitors with a body scanner (Rapiscan Secure 1000) in an effort to halt drug
smuggling. The low-intensity radiation permitted officers in the visiting area to
see through visitors' clothing, but not beneath the skin. Critics were concerned
about unnecessary exposure to radiation as well as the potential for sexual harass-
ment. For example, there were occasions when male officers would chuckle to
each other within earshot of the visitor about the shape of a woman's body under
the scanner. In any case, litigation eventually forced the California Department
of Corrections to desist from using the scanner on visitors.

Meanwhile, in a growing number of high security prisons, the only visits a
family is permitted occur over remote video monitors. The visitor comes to the
visiting area, but the prisoner remains inside the cellblock, and video monitors
are utilized to put the visitor and prisoner in touch with each other. In prisons
where visits are limited to this type of video arrangement, I have heard from prisoners that they tell their family members not to visit because they do not believe
that the video image is really their loved one, or they believe the video is being
recorded and the tape will ultimately be used against them. In other words, the

net effect of video visits, just as in the case of the body scanner, is a decrease in the number and quality of visits.

Often the rationale given for restrictions of visits with prisoners appears almost logical at first glance. For example, "zero tolerance" was the stated rationale for a policy of punitive visit restrictions that held sway in the Michigan Department of Corrections (MDOC) from 1995 until it was ruled unconstitutional in federal court a few years ago. In *Bazetta v. McGinnis,*[7] state prisoners claimed the MDOC's visit restriction policy violated their Eighth Amendment protection from cruel and unusual punishment. The policy stipulated that any prisoner with two substance-related infractions during his or her entire prison term lost the right to have visits except with an attorney or a clergyperson (the prisoner could apply for reinstatement after two years). The aim of the policy was "zero toler-ance" for substance use in the prisons.

The Michigan prisons, like many others around the country, had been conducting random urine tests for drugs for several years. The infractions that triggered visit restriction usually involved a "dirty" urine test. On far fewer occasions, they involved contraband drug paraphernalia. But in several cases I reviewed in preparation for my expert testimony in the case, an infraction resulted from a prisoner hoarding Motrin tablets beyond the prescription's expi-ration date. Since there is a significant "co-pay" when a prisoner sees a physician, this woman wanted to keep a supply of Motrin on hand so she would not have to pay to have the next doctor tell her once again that she had a back injury and needed to take Motrin when the pain became intolerable. One male prisoner was given a disciplinary ticket for "refusing" to produce a urine specimen when, because of an enlarged prostate, he was unable to urinate on command.

Restricting visits between prisoners and their families is simply another wrong turn in penology. There are other ways to bolster security. And why should all prisoners lose visiting privileges on account of the bad behaviors of a few, such as drug smuggling? (Interestingly, staff are rarely searched as they enter and leave prisons, and I have been told by very many prisoners that staff are often the conduit for illicit substances.)

When I admit an emotionally disturbed patient to a psychiatric hospital, and that patient becomes disruptive and difficult to manage, I contact the family to find out if there is something going on outside the hospital that is upsetting the patient and causing him or her to behave badly on the ward. If it is appropriate (i.e., in the absence of domestic violence or other toxic or unsafe situations), I encourage the family to visit the patient, or at least to remain in phone contact. And I may request a family therapy session. In other words, clinicians assume that there are reasons for a person to act out, and more likely than not, those reasons involve family and close associates on the outside. In addition, support from loved ones is probably the biggest factor in a disturbed individual's healing. The same logic holds in the prison setting. If an individual is trying to halt a drug habit, cope with depression, or simply control his temper, continuous support from family members would be a critical ingredient in her or his success. And if a prisoner is acting out enough to be placed in punitive segregation, then contact with and support from family members is likely a prerequisite for improved behavior. With prisoners who act out and get sent to punitive segregation or the SHU, and with prisoners who have substance abuse problems or mental illness, every effort should be made to increase their visitation, not restrict it, because contact with loved ones is the best support there is in helping them to stop acting out. Of course, security has to be maintained at all times, and to accomplish this, the mental health staff and drug counselors have to collaborate effectively with custody staff.

The prison visitation issue warrants a prominent place in the public debate about crime and punishment. There is a contradiction between the good we know quality visitation does and the inexplicable campaign in some departments of correction to obstruct visiting.

PRISONIZATION, OF COURSE, BUT TO WHAT EXTENT?

Craig Haney describes the chilling process of "prisonization," something that happens to all prisoners to a certain extent. According to Haney, "The process of prisonization involves the incorporation of the norms of prison life into one's habits of thinking, feeling and acting...the longer persons are incarcerated, the more significant is the nature of their institutional transformation."[8] The process includes all the phenomena sociologists have described as "institutionalization," where the institution is the prison. There is loss of the identity one had in the community as one becomes an anonymous prisoner known by a number. One's clothing choices are vastly restricted, one's grooming is proscribed, there are rules governing just about every aspect of one's existence, and there are officers who surveil, give orders, control one's life, and mete punishments on a regular basis. There is a large list of formal rules, which can seem very petty, and there are frequent tickets for rule-breaking, where punishment can involve solitary confinement in a segregation cell. There are also unwritten rules—for example, the "prison code" that requires one to act tough, not show feelings, definitely hide weakness and neediness, not talk to officers, and never "snitch."

I have written about the way the prison code and the institutional dynamics reinforce the most toxic aspects of masculinity, and ill-prepare an individual for successful reintegration into family and community upon release.[9] Prison rape is a pervasive fear in correctional settings. It happens too often, with tragic psychiatric consequences.[10] But one of the underreported fallouts of prison sexual assault and rape is the way prisoners learn to posture like a tough guy in order to avoid being sexually assaulted. Even while avoiding rape, they are learning habits that make it difficult for them to be gentle and intimate after they are released from prison. This is another unfortunate consequence of prisonization.

Prisonization is a phenomenon that affects all prisoners to a certain extent, but the most damaging aspects of prisonization are exacerbated by crowding, harsh conditions, a lack of meaningful activity, long stints in isolation, and too few visits from loved ones. I hear from prisoners that the way to survive a prison term and then return to the community and be a success is to "keep your head out of the prison"—in other words, maintain one's identity as a citizen in the free world, a loved member of a family, a son or daughter, a father or mother. I ask prisoners who seem very successful at keeping their heads out of the prison how they accomplish that amazing feat. They tell me they read newspapers and current books so they can stay up with what is going on in the world, they maintain contact through letters and visiting with as many loved ones and friends as they can, and they work incessantly on maintaining meaningful contact with their children—that way, there is less risk that they will be isolated and lonely when they are released, and their family remains functional. And they take part in every program they are eligible for—anger management, training in a trade, classes, even music lessons. They want to increase their skills so they can succeed at "going straight" after they are released.

Let us hypothetically add to the mix one after another of the unfortunate realities of modern prisons that I outlined in previous sections. Consider the plight of one of the very mature and effective prisoners I just described—the one who reads voraciously, keeps in touch with lots of people in the free world, sustains contact with his wife and children, and takes advantage of every program for which he is eligible. Place that prisoner in an overcrowded prison where, instead of having a cell to himself where he can retreat and read or write letters, he has to sleep on one of 150 bunks in a converted gymnasium, experiences high noise levels day and night, has the programs where he is enrolled cancelled in the middle of his tenure, and then is sent to segregation for a long time because he voiced his indignation too vociferously. And then, in punitive segregation, his visits are very restricted and he has to see his mother and children through a lexsan/plexiglass window and talk to them over a wall phone. Each of these successive indignities reduces by a certain proportion the likelihood of his remaining task-oriented, keeping his head out of the prison, and spending every day he is in prison preparing to "go straight." In the hypothetical case in which all these stressors take their toll on a prisoner, there is much less likelihood that he or she will succeed at "going straight" after release and avoid future involvement in the criminal justice system.

WHAT IS TO BE DONE WITH THE PRISONERS WHO ARE BROKEN?

Alarming statistics are surfacing about today's prisons. There are an unprecedented number of people in prison (nearly 2.5 million in jail and prison at any given time, but that number needs to be multiplied many times over to encompass all the people who have served time and are now in the community); even as the prison population has multiplied, the proportion of prisoners suffering from serious mental illness has actually grown;[11] the prisons are massively overcrowded; the prison suicide rate is very high, but an even more disturbing statistic is that approximately half of the successful suicides in prison occur among the 6–8 percent of prisoners confined in segregation at any given time; the recidivism rate is rising, and rising even faster is the rate of parole violations. The data about increasing recidivism and parole violation rates is especially alarming.

For example, there is the phenomenon of "maxing out of the SHU." In most cases, a prisoner is sent to the SHU for some prison-related misbehavior or risk. The prison sentence is meted by the court, but the SHU sentence is meted within the prison's classification and disciplinary systems. So many prisoners are relegated to long-term isolated confinement that a certain number of them reach their fixed (court-assigned) release date prior to finishing their stint in the SHU. They are released into the community straight out of a cell where they had been isolated and idle for years. Not surprisingly, a significant proportion of them return to drugs and alcohol and commit serious crimes. What is surprising is that there are not more who do so. Most ex-inhabitants of supermaximum isolation cells actually keep to themselves after they are released from prison, their will to relate to others having been broken. But when any ex-resident of supermax commits a violent crime, there are headlines, and of course, there are heated accusations about where the fault lies.

The "tough on crime" faction loudly proclaim that the heinous deed is incontrovertible proof the violent criminal element is incorrigible, and call for a halt to "coddling" and the building of even more super-secure prisons where we can "lock-'em-up-and-throw-away-the-key." The other side in the debate, prison reformers and human rights advocates among them, just as passionately believe that the error was to lock prisoners in cold storage in the first place—long-term isolated confinement causes human breakdown of all kinds, including psychosis, suicide, and, in far too many cases, intensification of uncontrollable violent impulses.

To advocates of rehabilitation as a primary aim of incarceration, the crime spree of an ex-SHU inhabitant means that the corrections department has failed in its mission to reduce violence and "correct" the errant felon. After all, the first principle of interventions aimed at reducing violence is to make certain that the interventions themselves do not actually raise the prevalence of violence; and many commentators are coming to the conclusion that the advent of the supermaximum security prison has increased rather than decreased the rates of violence in the prisons and on the streets.[12]

With recidivism rates and parole violation rates on the rise, the question is: Why do so many ex-prisoners fail in their attempts to reenter the community after a stint in prison? Either criminals, on average, are more hardened and incorrigible than they once were, so they merit longer terms and harsher punishments; or the things we do to the growing number of people we put in prison are breaking them as human beings and making it even more likely they will fail at putting their life together again when the time comes for them to return to the community—and 93 percent of prisoners do eventually return to the community. I believe there are always criminals among us, but their number is not especially high right now, from a historical perspective. A subset of ex-prisoners—individuals who have spent very hard time in prison and been subjected to crowding, enforced idleness, high violence rates, a great risk of rape, long periods in a segregation cell, and restrictions of visiting—tend to repeatedly be rearrested, and chronically fail in all their attempts to reenter the free community. These are people who have been broken by prison. When it comes to remedies for this glaring social problem, the same kind of foolhardy thinking that resulted in the unnecessarily harsh conditions of confinement lead to false solutions. For example, law-and-order buffs call for even longer sentences and the construction of more prisons. Their strategy would only result in more prisoners being broken by the system and subsequently failing in their attempts to "go straight." It is time to rethink the reasons why so many ex-prisoners get trapped in the cycle of crime and incarceration.

NOTES

1. Willie Russell et al. v. Christopher Epps/Mississippi Department of Corrections, U.S. Dist Ct, No. Dist. of Mississippi, Eastern Div., Civ. No. 1:02CV261-D-D.

2. Ojeda, Almerindo "What is Psychological Torture," Chapter 1 of this volume.

3. Paulus, P. B., McCain, G., and Cox, V. C. (1978). "Death rates, psychiatric commitments, blood pressure, and perceived crowding as a function of institutional crowding." *Environmental Psychology and Nonverbal Behavior* 3: 107–117.

4. Pizarrro, J., & Stenius, V. (2004). "Supermax prisons: Their rise, current practices, and effect on inmates," *The Prison Journal* 84(2): 248–264.

5. Grassian, S., "Overview: Neuropsychiatric effects of isolated confinement," Chapter 6.

6. Holt, N., & Miller, D. (1972). Explorations in Inmate-Family Relationships. Sacramento: Research Division, Department of Corrections, State of California; Schafer, N. E. (1994) "Exploring the link between visits and parole success: A survey of prison visitors." *International Journal of Offender Therapy & Comparative Criminology* 38(1):17–32.

7. Bazetta v. McGinnis, U.S. Dist. Ct., E.D. Michigan, So. Div., No. 95-CV-73540-DT, 2001.

8. Haney, C. (2003). "The psychological impact of incarceration: Implications for postprison adjustment," in J. Travis & M. Waul, Eds., *Prisoners Once Removed*, Washington, DC: The Urban Institute Press, pp. 33–65.

9. Kupers, T. (2005). "Toxic masculinity as a barrier to mental health treatment in prison," *Journal of Clinical Psychology* 61(6): 713–724.

10. Visit the website of Stop Prisoner Rape, http://www.spr.org.

11. U.S. Bureau of Justice Statistics. (2006). Special report: Mental health problems of prison and jail inmates. Available at http://www.ojp.usdoj.gov/bjs/pub/pdf/mhppji.pdf, September. Washington, DC: USDOJ.

12. Briggs, C.S., Sundt, J.L., & Castellano, T.C. (2003). "The effects of supermaximum security prisons on aggregate levels of institutional violence," *Criminiology* 41(4): 301–336.

CHAPTER 8

THE NEUROBIOLOGICAL CONSEQUENCES OF PSYCHOLOGICAL TORTURE

Rona M. Fields

TORTURE

Torture is speciously categorized as *physical,* when it is evidenced in damaged tissues, impaired sensory organs, broken bones, and/or major organ failures; or as *psychological.* This is a distinction without a difference. Coercion of any type in itself implies threat, fear, and powerlessness, all of which can and often does impact on brain, spinal cord, and organ integrity and therefore has medical consequences. Given the intricate mind-body connection known in science and philosophy for centuries if not millennia, physical versus psychological is an irrelevant predicate for differentiating between acceptable and prohibited information-gathering tactics.[1]

Threat, fear, and trauma—any and all of which are experienced physiologically as well as psychologically—can be tracked through the neurophysiology of the brain. This chapter tracks mind-body integrity primarily through three processes that result in permanent brain damage: pain, environmental stressors, and sleep deprivation. Torture, whether inflicted by physical means such as beatings, or psychological through, for example, environmental manipulation, inflicts pain experienced in the brain and extending from there to all of the different organs and physiological processes.

BACKGROUND: APPLICATION OF EXPERIMENTAL PSYCHOLOGY

The physiological and lasting effects of psychological torture are documented in studies and published in many articles and books. Some of the classic studies were published in the sixties and early seventies. The more recent research involves the use of scanning techniques—PET scans and MRIs—to track the blood flow and metabolism of parts of the brain in process and in consequence.

In 1971, findings reported by this author in a series of publications indicated that prolonged stress through sleeplessness, time disorientation, threat and physical abuse, sensory deprivation, limitations of oxygen intake, hypnosis, drugs, and overcrowding ("cage-like confinement") of an apparently random selection of a thousand Catholic men and boys in Northern Ireland resulted in measurable organic damage. In further studies on the Northern Irish detainees, this author found that two-thirds of the 125 subjects in the first sample, tested between 1971 and 1973, had measurable brain damage within two years of their release from the imprisonment. Some of the damage is attributable to their efforts to self-medicate with alcohol and drugs—often prescription antidepressants and antianxiety medications taken together. In the Northern Ireland detention camps, there was regular and frequent distribution of these substances to "calm" the inmates[2] (see http://www.ronafields.com).

Studies in clinical and social psychology, sociology, and developmental psychology also report animal and laboratory experiments predicting outcomes such as these described in clinical reports on torture survivors. In fact, the CIA/DOD manual for Foreign Intelligence Assistance Training bases many recommended techniques for interrogation on these same experiments.

Prior to this author's study of Irish men and boys subjected to depth interrogation techniques and detention, there were studies on survivors of World War II concentration camps with which to compare findings. In concentration camp survivor studies, most notably books by Eitinger and Strom, periodic medical examinations had included the use of the Bender Gestalt, a neuropsychological screening instrument used in the Northern Ireland studies. The studies by Drs. Eitinger and Strom said that these and similar findings on other tests aroused speculation but no conclusions. Eitinger and Strom, upon seeing the Bender-Gestalt protocols on which some of the Northern Ireland findings were based, reconsidered the neurological effects in their studies that had been attributed to starvation and physical abuse. They gave the K-Z syndrome, or Concentration Camp Syndrome, a new dimension—psychological abuse.

Viktor Frankl, in his work *The Doctor and the Soul: From Psychotherapy to Logotherapy,* recognized the impact torture had on survival itself. Robert Lifton, not long after writing on brainwashing, similarly identified the role that psychological torture can play in physical sequelae. In a case presented to the Superior Court of New York in 1973 (*New York vs. Eugene Hollander*), Lifton and this author testified as experts that the psychological consequences of the subject's concentration camp experiences seriously impaired his judgment and behavior. Neuropsychological screening tests indicated frontal lobe damage (impaired judgment and executive function), and psychiatric examination suggested organic seizure activity.

At the Western Psychological Association annual convention in January 1972, a panel presented the use of interrogation techniques. One example cited by the panel was Vaccaville State Prison's medical facility in a special "behavior therapy" program for inmates. At the time the panel was presented, Donald Defreeze was an inmate subjected to these treatments. Several years later, under the alias "Cinque" he led the Symbionese Liberation Army in kidnapping Patty Hearst and applied the same techniques to intimidate her into collaboration in their violent, antisocial campaign.

The techniques used in psychological torture have been refined for many decades. During the Algerian war, the French used many of the techniques now classed as "psychological torture" to interrogate and debase suspected Algerian resistance fighters. The French argument was that by compelling information from captives, they were saving lives, because they could learn about pending and contemporaneous attacks and dangers. This became a rationalization for interrogation torture beyond the time of the Algerian War and well beyond the geographic confines of the French Empire. The classic study by Frantz Fanon, himself a doctor, in *The Wretched of the Earth* (1968) details many of the torture techniques as well as the overall campaign to intimidate the Algerians into compliance with their occupation.

By the mid 1960s, the British Special Air Service (SAS) had begun writing manuals on their experience with gathering information from counterinsurgents in Borneo. The Foreign Intelligence Assistance Program, in collaboration with the Central Intelligence Agency and the Department of Defense, infused their manuals with the techniques used by the SAS. Coincidentally, British SAS veterans taught the depth interrogation techniques used in Northern Ireland to the Special Branch of the Royal Ulster Constabulary (RUC). Prolonged stress, sensory deprivation, sensory overstimulation, hooding, sleep deprivation, threat of killing, staged executions, isolation, and finally incarceration in cages were used on activists in the Northern Ireland Civil Rights Association, labor unions, presumed members of the Irish Republican Army (IRA) and later, the Ulster Defense Association (UDA). In Latin America, the techniques originally described by the SAS were invoked against members and supporters of reformist governments democratically elected and against organizations seeking to overthrow military dictatorships.

The SAS and later CIA and FIAP manuals make frequent references to the tactics and strategies of how to inflict pain—without leaving marks—to make their "subjects" yield information. However in some places, and there is reason to believe so in Northern Ireland particularly, details of the manuals themselves were leaked to the public. The intent of the "leak" was to widely impose fear and threat per both Britain and the U.S. "psyops," or psychological operations. The psyops techniques frankly borrowed from psychological experimental studies aimed at producing stress or inducing "brainwashing." Retired SAS Brigadier

Frank Kitson refers to these kinds of deliberate leaks as effective techniques in *Low Intensity Operations* (1971).[3, 4]

In 1976, at the American Psychological Association (APA) convention in Washington, DC, a panel consisting of Chilean psychologist Katya Raczynski, South African lawyer Joel Carlson, and a representative from Amnesty International (for which this author served on the medical commission) presented on psychological torture. Dr. Raczynski, Mr. Carlson, and Dr. Fields presented case material and data attesting to the use of psychological research in the torture and coercion of prisoners in South Africa, Chile, Northern Ireland, and Portugal. With the help of Chilean and Argentinean colleagues and 25 years of studies, the results of psychological and psychiatric research on torture concluded that there are permanent, damaging effects of these experiences on the brain and on the physical condition of victims.

Awareness of an aversive stimulus approaching, such as a barking dog, a snake, a rat, or other predators can evoke a remembered pain sensation and is itself stressful. This reaction has its counterpart in the hippocampus and is recognized as the kindling effect that communicates to the pain process. It is located very proximal. Initially, along with other researchers on torture survivors and brainwashing victims, we assumed that the organic consequences were linked to the shortage of oxygen in the blood supply to the brain. Now we know that the emotional experience of fear, dread, and threat to bodily integrity all have organic consequences in the brain, including reduced oxygen in red blood cells, metabolic interruptions, nutritional deficiencies, and cardiovascular disorders.[5]

Results from experimental psychology have been used by various governmental and nongovernmental organizations. For example, in the early 1970s, Peter Suedfeld, a psychologist, engaged in experimental work on sensory deprivation. The CIA Foreign Intelligence Assistance Program cites Dr. Suedfeld's work from this era, and the U.S. Department of Defense lists his studies in both the CIA and FIAP manuals. Twenty years later, Dr. Suedfeld wrote a book about torture and the psychological consequences on the victims, though he did not include findings from his own earlier experiments on sensory deprivation and sensory overstimulation performed on his students at the University of Michigan and the University of Toronto. In some of Dr. Suedfeld's early student experiments, the subject was exposed to "white noise" that covers all sound while held by cuffs in a fixed stationary position, with a visor-like device affixed to his head with translucent eye covers that admitted only diffuse light. Chimpanzees reared under similar conditions of partial sensory deprivation developed an abnormal characteristic. Such chimpanzees were unable to locate pain stimuli. Other studies on torture techniques remain classified.

In his 1968 book, *A Time To Speak: On Human Values and Social Research,* psychologist Herb Kelman addresses the social scientists' knowledge of behavior control and the potential ethical dilemma posed by the manipulation of human behavior. One of the major themes of his work on morality in social science is the need for scientists to take responsibility for their work and the application of that work. On the applied researcher, Kelman says:

> the researcher is merely gathering facts, he is nonetheless participating quite directly in the operations of the organization that employs him...his findings will be applied to the formulation and execution of the organizations' policies...the investigator [thus may be] helping the organization as it attempts to manipulate the behavior of others." (p. 2)

He poses the ethical dilemma thus:

> an ethical problem arises not simply from the ends for which behavior control is being used but from the very fact that we are using it. (p. 15)

Kelman addresses the issue of psychological experiments that deceive the subjects as part of the design, such as the *Obedience to Authority,* the Milgram and the Suedfeld studies, or the use of students in experiments for course grades or other incentives.[6]

There is increasing awareness that a number of scientific and clinical disciplines are converging on the centrality of affective processes in essential human survival functions. Affect, including unconscious, as well as the unique, early forming defenses against overwhelming traumatic emotional experiences, are now a central focus of clinical, forensic and experimental sciences (J. Pincus 2001).

Recent interdisciplinary information on affect and affect regulation is directly relevant to a deeper understanding of early forming self-pathologies. Developmental studies (S. Ewing-Cobs, L. Kramer 1998) are now exploring the intersubjective, bodily based, nonverbal affective communication. Neurobiological research is describing the bodily based affect regulatory mechanisms of attachment and trauma. Experimental models of the enduring impact of early relational trauma on the later capacities of the right brain to implicitly regulate an array of affective and motivational states are generating complex models of psychopathogenesis. Current models emphasize the primacy of affect, perhaps even more than explicit cognitive insight, as, potentially, the central mechanism of therapeutic change. In addition to deepening our understanding of the rapid appraisal of emotional information that occurs beneath awareness, studies of right-brain unconscious communication are also emphasizing the essential role of affect and the body in the change process.

PAIN

Pain is the most universal human experience and, perhaps, the least universally defined. The subjectivity of the experience of pain is compounded because it is not transmitted via a single sensory sequence, nor is it measured in intensity through the space of brain activation or the single site of brain activation. It is difficult to measure.

Pain is not a simple sensation. For example, pain accompanies tissue damage, but not all tissue change is felt as painful. A growing tumor, tuberculosis, or hardening of the arteries may be completely painless. When tissue damage becomes painful, the disease process has attacked either the sensory pathways or their connection with the medial thalamus. When excitation in those relays becomes excessive, there is thalamic pain that may continue even after the somatosensory nuclei have been removed. Sensory pathways project to the reticular formation in the lower brain stem from which relays can reach the centrum medianum directly. The destruction of this nucleus abolishes pain. This has been confirmed through studies of patients who have, because of cancer or Traumatic Brain Injury, experienced partial or complete destruction of the sensory thalamic nucleus. Only complete destruction succeeds in halting these relays and thus ending pain.

Neurotransmitters that register pain have been identified in the brain. Some brain neurons use acetylcholine; others use catecholomines, such as noradreenaline and dopamine or indolemines (seratonin), as transmitters.

It is possible to differentiate between neural systems according to the substances that serve as transmitters. The neurons synthesize transmitter substances from a precursor through a series of enzyme reactions, store them in vesicles of presynaptic nerve endings, and release them into the synaptic cleft on arrival of a neural impulse.

Neurotransmitters for inhibitory and stimulatory functions are abundant and complex in the brain. At first glance, it might seem unlikely that a structure like the hippocampus should serve as a relay station for as many different psychological activities as it does: sensory recall, the revival of appraisal (affective memory), the initiation of directed action and the physiological changes that go with it, and the revival of motor memory.

Neurotransmitters alter membrane conductance by engaging specialized receptors at the synapse, thus changing the excitability of a single excitable element for a brief period of time. In contrast, peptides directly alter the conductance of a membrane that is already activated by a transmitter. These are neuromodulators. Still another type of transmitter has been observed in axons that are not in synaptic contact with the neurons they influence. These are neurohormonal transmitters. Both neuradrenaline and serotonin fibers in the cerebellum have a synaptic and non-synaptic mode of transmission. They are both neurotransmitter and neurohormonal functions.

The released transmitter molecules bridge the fluid-filled gap between the presynaptic axon terminal and the cell membrane of the postsynaptic receiving neurons and are taken up by protein molecules precisely tailored to their configuration. Conduction over other synapses may require amino acids such as gamma aminobutyric (gaba) glycine, glutamic acid, and others. Certain peptides and some hormones and corticoids can mediate nervous conduction, but these substances have a different mode of action.

The amygdala mediates different *emotional actions*. This structure can mediate so many different activities because it serves as a relay station for several neural systems, including the limbic or involuntary system. A sensory appraisal is different from other functions because it indicates not the quality of things around us but their effect on us. On the level of somatosensory experience, what is bad or harmful is experienced as pain.

Arnold (1960) hypothesized fibers that mediate pain or pleasure, and that this system of fibers, the appraisal system, connects with the area called the brain reward system. She calls the appraisal system an "internal sense" like memory or imagination, assuming that such feelings could not be mediated by known peripheral fibers. When peripheral fibers were identified that produced pain on stimulation, physiologists decided that pain is a somatic sensation like touches or muscle strain. But Arnold contends that pain and pleasure are different from sensations. Sensory functions stand on their own, while pleasure or pain are always *reactions* to some sensory experience. Sensory experiences excite fibers of a peripheral appraisal system that activates all gradations of pain or pleasure. Hence, according to Arnold and others, pain and pleasure are feelings rather than sensations. As such, they are precursors to emotional experience and behavioral response.

ENVIRONMENTAL STRESSORS

There are only a few things we can immediately appraise as good or bad for us. We react to them with a range of feelings, from pleasure to pain. We are reflectively aware when we make a judgment of beneficial or harmful. All of these sensations are experienced via the somaesthetic system and affect us directly. We experience an action impulse that flows from it on the level of somatic sensations. Or, we experience pleasure with its readiness to enjoy or pain with an impulse to ease it. On the level of object relations, we are attracted to anything we appraise as good and repelled from anything we have appraised as bad.

A sharp tone or penetrating odor is immediately felt as unpleasant or even painful because it affects fibers of the appraisal system in addition to auditory or olfactory receptors. In contrast, anything we see or hear that is not near enough to touch us, we appraise as good or bad only because we have experienced its effects in the past. This has been identified in literature on animal experimentation as "shock effect." It is clear that the analgesic effect of exposure to inescapable stress is mediated by endogenous opioids and that this response is reversible by naloxone. There is an endorphin response to inescapable shock in animals.

In humans, when the experience of pain and helplessness is repeated by sugges-tion or memory, we relive the feelings we had on similar occasions. The fact that we relive rather than remember is achieved through a different brain circuit called affective memory. Viewed on a PET scan, this may be represented by the kindling effect in the thalamus, which transmits through the amygdala to the hippocampus and finally through the neural pathways to the parietal lobe, where sensory information converges and becomes an integrated and coherent percep-tion. Spindle cells in the frontal lobes contained in special circuits make the inter-pretation and broadcast the messages that become emotions.

The brain chemistry for pleasure and pain is apparent in the chemical reac-tions to analgesics. The serotonin system mediates the effect of morphine's and other opium derivatives' electrical stimulation of the periacquaductal gray, and the midbrain raphe suppresses pain. This effect is reversed by naloxone, a mor-phine antagonist. Morphine not only abolishes pain, but also produces a kind of elation—a high. After painful stimulation, intravenous morphine depresses the firing of the fine "c" and "a-delta" pain fibers of the spinal cord. It does not reverse the depressed firing of pain fibers after a direct action of morphine on these fibers. However, the serotonin system is also involved in the depression of pain fibers. Microinjections of serotonin depress the spinothalamic neurons that respond to various intensities of touch. When the spinal level of serotonin is low-ered and the brainstem level is maintained, morphine analgesia is resumed. Apparently, the brainstem raphe nuclei inhibit the spinothalamic pain neurons. Electrical stimulation of the raphe nuclei produces analgesia. Their ablation pre-vents the analgesia produced by morphine. Painful stimuli inhibit about a third of brainstem raphe cells, while exciting less than a third and leaving less than a third unaffected. Contrary to expectation, the iontrophetic correct application of serotonin to these nuclei did not excite these cells, but inhibited some and left others unaffected. The analgesia produced by electrical stimulation probably acts via the brainstem raphe nuclei, which send seratonin in energic relays to the spinal cord. Morphine reduces the medial thalamic, limbic cortex, and hippo-campus responses. There is an increased firing of neurons in the medial thalamic after painful stimuli. The morphine antagonist maloxone prevents this effect. When the spinal level of serotonin is lowered while the brainstem level is main-tained, morphine analgesia is reduced. The two-midbrain raphe nuclei excite the brainstem raphe, and so does stimulation of the periaquaductal gray.

The circuit affected by morphine has an afferent as well as an efferent link. The efferent link seems to be part of the medial appraisal system, which consists of three different fibers that mediate a positive appraisal of touch or stroking. This afferent appraisal system seems to make contact with the midbrain raphe, the medial thalamus, the limbic cortex, and the hippocampus. Morphine reduces the increased firing of neurons in the medial thalamus after painful stimuli. The connections of the raphe complex with the limbic system and hippocampus seem to mediate positive appraisal of the bodily state after morphine induces a feeling of well-being, ease and relaxation. Via the hippocampus, fornix, and midbrain, fibers of the action circuit seem to connect with the periacquaductal gray, the midbrain and the brainstem raphe, and the spinal cord. Since microinjections of serotonin in the midbrain raphe inhibit all cells and microinjections in the brainstem raphe inhibit most of them, it is quite likely that the fibers of the action circuit connecting with the raphe do not use serotonin as transmitter, but rather, acetylocholine.

Differences in the use of brain chemicals have everything to do with the effectiveness of analgesics and delivery systems for some. The use of analgesics and antidepressants/antianxiety drugs on persons in detention on whom episodic depth interrogation is continuing can contribute to the long-term exacerbation of the physical effects and the ineffectiveness of painkillers on these individuals. There is also the beginning of useful theory on why treatment with antidepressants may be totally ineffective for chronic pain syndrome patients, and also some clues for countering long-term drug dependencies. Addicts experience tremendous pain when they are withdrawing. The prolonged activation and excitation with immediate inhibition of the pain circuits produces distortions. This is apt to contaminate any revelations or information communicated by an individual who has been coerced using pain inducing psychological "torture" (sensory over stimulation, sensory deprivation, thermal extremes). On the other hand, emotional conflicts and depression play a role in the subjective awareness of pain in organic states. Similarly, pain on a functional basis may be generated or intensified by depression. Antidepressants, by elevating the affective state, may alter the degree of pain. Studies of patients experiencing pain and depression have suggested that while antidepressants are effective for those whose pain and depression was coincidental, those who had experienced pain before the onset of depressive symptoms did not lose their pain entirely (see http://www.ronafields.com).

The sensory system is the primary focus of attack in torture because of the potential to produce pain and long-term pathologies. Assaults on the sensory system generate increased sweat and blood flow, and begin synthesizing the major chemical components of pain, along the dorsal fibers of the brain, until it reaches the dorsal horn of the spinal cord, from which it distributes information to the afferent sensory system traveling along the spinal cord to the brain. The thalamus recognizes sensory experience and from there to the cerebro-cortex, which recognizes and localizes pain.

Acute pain in itself interferes with breathing (limbic system), causes nausea because it is affecting the gastrointestinal system, causes strain on the heart, and can induce stroke. Indeed, the muscular-skeletal, gastrointestinal, cardiovascular, skin and genitourinary system are likely to be adversely affected and become dysfunctional. The technique of filling the victim's stomach with water almost to the point of asphyxiation inflicts some of the most intense pain the visceral system can experience. This is what happens in "water boarding." This technique has been included as "psychological torture," despite its very obvious physical incitement. The Nazi doctors used water boarding and extreme thermal manipulations ostensibly to provide data for survival of downed German fliers or soldiers under extreme climate conditions. But in fact, the technique was often used on captured members of the resistance or underground to weaken them into providing information. Electric shock to particularly sensitive body parts (including hands, feet, genitals, and nipples) also was used by the Gestapo and then became part of the repertoire of the Apartheid government in South Africa. These techniques were used on about a dozen detainees in Northern Ireland and various Latin American countries. A variation of the technique, Electro-convulsive Shock (ECT), was used in the CIA MKULTRA "experiments." Intended to inflict pain and "confessions" in fact, the effects of electric shocks elicit anything the victim believes the tormentor wants to hear. ECT leaves histological markings and severe psychological damages.[7]

The SAS had been actively involved in Northern Ireland since at least 1970. Political murders have been attributed and proven their culpability. These are typical techniques for intimidating the larger population and prospective opponents. The techniques are described in the FIAP and in retired SAS Brigadier Frank Kitson's book, *Low Intensity Operations.* Referenced in the later censored, and then withdrawn, *Society on the Run* (Fields 1973), an SAS informant described training the RUC Special Branch in interrogation techniques previously used in Malaysia and Borneo. There are references in declassified CIA material to joint operations with British forces in Latin American security forces training programs.

Prolonged and/or extreme stress reduces the supply of oxygen in red blood cells. Combined with dehydration, all organs are adversely affected. Aerobic exercise and sleep stimulates development of neurotransmitters and brain cells, increasing ability to concentrate and make judgments. This in itself can increase cognitive performance, but it also deters degeneration. Early studies of stress effects also indicated that prolonged stress contributes to arteriosclerosis, the buildup of plaques in the arteries, and ultimately to vascular dementia. One of the immediate consequences of this shortage of oxygen and the interruption of circulation to the brain is loss of consciousness, sometimes diagnosed as syncope and other times as ischemic stroke. The loss of oxygen in the blood supply to the brain can be a spike in blood pressure (and the latter diagnosis is used), or an oxygen deprivation imposed by breathing problems can result in an arterial blockage. For example, during a stroke, a specific part of the brain does not receive adequate nutrients. If ischemia from tissue starvation occurs, but the ischemic tissue has sufficient collateral supply, then functional impairments are temporary with eventual recovery. After several minutes of deprived blood supply, infraction (damaged or dead tissue) occurs.[8]

Techniques of coercion most likely to induce these low-oxygen conditions include the "hooding treatment," in which a usually foul-smelling black bag is placed over the victim's head and secured around the neck, severely limiting oxygen intake physically while increasing stress and discomfort, thus impacting on the oxygen supply in several simultaneous ways. Often in practice, this is accompanied by positions of prolonged physical stress.

In the case of the prisoners in Northern Ireland, they were forced to assume a position of discomfort while hooded, and if they seemed to be passing out, they were beaten awake. In this process there are several factors that can contribute to the shortage of oxygen besides the hooding and constriction it imposes. Beatings and falls may induce a Traumatic Brain Injury, and prolonged positions of discomfort inhibit circulation in itself and cause pooling of blood and fluids at ankles and feet, numbing sensation and collapsing veins. Prolonged standing in one place, particularly on damp concrete, can cause blood to pool in the lower extremities, inducing blood clots and arterial plaque. Keeping arteries flexible—which requires movement and oxygenation—is critical for providing the collateral tissue needed to regenerate brain cells (Taylor 1978). Hours of extreme physical stress and deoxygenation adversely affect temporal and prefrontal cortices. This is manifested in control functions such as memory, multitasking, planning, and attention (essentially frontal lobe executive processes), and visual motor coordination and perceptual motor integration.

Ironically, the effects of stress as well as the neurological consequences of pain inhibit memory and executive function. This practically ensures that the individual subjected to these conditions will be unable to accurately remember the information for which he or she is being coerced. Stress conditions have the effect, over a period of time, of reducing the independent individuality and increasing suggestibility, making the victim more receptive to the interrogator's demands for what information is wanted (which may not always be the truth).

Stress conditions used in Northern Ireland and elsewhere required the victim to lean at a 45-degree angle on toes, with legs wide apart and fingertips against the wall. This is not particularly painful, because the victim soon becomes numb. The main effect of the position is to induce extreme fatigue with the consequent lowering of the oxygen level in the blood, inducing a sensation of numbness and ultimately subservient compliance.

The immediate history of stress treatment originates with the Russian KGB. Prisoners were arrested and taken to the detention prison, where they underwent an introductory routine that included removal of all clothes and possessions with no explanation. They were placed in solitary confinement in a featureless room for an indefinite period, totally isolated from human contact except during interrogation. They had to sit or stand in a fixed position all day, and were allowed to attempt to sleep only at designated times and always in a fixed position facing light. Any deviation from this was punished severely. Throughout the process, they were fed an inadequate diet. Ironically, they were routinely weighed by apparent medical personnel and could recognize their weight loss over time directly. The Northern Irish victims were compelled in this position from nine to more than 43 hours at a time.

There were common elements between the Russian and the British stress procedures. However, hooding and noise were not part of the Russian procedure and appear to have been developed from a line of research initiated in the early 1950s —sensory deprivation. Earlier, hooding was used by the British in the Palestine mandate between 1945–48, against prisoners believed to be Irgun and Stern Group on the one hand, and Palestinian Communists on the other. That and wall standing—positions of great stress—were among the tactics used for interrogation. Survivors of the 1952–56 Mau-Mau insurgency in Kenya report experiencing similar depredations when they were put through interrogations and imprisoned.[9]

Research on sensory deprivation, extreme stress, and suggestibility began as an attempt to understand brainwashing—a feature of Chinese coercive or torture strategies used during the Korean War. Under the belief that by training soldiers and Marines to withstand these conditions, U.S. forces would be protected from the damaging consequences if they were captured. Many of these techniques were studied in the experimental psychology laboratory by the Canadian psychologist D.O. Hebb (1949), in development of a theory that there is an optimum level of arousal for cognition (Solomon et al. 1961). This theory, described in more detail later in this chapter, derived from Moruzzi and Magoun's work (1949) on the reticular formation that has been thoroughly discredited, as described above by all scientific studies. Nonetheless, it remains a standard in the arsenal of the CIA and DOD Foreign Intelligence Assistance Training Program and, apparently, in the tactics of U.S. interrogators in Guantánamo and Iraq.

There is no physical brutality without a component of psychological torture, and vice versa. Those treatment techniques that incorporate the physiological contingencies in concert with specific attacks on the cognitive process appear to produce the most permanent and long-term damage. In this way, the hooding serves at once the function of deleting sensory experience and limiting the supply of oxygen and blood sugar to the brain through restricting breathing, producing mental damage, circulatory disrepair, and a host of anxiety symptoms. This reduction of oxygen has effects similar to drugs on states of consciousness, often extending well beyond the period of immediate reaction.

SLEEP DEPRIVATION

Sleep deprivation is the technical bridge between extreme stress and sensory/environmental manipulation. It affects the brain and central nervous system in several ways; first by depriving oxygen supply and interfering with circulation of nutrients, and then by weakening resistance and bringing the victim under control of the interrogator. Sleep deprivation directly affects the chemical processes that facilitate neurotransmission and serotonin, and finally, because it inhibits the regeneration of brain cells, results in shrinkage of the gray matter, particularly in the hippocampus and amygdala where memory functions are based.

Sleep, and achieving a regular circadian rhythm, is essential for metabolism. The metabolic process not only breaks food into energy, but it also masters the glandular/hormonal system, and is associated with neurotransmitter abnormalities that have behavioral symptoms such as aggression and mood swings.

One of the more promising research directions in neuropathology connects toxicity with sleep anomalies. Pincus and Tucker (1978) elaborate on the effect of lithium in alleviating mania and depression. Hypothalamic dysfunction in depression, they write, is suggested by sleep disturbances, slowed heart rate, lowered body temperature, hyperarousal, elevated skin galvanic responses, and muscle tension. There is a notable decrease in non-rapid eye movement (REM) sleep and increased relative and total time spent in REM sleep. The relationship between the chemistry of clinical depression and its manifestations in sleep behavior with the use of sleep deprivation in psychological torture demonstrates the dysfunction in the hypothalamus that can persist long after the period of interrogation and evolve into chronic and deteriorative diseases of the central nervous system as well as chronic clinical disorders.

Sleep patterns are regulated by the secretion of neurohormones that control the degree of wakefulness. These hormones are normally secreted in rhythms corresponding with periods of lightness and darkness. With diffuse brain dysfunction such as that induced by enforced wakefulness, the neurohormones lose their circadian rhythm and are more likely to resolve in depression than in REM sleep. There is some relationship between the duration of sleeplessness and the duration of metabolic disturbance. There is not a valid estimated relationship between duration of sleeplessness and cellular destruction. However, just as sleep disturbances contribute to hallucinations, clinical pathologies, and abnormalities in blood pressure and oxygenation, consequences can be severe and long term. Along with sleep deprivation, sometimes in tandem with it and sometimes as a separate "treatment" is isolation, and even the manner of arrest.

The KUBARK manual, part of the CIA/DOD documents developed in the 1950s and 1960s, instructs how to psychologically disarm somebody when arresting them.

> The manner and timing of arrest should be planned to achieve surprise and the maximum amount of mental discomfort. He should therefore be arrested at a moment when he least expects it and when his mental and physical resistance is at its lowest ideally in the early hours of the morning. When arrested at this time, most subjects experience intense feelings of shock, insecurity and psychological stress and have great difficulty adjusting to the situation. (p. 85)

It should be noted that immediately upon awakening, blood pressure spikes, and shock impact at that time can be extensive and damaging physically. When the KUBARK manual discusses conditions of imprisonment, it lauds solitary confinement as a means of extracting confessions. Solitary confinement acts on most persons as a powerful stress. A person cut off from external stimuli turns his awareness inward and projects his unconsciousness outward. The symptoms most commonly produced by solitary confinement are hallucinations, delusion, identity confusion, and typical symptoms of sensory deprivation, including pain.

There is a difference between functional anomalies and organic damage. Hallucinations and delusions in schizophrenics have been demonstrated to have organic consequences, including the shrinking of gray matter. How this happens functionally remains a matter of conjecture, but we do know that the process itself has a kindling effect on the hippocampus and a corollary shrinkage of the gray matter: we can see in sequential MRIs increased ventricular space. The same is true for flashbacks. The continued reinforcement of the pain pathways by the neuromuscular portion of the revivification of the experience probably contributes significantly to the physical as well as the psychological deterioration over time. It is important that the torture survivor learns progressive relaxation or self-hypnosis techniques to combat these reiterations of the original assault on their system. While there is much debate on treatments for PTSD and contradictions in studies of treatment outcomes, the neurological evidence on the consequences of repeated flashbacks and revivified trauma is clearly damaging. One treatment combination that needs to be more thoroughly researched and tested is the progressive relaxation with gradated exposure. Known as behavior therapy in the sixties, this was proved successful in overcoming phobias and anxieties.

LONG-TERM CONSEQUENCES

There are long-term consequences to psychological torture, most prevalent of which is chronic depression. More than two-thirds of the Northern Irish survivors of psychological torture had chronic depression. Among the first 1,800 internees who had suffered sensory deprivation torture, at least three committed suicide and an uncounted number required treatment in mental hospitals. Similarly, the South African, Chilean, and Argentine survivors required medical and psychiatric treatment for chronic depression as well as degenerative diseases of the spinal column, joints, and brain seizure activity. Medical scientists who studied Holocaust survivors and concentration camp survivors over the long term had considered their degenerative diseases and premature deaths a consequence of their starvation and physical brutalization. Findings on survivors of psychological torture suggest that perhaps the psychological toll on the concentration camp survivors contributed in large part to their physical deterioration and diseases. When prolonged sleeplessness and dietary insufficiencies added to the survivors' physical breakdown, there was premature aging, and premature dementia as well.

Sleeplessness or sleep deprivation is at the intersection between the psychological and the environmental stressors that impact the central nervous system, resulting in neurological damage. Thermal extremes, positions of discomfort, and threat and fear of threatened actions (for example, threatened with or by snarling dogs); guards or inquisitors playing "Russian Roulette" with revolvers or semiautomatic handguns and a bullet; stun guns; forced nudity, noxious sexual behaviors, and noxious odors; forced ingestion of noxious substances and/or contaminated water; simulated execution; sham executions; witnessing the torture of others, solitary confinement, sensory deprivation, and sensory overstimulation are all psychological stressors used in torture and have a biological impact.[10]

DISTINCTIONS WITHOUT DIFFERENCES

As the science of neuropsychology has rapidly evolved during the past decade along with electronic imaging of brain processes, there is no longer any basis for arguing that there is a kind of coercion and behavior change that neither does organ damage nor endangers life itself. The intention of coercion is to cause pain, and the success of that effort can be measured in organicity. Clearly the autonomic nervous system is involved in the pain process and is consequently affected by it even as the parts of the brain involved in appraisal and arousal are immediately responding to threat. Studies by Eitinger and Strom of concentration camp survivors and many of the classic studies of psychosomatic disorders (Lennart Levi, et al.) demonstrated the systemic sequelae of high stress levels on basic gastrointestinal and circulatory system functioning.

Decades of experimentation with mind-manipulating drugs likewise demonstrates that behavior change is intricately connected with brain activity, and that specific aspects of behavior are demonstrated by stimulation and ablation of the limbic system (Pincus and Tucker 1978). Arnold in her landmark studies of emotion and personality (1960) and later in *Memory and the Brain* (1984), Monat and Lazarus's *Stress and Coping* (1977), and Spielberger and Sarason's *Stress and Anxiety* (1975–82) have long since made the case for the interconnectedness of mind-body and the medical sequelae to psychological phenomena. Studies of Closed Head Trauma victims and Traumatic Brain Injury are illustrative of the relationship between voluntary brain functions and actual decreases in brain mass in frontal, prefrontal, temporal, and lower hippocampus. All of these studies and the most recent brain imaging studies that measure blood flow and metabolism in parts of the brain validate earlier hypotheses about measurable brain damage in survivors of psychological torture and coercion. After injuries (physical as well as psychosomatic), the brain and spinal cord rewire themselves, forming pain pathways that can become overactive immediately or years later.

This knowledge is at the core of physical therapy, and the need for physical therapy to commence as soon as possible even during the acute phase in many instances. Torture survivors not only lack access to therapy, but often are too humiliated by their experience to seek help upon release. More often they become socially isolated because they have been detained and tortured and thus vulnerable. The social stigma is the second wound.

SOMATIC, PSYCHOLOGICAL, AND SOCIAL CONSEQUENCES

The somatic, psychological, and social consequences of psychological torture are contained in Table 8.1.

Some of these consequences are permanent, while some survivors may suffer fewer sequelae sporadically. The symptoms are not necessarily recognizable as consequences of specific acts of torture, and some may turn up more than six months after cessation of torture.

In many ways, post–psychological torture symptoms resemble Posttraumatic Stress Disorder. Indeed, that diagnostic category was predicated on concentration camp survivors, combat veterans, and extraordinary stressful events. In many instances, however, the residual clinical syndrome may be Depression, Dissociative Disorder, or Chronic Pain Syndrome. Before brain imaging was possible for diagnostic purposes, these were considered to be behaviorally originated. Now that so much more is known about the brain and behavior we can recognize these diagnostic categories as having their etiology in the brain processes consequent to torture.

For several years, the International Rehabilitation Center for Torture Survivors in Denmark provided valuation and treatment on site for those fortunate enough to get to Denmark. The center also served a very important function in maintaining an archive of books and articles relating to the subject, including treatments and effectiveness. In Chile and Argentina, local medical and psychological professionals made themselves available to evaluate and work with torture survivors.

The larger problem remains a societal one. Torture has become a phenomenon of civil society and is either ordered or tolerated by governments. This further complicates provision of rehabilitation services to the victims who, along with their families, need treatment and can be in need for many years afterward. If the government does not change and/or if, as happened in Chile and Argentina, those committing these acts receive immunity from prosecution, any modicum of rehabilitation for the victims is compromised by the daily reminder of their own powerlessness in the face of the continuing power of their tormentors. The psychological consequences of impunity exacerbate the damage (Fields, *Impunity versus Healing: The Exacerbation of Torture,* 1996; *Culpables para La Socieded: Impunes por La Ley,* 1988; and *Persona Estado Poder: Estudios sobre Salud Mental Chile 1973–1989*).[11]

Table 8.1
Somatic, Psychological and Social Consequences of Torture

Sequelae	Symptoms
Somatic	– Gastrointestinal disorders, gastritis, ulcer-like dyspeptic symptoms, regurgitation pains in the epigstrium, spastic or irritable colon
	– Rectal lesions, sphincter anomalies
	– Skin lesions, histological lesions
	– Dermatological disorders, dermatitis, uricaria
	– Tendonitis, chronic rheumatoid arthritis, osteoarthritis, and chronic joint pain and deterioration
	– Brain atrophy and organic brain damage
	– Dental disorders
	– Gynecological disorders
	– Hearing impairment, lesions of the eardrum, collapsed ear canal
	– Visual impairments
	– Arteriosclerosis
Psychological	– Chronic Stress Syndrome
	– Suicide
	– Psychiatric breakdown requiring hospitalization
	– Anxiety, fear, depression
	– Psychosis, borderline psychosis (Dissociative Disorder)
	– Instability, irritability, introversion
	– Difficulties in concentration
	– Chronic fatigue, lethargy
	– Restlessness
	– Communication difficulties, especially expressing emotion
	– Memory and concentration loss (may be a consequence of organicity)
	– Loss of sense of identity
	– Insomnia, nightmares
	– Hallucinations (may be a consequence of organicity)
	– Impaired memory (may be a consequence of organicity)
	– Visual disturbances (may be a consequence of retinal damage, ruptured blood vessels, interrupted blood/oxygen supply to the optic nerve
	– Headaches (may be a consequence of organicity)
	– Alcohol and drug abuse (self-medicating)
	– Vertigo (may be a consequence of organicity)
	– Paraesthesia
	– Sexual dysfunction
Social	– Impairment of social personality
	– Inability to function in intimate relationships
	– Impaired family relationships
	– Inability to socialize
	– Inability to work
	– Inability to socialize

Like combat veterans, torture survivors are varied. In Argentina, the vast number of torture survivors in itself provides some social supports. Argentina also has more psychotherapists per capita than any other country. But while there are some scattered treatment centers in the United States (in Minnesota, New York, California, and one in Washington, DC), they are focused on providing psychotherapeutic services rather than medical care. Torture survivors require both.

There is no psychological torture without physical consequences and there is no psychological treatment that is, in itself completely successful. Validating torture for forensic purposes remains largely in the domain of medical documentation through visible and quantifiable objective damage to the head and body. The use of PET scans, SPECT, and MRIs can provide the physical reference for behavioral anomalies by tracking brain process changes (*The Neuropsychology Handbook: Vols. 1 & 2* 1997). It is quite common that the clinical residue is a perversion of the torture experience itself and, of course, the social/political environment into which the victim emerges.

NOTES

1. The United Nations Convention Against Torture defines torture as "any act by which severe pain or suffering, whether physical or mental, is intentionally inflicted on a person for such purposes as obtaining from him or a third person information or a confession, punishing him for an act he or a third person has committed or is suspected of having committed or intimidating him or a third person or for any reason based on discrimination of any kind, when such pain or suffering is inflicted by or the instigation of or with the consent or acquiescence of a public official or other person acting in an official capacity . . . evidence of torture can be both physical and/or psychological."

2. The *Congressional Record*, February 16, 1972, entry by Congressman Ron Dellums is probably the earliest publication in the United States to detail some of the interrogation tortures that were then in use in Northern Ireland and included descriptions of the CIA and DOD techniques also in use in prisons in the United States. It includes the author's 1971 papers (presented at the convention of the Western Psychological Association) as well as 1972 publications. The entire text is available on line at the author's Web site, http://www.ronafields.com, and also at the Web site for the DC Psychological Association, http://www.dcpsychology.org.

3. The *Human Resource Exploitation Training Manual-1983* was used in a number of Latin American countries from November 1982 through March 1987. It references techniques used by the British SAS in the sixties, but this author also witnessed the use of the CIA/DOD techniques by the Special Branch in Northern Ireland in the seventies. It has an added section placed there in 1984 that indicates that torture is not authorized or condoned. There are detailed directions on the apprehension of the subject through a process of psychological victimization including blindfolding and, with others present, a medical examination including bodily cavities. This precedes the questioning, which transpires after there is evidence of disorientation and regression. The manual goes into types of

personalities more extensively than the first manual. In the section on coercive techniques (which are officially disavowed) there are a number of written-in changes, yet all of the "unacceptable" instructions remained. The manual goes on to describe in detail how to induce regression through prolonged exertion, hot, cold, moisture, deprivation of food or sleep, etc. A section is crossed out about the importance of having a psychologist available because a subject may "sink into a defensive apathy from which it is hard to arouse him." This illustrates why this coercive technique may produce torture. A series of psychological pressures are detailed that will lead to disorientation and lack of control.

4. The KUBARK Counterintelligence Interrogation Manual issued in 1963 KUBARK refers to some branch of U.S. intelligence that was involved in foreign settings. KUBARK was governed by regulations that came out of existing legislation involving intelligence gathering and operations. The purpose of this manual is to obtain information from unwilling sources, using scientifically based means, and by violating the subject's rights to freedom of movement for some period of time. The Espionage Act passed by the U.S. Congress extended its power to control its citizens regardless of where they might be. It allowed federal court prosecution of persons apprehended for activities in other countries. The manual includes an annotated bibliography that contains the work of Lifton, Singer, Schein, and others who did research on brainwashing and the North Korean, Chinese, and Russian methodologies. It includes work by American psychologist M. T. Orne as expert on hypnosis and interrogation (1961). Orne was involved in CIA experimentation to develop techniques of brainwashing. In 1984, he testified in a trial that he was not allowed to discuss the work he had done (*Commonwealth of Pennsylvania v. DiViola,* 1984). Imbau and Reed are referenced for their 1963 manual, as were specific techniques and the general approach referenced in interrogation/investigative interviewing texts. The section on coercive interrogation recognized that moral issues are brushed aside as "not the province for the manual." This manual goes on to advocate the use of hypnotic drugs to hypnosis resistant subjects.

5. Some case studies on Northern Irish survivors of the "depth Interrogation" recognized by the European Commission on Human Rights as cruel and inhuman treatment that fell just short of the then definition of "torture" are posted at the author's Web site, http://www.ronafields.com. This is excerpted from the book that was, one month after its publication, ordered off the market by British Military Intelligence and 10,000 copies shredded. This author wrote *Society on the Run,* which was to have been subtitled, Psychological Genocide (1973), Penguin Ltd. Education, Hammondsworth, UK. She was subsequently put under "D" notice and was banned from the British media, and her book was banned from the market and 10,000 copies were shredded. Of the printing of 15,000, only 5,000 survived in circulation (see http://www.ronafields.com).

6. The American Psychological Association Ethical Code has undergone many changes in the years between 1970 and the present. Since the APA code, contrary to the philosophical principles of Axiology, proceeds from the *is* to the *ought,* it is more a case book on practice than a guideline for values. In contrast, the medical profession sets in the American Medical Association (AMA), for instance, a standard of values, there has been no question of the appropriateness or of the responsibility for physicians, including psychiatrists engaging in torture or taking responsibility for research that inflicts pain.

In 2006–7, serious conflict arose in the APA that echoed the issues raised by the *Congressional Record* articles of 1972. A series of resolutions in APA Council and the Ethics Committee has attempted to resolve these conflicts. At the time of this writing, it has only been resolved in so far as to say that psychologists cannot ethically participate in nor actively devise such actions. *A Time to Speak Out: On Human Values and Social Research* (1968; San Francisco: Jossey-Bass Inc.) sets some much needed standards for psychological search and has not yet been adopted fully in practice by the APA 20 years after its writing.

7. Alan W. Shevlin and Edward M. Opton, *The Mind Manipulators,* Paddington Press, New York and London 1978. The authors thoroughly document years of CIA/DOD experiments using domestic and foreign research on mind manipulation and the experimental use of many of these techniques on prisoners in U.S. facilities. Several of these techniques were similar to, if not identical with, those used by the British in Northern Ireland and elsewhere earlier. They list, among other techniques, brainwashing, drugs, lobotomy, psychosurgery, castration, behavior modification, aversion therapy, ECT, and others.

8. In 1975 Hans Selye revised his classic *The Stress of Life* and extended his earlier work on stress to extend his theory's application to all of the disorders of the biologic mechanisms and into the psychosomatic foundations of many chronic disorders. At the time of his writing he could only theorize on dissection findings on animals, post mortem and surgical findings on humans. The following year Alan Monat and Richard Lazarus published *Stress and Coping: An Anthology* (1977), which focused on the psychological processes of stress and psychological stressors. In that volume, Mark Zborowski focused his research on pain as a stressor and culturally related attitudes toward pain. Each essay in that volume focuses on social or cultural aspects of stress and stressors, while the Selye book is physically and medically oriented. None of the essays duplicates the Lennart volume, and both books complement each other.

9. Terrrorism and torture are inextricably bound together for studies on the psychological, medical and social consequences of extreme conditions. This was well established in the content of one of the earliest publications on Posttraumatic Stress Syndrome, the Special Issue of *Evaluation/Change: A Forum for Decision Makers* (1980), subtitled *Services for Survivors* (Susan Salasin [Ed.]). Besides the authors' comparison study of the survivors of a hostage-taking terror attack with Northern Irish survivors of interrogation torture, essays and research reports include Callvin Frederick's important study of the difference between man-made and natural disasters in the psychological consequences for victims and the argument about transference and pathological transference by Martin Symonds and Frank Ochberg's "Stockholm Syndrome." Contents of this compendium reflect the state of the art in treatment strategies and etiologies of the then-new diagnosis, Posttraumatic Stress Disorder. Peter Taylor's book, *Beating the Terrorists? Interrogation in Omagh, Gough and Castlereagh* (Penguin, 1980), documents the increased use of beatings after the European Commission and European Court hearings on brutality in Northern Ireland. He uses interviews with physicians who examined former prisoners and the affidavits and interviews with former prisoners for documentation.

10. When this research began, there were few or no resources in neuropsychology to use as references in planning the research. There were few psychological tests, and the

noninvasive medical repertoire was not extensive. In fact, frequently physicians—even neurologists—would refer patients to a psychologist for testing because our tests were more likely to distinguish among Alzheimer's, Parkinson's stroke, etc. In 2006, the American Psychological Association publications issued *Clinical Psychology: A Pocket Handbook for Assessment.* However, under the circumstances in which the author's initial researches were conducted—in war zones and detention facilities—only the conventional screening tests were practical. At the time, the Halstead-Roitan Battery required laboratory administration, but was used in Scandinavia and Canada particularly following head trauma. The Applebaum, Uyehara and Ellin volume, *Trauma and Memory: Clinical and Legal Controversies* was issued in 1997 and focused on memory function and means for assessing and specifically focuses on the neuropsychology of memory function. Obviously, this book and the studies reported therein was unavailable in the seventies. What was available and became classics in the field was the series edited by Lennart Levi. A series of volumes titled *Society, Stress and Disease,* based in a symposium sponsored by the University of Upsala and the World Health Organization (1971; New York, Toronto, and London: Oxford University Press). With its essays on the effects of experimental, clinical and epidemiological evidence concerning psychiatric and psychosomatic diseases provoked by psychosocial stressors, this volume of proceedings brought together research on the psycho-physiological consequences of exposure to extreme environments such as concentration camps. In 1973, Lennart Levi and Thomas Hammerburg also served on the Medical Commission of Amnesty International in the Campaign to Abolish Torture. This author's participation in the commission as one of two psychologists on that body and her subsequent Amnesty International/Norway fellowship at the Peace Research Institute Oslo contributed greatly to her development of a protocol for the psychological examination of torture survivors and the outlines of a protocol for treatment.

11. Papers, chapters, and books, including this author's paper, "Impunity vs. Healing," many of which were published in Chile and Argentina between 1990 and 2006, documented the continuing pathologies consequent to torture by the direct victims and by the families of the "disappeared." These crippling sequelae were attributed to the practice of impunity, which granted immunity to the official who ordered torture and murder and to their subordinates who executed these strategies also prevented the system of justice from acknowledging the damage done in the name of the state and, of course, no penalties and no apologies. Some authorities contend that the Truth and Justice Tribunals constituted in South Africa had a healing effect. Much of the healing is attributed to the survivors of those who were murdered by the apartheid regime. The South African tortures and justice system are dealt with by Joel Carlson, for 20 years a defense lawyer for Black South Africans, in *No Neutral Ground* (1973).

BIBLIOGRAPHY

American Psychological Association (2006). *Clinical Psychology: A Pocket Handbook for Assessment.*

American Psychological Association (1970, 1976, etc.). *American Psychological Association Ethical Principals.*

Applebaum, P., Uyehara, L.A., & Elin M.R. (1997). *Trauma and Memory: Clinical and Legal Controversies.* New York: Oxford University Press.

Arnold, M.B. (1960). *Emotion and Personality* Volumes 1 & 2. New York: Columbia University Press.

Arnold, M.B. (1962). *Story Sequence Analysis: A New Method of Measuring Motivation and Predicting Achievement.* New York: Columbia University Press.

Arnold, M.B. (1984). *Memory and the Brain.* Hillsdale, NJ, and London: Lawrence Erlbaun Associates.

Belcher, J., and West, D. (1975). *Patty/Tania* New York: Pyramid.

Carlson, J. (1973). *No Neutral Ground.* New York: Thomas Y. Crowell Company.

Central Intelligence Agency (July 1963). *KUBARK Counterintelligence Interrogation* (until 1997, a classified internal CIA publication).

Central Intelligence Agency (1983). *The Human Resource Exploitation Training Manual: An Interrogation Manual* (until 1997, a classified internal CIA publication).

CODEPU (1998). *Estudios Sobre Salud Mental Chile 1973–1989,* Vols. 1–4. Santiago, Chile: CODEPU.

CODEPU (1973–1989). *Persona Estado Poder: Estudios sobre Salud Mental Chile 1973* Santiago, Chile: CODEPU.

Dellums, R. (1972). *Congressional Record,* February 16.

Eitinger, L., & Strom, A. (1973). *Mortality and Morbidity After Excessive Stress; A Follow up Investigation of Norwegian Concentration Camp Survivors.* Oslo: Universitetsforlage.

Ewing-Cobs, S. Kramer, L., et al. (1998). "Neuro-imaging Physical and Developmental Findings After Inflicted and non Inflicted Traumatic Brain injury in Young Children." *Pediatrics,* 102.

Fanon, Frantz, (1963). *The Wretched of the Earth.* New York: Grove Press Inc.

Fields, Rona M. (1971). Northern Ireland papers presented at the Western Psychological Association convention in San Francisco.

Fields, Rona M. (1972). *The Men Behind the Wires and Psychological Research; The Perversion of Human Welfare.* Washington, DC: Congressional Record, H.1192–1198.

Fields, Rona M. (1972). *Ulster: A Psychological Experiment,* New Humanist March Issue. London.

Fields, Rona M. (1973). *Society on the Run,* Hammondsworth, UK: Penguin Ltd. Penguin Education.

Fields, Rona M. (1976). *Society under Siege.* Philadelphia, PA: Temple University Press.

Fields, Rona M. (1980). *Northern Ireland.* New Brunswick, NJ: Transaction/Society Press.

Fields, Rona M. (1977). Repression and Repressive Violence. In M. Hofnagels (Ed.), *Psychological Genocide.* Amsterdam: Swets.

Fields, Rona M. (1989). Terrorized into Terrorist: Pete the Para Strikes Again. In A. O'Day & Y. Alexander, *Ireland's Terrorist Trauma: Interdisciplinary Perspectives.* London: Wheatsheaf Press.

Fields, Rona M. (1996). *Impunity versus Healing.* Seminario Internacional: Impunidad Y Sus Efectos en los Processos Democraticos," International Convention for Human Rights; Santiago de Chile, December 13–15, 1996.

Fields, Rona M. (2002). Palestinian Suicide Bombers. With Salman Elbadour and Fadel Abu Heim. In Chris Stout (Ed.), *The Psychology of Terrorism: Clinical Aspects and Responses,* vol. 2, Westport, CT: Praeger Publishers.

Fields, Rona M. (2004). The Remarkable Normalcy of Dying to Kill in Holy War. In Thomas G. Plante (Ed.), *Mental Disorders of the New Millennium: Public and Social Problems,* vol. 2. Westport, CT: Praeger Publishers.

Fields, Rona M. (2007). Xenophobia: The Social Psychological Consequence of Terror Trauma. In E. Carll (Ed.) *Trauma Psychology: Issues in Violence, Disaster Health and Illness,* vol. 1. Westport, CT: Praeger Publishers.

Frankl, V. (1982). *Man's Search for Meaning: From Concentration Camp to Logotherapy.*

Hebb, D.O. (1949). *The Organization of Behavior.* New York: Wiley.

Hebb, D.O. (1970). *The Motivating Effects of Exteroceptive Stimulation,* American Psychologist 25(4): 328–336.

Horton A.M. Jr., Wedding, D., & Webster, J. (Eds.) (1997). *The Neuropsychology Handbook,* vols. 1 & 2, New York: Spring Publishing Company.

Kelman, H. (1968). *A Time to Speak Out: On Human Values and Social Research,* San Francisco: Jossey-Bass Inc.

Kitson, General Sir Frank (1971). *Low Intensity Operations: Subversion, Insurgency and Peacekeeping.* Faber and Faber.

Korden, D. (1988). *Culpables para La Socieded: Impunes por La Ley.* Buenos Aires, Argentina: Eatip.

Levi, Lennart et al. (1962). *Principles of treatments of psychosomatic disorders,* New York: Oxford University Press.

Levi, Lennart (1971). *Society, Stress and Disease.* New York: Oxford University Press.

Lifton, Robert, (1973). *New York vs. Eugene Hollander,* Superior Court of New York.

Lifton, R. (1961). *Thought Reform and the Psychology of Totalism: A Study of "Brainwashing" in China.* W.W. Norton and Company.

Milgram, S. (1974). *Obedience to Authority: An Experimental View.* New York: HarperCollins.

Monat, A., and Lazarus, R (1977). *Stress and Coping: An Anthology* New York: Columbia University Press.

Moruzzi, G., & Magoun, H. (1949). *Brain stem reticular formation and activation of the EEG* Exectroencephalogr. Clin. Neuro. 1: 45–473 (Dept. of Anatomy, Northwestern University Medical School, Evanston, IL).

Orne, M.T. (1961). The Potential Uses of Hypnosis in Interrogation. In A.D. Biderman & H. Zimmer (Eds.), *The Manipulation of Human Behavior.* New York: Wiley.

Peters, E. (1985). *Torture.* New York: Basil Blackwell.

Pincus, J. (2001). *Base Instincts: What Makes Killers Kill?* New York: W.W. Norton & Co.

Pincus, J. & Tucker, G.J. (1978). *Behavioral Neurology,* 2nd Edition. New York: Oxford University Press.

Salasin, S. et al, (1980). Services for Survivors. *Evaluation/Change: A Forum for Decision Makers.* Minneapolis, MN: Program Evaluation Resource Center, Medical Research Foundation.

Schrag, P. (1985). *Mind Control.* New York: Pantheon Books.

Selye, Hans (1975). *The Stress of Life.* New York: McGraw-Hill.

Solomon, P., Kubzansky, P.E., Leiderman, P.H., Mendelson, J.H., Trumbull, R., & Wexler, D. (Eds.) (1961). *Sensory Deprivation: A Symposium Held at Harvard Medical School.* Cambridge, MA: Harvard University Press.

Speilberger, C. and Sarason, I. (Vols. 1–8, 1975–1982). *Stress and Anxiety* (Series in Clinical & Community Psychology). Washington, DC: Hemisphere Publishing Corporation.

Suedfeld, P. (1990). *Psychology and Torture* (Series in Clinical and Community Psychology). New York: Hemisphere Publishing Corporation.

West, D. & Belcher, J. (1975). *Patty/Tania.* New York: Pyramid Communications, Inc.

CHAPTER 9

DOCUMENTING THE NEUROBIOLOGY OF PSYCHOLOGICAL TORTURE: CONCEPTUAL AND NEUROPSYCHOLOGIGAL OBSERVATIONS

Uwe Jacobs

INTRODUCTION

The massive use of so-called "psychological torture" techniques by the United States in the so-called "War on Terror" has sparked enormous debate in the body politic and among medical, legal, and psychological professionals.[1] The central question for this chapter is whether and how the neurobiological consequences of such torture may be documented in the interest of redress and prevention. I will examine this question by suggesting some general conceptual ideas and by considering some technical requirements for such documentation. I hope that this may clarify how this type of activity needs to be framed in a larger context and what some of its technical constraints are. I also hope to show that the notion of psychological torture is itself artificial, and that it is of interest mainly for those who hope to conceal and deny the practice of torture.

BACKGROUND

At the time of this writing, a special effort of torture prevention through documentation is ongoing worldwide. Medical, legal, and psychological experts are training their colleagues on the international guidelines of documenting the consequences of torture as detailed in the Istanbul Protocol,[2] which is published by the UN High Commissioner for Human Rights. The International Rehabilitation Council for Torture Victims (IRCT) is conducting this project and calls the protocol "the first set of internationally recognized guidelines to establishing independent valid evidence that can be used in court cases against alleged torturers. Since its inception in 1999, the Istanbul Protocol has become a crucial instrument in the global effort to end impunity for perpetrators" (IRCT Web site at http://www.irct.org).

A recent publication by Physicians for Human Rights (PHR) and Human Rights First provides a comprehensive analysis of the torture methods euphemistically described as "enhanced interrogation techniques" by the U.S. government, discussing the unlawfulness and the adverse consequences of such torture.[3] Its title *Leave no Marks* summarizes the principal intent and the salient feature of the subject under discussion. The publication followed an earlier one from 2005, *Break Them Down,* which PHR considers "the first comprehensive review of the systematic use of *psychological torture* by U.S. forces"[4] (emphasis added). A descriptive, operational definition of psychological torture is provided by Ojeda (see Ojeda, Chapter 1). Others in this volume discuss new brain imaging methods of studying the effects of traumatic stress (see Catani, Chapter 10). This paper is concerned with more general conceptual issues that arise from trying to formulate a neuropsychological understanding of hands-off torture and from the attempt to document psychological torture in a forensic context.

MIND-BODY DUALISM AND THE IDEA OF PSYCHOLOGICAL TORTURE

The list of techniques subsumed under psychological torture by Ojeda have the intent of inflicting pain and distress without causing visible, physical injury. These torture methods have also been described as "hands-off torture" (see McCoy, Chapter 3)[5] and "torture lite."[6] What is remarkable and requires immediate mention is that most, if not *all* of these techniques are, in actual fact, far from nonphysical. Firstly, all torture and interrogation requires physical confinement and cannot be administered unless the victim is detained and under complete physical control. Secondly, the conditions of confinement constitute physical restriction or manipulation of movement and sensation. Thirdly, most of the techniques themselves are physical interventions, such as shaking a victim or shouting at him every time he is falling asleep in order to keep him awake, or manipulating the physical environment by keeping the temperature too high or too low, keeping the light on 24 hours per day, etc.

In short, the methodology of so-called "hands-off torture" requires extensive physical manipulation, even though understanding the mechanisms of stress inducement requires psychological knowledge. Thus, to think that psychological torture is *not* an assault on the body is a conceptual error from the outset. To realize that this is the case only requires considering what is being *manipulated,* without even invoking the fact that biology gives rise to all mental processes.

Consider the physicality of a seemingly nonphysical cruel mind game: a mock execution, for example, will induce in the victim a state of extreme somatic-emotional arousal that may be accompanied by sobbing, shaking, sweating, and loss of bladder and sphincter control. This is a forced alteration of the victim's bodily state and may be experienced by the victim as a greater assault on bodily integrity than a beating.

Most importantly, what all torture has in common, regardless of physical or mental appearances, is its assault on the brain. Indeed, *to make a concerted assault on the brain is the primary aim of torture.* Extreme fear and despair, which are the states torture seeks to induce for the purpose of breaking resistance, political demoralization, or surrender to the interrogation process, are emotional states that are anchored in brain states. In light of our modern understanding of the biological underpinnings of psychiatric and neuropsychological disorders, there is little justification for a distinction between physical and nonphysical torture methods, at least to the extent that we have the long-term consequences of torture in mind. From this point of view, one may legitimately question the very notion of psychological torture as distinct from ordinary physical torture. One may also ask why tormenting someone systematically and for an extended period of time should have no long-term consequences only because no obvious tissue damage was inflicted. This notion underlies the employ of psychological torture, even as it seems patently absurd after only a moment's reflection.

However, the common-sense distinction between physical and nonphysical torture is rooted in one particular practical consideration. What lends legitimacy to making distinctions between the two classes of torture is not the presumed absence of physical intervention in some torture methods, but the absence of physical markers that may become subject to direct physical examination by a physician. The investigation of nonphysical torture requires indirect examination that seeks to document the correlates of biological changes brought about in the brain. While both physical torture methods and psychological torture methods produce changes in the brain, only physical torture produces visible markers on the body. Avoidance of such physical markers is what makes hands-off torture attractive to torturers.

THE ORGANISM IN DISEQUILIBRIUM: A BIOLOGICAL PARADIGM FOR MENTAL TORTURE

What happens in psychological torture may be appreciated when we consider the balance that our system needs to be maintained in order to function and how this balance can be systematically undermined. Every organism requires special conditions under which it can survive. If it is transported to another, different place, it may die. Life requires homeostasis, for example, the maintenance of constant conditions. There is a complex effort going on in our bodies at all times just to maintain a temperature of approximately 98.6° F. The maintenance of homeostasis in interacting with the environment is, however, just as necessary on the social and psychological level as it is on the level of biology. In properly engaging with its environment, the organism maintains sustainable levels of arousal within a certain spectrum. If arousal is too low, there is coma or death. If it is too high, there is panic and disorganization.

High levels of arousal without the appropriate action that allows arousal to readjust is what we know as "stress."[7] Chronic hyperarousal is the central and most pernicious aspect of clinical stress conditions such as Posttraumatic Stress Disorder (PTSD). This is a condition in which what was once a situation-induced arousal pattern has become self-maintained by the person suffering from the condition. The arousal-inducing situation under discussion here is torture, and the classic paradigm follows the infliction of extreme physical pain through special kinds of bodily injury, such as electric shocks, stretching of limbs, crushing injuries, etc. The paradigm of psychological torture follows a different paradigm, namely the disruption of behavior that would allow an appropriate response of the individual to organismic need states and to stimuli from the environment. Psychological torture thus prevents the maintenance of balance, or homeostasis. The response of sleep is disrupted by forcible sleep deprivation, avoidance of noxious stimuli is forcibly prevented, etc.

At one end of this spectrum of disruption is stimulus overload. The constant bombardment with stimuli in a manner that does not exist in the natural environment will induce increasing stress and disorganization. In such an environment, humans and other animals resort to certain typical defense maneuvers in order to reduce stress, including evasion, habituation, and distraction, usually in that order. If we cannot evade the noxious stimulus by leaving, we can hope that our response will flatten through habituation. If this is not possible because the stimulus is too strong or noxious, we will then try to distract ourselves and refocus on something other than the noxious stimulus. A key component of inducing extreme distress is to interfere with these defenses. The prisoner is confined so that he cannot leave; exposed to multiple stimuli of extreme intensity so that he cannot habituate; and redirected any time he attempts to secure control or constancy via selective focusing.[8] Prisoner 063 at the Guantánamo Bay detention facility was reportedly put on a swiveling chair at the recommendation of Major John Leso, a psychologist who was assisting his interrogators, so that he would be unable to fix his gaze. The prisoner was presumably trying to erect a barrier between himself and his interrogators by maintaining control of this bodily function and refocusing inward (on the interrogation of Prisoner 063, see Gutierrez, Chapter 11).

At the other end of the spectrum is stimulus deprivation. One of the necessary conditions for many animals is constant contact with other animals of the same species. Another more basic requirement is stimulation in general. Living organisms evolved in natural environments that feature constant and constantly changing stimuli. Without being stimulated and without contact, living organisms deteriorate and die. Since stimulation under natural conditions occurs constantly, it requires enormously artificial efforts to prevent it from occurring. The prisoner is kept in isolation in an environment that is kept constant by shutting out sounds and natural light; items in his small environment are kept to a minimum to prevent cognitive self-stimulation. Stuart Grassian (see Grassian, Chapter 6) has described the deleterious effects of isolation on prisoners that were first comprehensively documented by German researchers in the nineteenth century and more recently in the American penal system.[9]

Without cognitive stimulation, the entire arousal system becomes disorganized. As Donald Hebb pointed out half a century ago, it is astonishing to what extremes people go just to get cognitively stimulated.[10] Experimental volunteer subjects under conditions of sensory deprivation began to hallucinate and to have other psychotic symptoms after hours in a silent room. In another experiment, they would request listening to the same boring tape over and over again rather than have no stimulation at all after only a few hours of isolation. And yet, when they were given cognitive testing, they found it confusing and fatiguing, and they performed very poorly. In short, sensory deprivation produces rapid cognitive disorganization as well as emotional distress. Under sensory deprivation humans are like fish on dry land and cannot survive.

In sum, much of what may be described as psychological torture involves a powerful assault on the basic conditions for mental survival that have a direct effect on the bio-psycho-social equilibrium of the victim. Looking at these methods of torture through a holistic lens facilitates the appreciation of the seriousness of such methods of tormenting prisoners and of the mechanisms by which lasting neuropsychological damage may be inflicted. The next question is whether this general understanding of the ways in which hands-off torture works may assist in the practical forensic documentation of psychological torture.

MIND-BODY DUALISM CONTINUED: WHAT CONSTITUTES EVIDENCE?

I submit that psychological torture has been used for two reasons: (1) to help the torturer convince himself that he is not, in fact, torturing, but acting in a civilized manner by applying an "enhanced interrogation technique"; and (2) to convince the public that what is going on in any given prison does not constitute torture and that no crime has been committed. In addition, select interrogators may derive sadistic gratification from the knowledge that they are inflicting suffering without leaving marks.[11] This kind of deniability appears to be related to a common bias, for example, the belief that physical reality is objective and therefore more real than mental reality, which is subjective and therefore less real. Lay persons and professionals alike do not think of psychology when they think of forensic science. In a court of law, a clinical diagnosis of PTSD that depends in part on a patient's self-report may be relegated to hearsay, whereas a scar from a wound remains a scar from a wound, even if it is not thought to have occurred under torture.

In order to understand this further, we may consider a few practical realities in the documentation of torture as it occurs in the real world. We know from experience that many, if not most, legitimate claims of torture feature no *diagnostic* physical evidence, but only evidence that is more or less *consistent with* the victim's story. To understand this technical difference requires reference to the current international guidelines codified in the Istanbul Protocol, which recommends a classification of medical evidence on a continuum of being *inconsistent* with, *consistent* with, *highly consistent* with, and *diagnostic* of specific allegations of torture. In other words, the doctor's medical findings can be more or less well explained by causes other than torture. One might say that diagnostic findings mean that there are no other plausible causes, and highly consistent findings mean that other causes are possible but unlikely.

However, even in lesions that might be considered diagnostic, such as the presence of multiple scars typical of cigarette butts extinguished on the skin of the victim, the counterclaim can be made that the claimant self-inflicted the lesions and/or had help from a confederate for those lesions on parts of the body he could not have reached himself. The acceptance of evidence still requires good faith, as always. The more general point here is that physical evidence becomes only physical evidence of torture in the context of the history taken by the physician and his/her expert *judgment* concerning the overall consistency of the physical and historical evidence. Outside of a history, there is very little evidence of torture because the history is required for establishing the so-called "nexus" between observed consequences and presumed causation.

Given the usual absence of "diagnostic" physical findings of torture and the reliance on history taking, there seems to be little objective justification for considering interview plus behavioral analysis (including psychological testing where possible) to be less important than interview plus analysis of physical signs. However, the fantasy of incontrovertible proof motivates much practice even when such proof can seldom be had. Conversely, it appears that the fantasy of maintaining deniability has facilitated the torture of thousands in Iraq alone, in spite of some torture having resulted in the deaths of victims,[12] the release of photographs, and all kinds of other proof. As far as medical and psychological evidence are concerned, however, the call for neurobiological documentation of psychological torture emanates from the desire to find proof through new, special, scientific methodology, realizing that a picture is often worth a thousand words.

NEUROBIOLOGICAL EVIDENCE OF PSYCHOLOGICAL TORTURE?

From the discussion above, it may be evident that, without interpretation in the context of a history taken or other factual evidence, there can be no *diagnostic* evidence of *psychological* torture specifically, although there might be diagnostic evidence of trauma. Certain physical evidence is subject to direct measurement and may be correlated to the discrete physical impact of an object or torture technique on the body. However, even the most sophisticated brain imaging technique may only yield evidence of trauma in general. If a brain can be shown to be traumatized, it cannot be said whether the trauma was torture, much less psychological torture in particular, without interpretation of history or other documented facts. This does not discourage the neuropsychological documentation of torture any more than the documentation of most physical evidence of torture, but it is merely a logical constraint to be recognized. In the same way that the historical context is critical for all other kinds of forensic documentation, here, too, there is a need to rule out other possible sources of traumatization by history. The ultimate source of distress is not directly traceable. On the other hand, an individual who was demonstrably not traumatized prior to confinement and now evinces neuropsychological signs and symptoms of trauma can be assumed to have sustained trauma during confinement.

NEUROPSYCHOLOGICAL EVIDENCE OF TORTURE IN PRACTICE

The attempt to catalogue all the general principles of documenting psychological and neuropsychological evidence of torture is beyond the scope of this chapter and has been detailed elsewhere.[13] It may be stated, however, that the utility of neuropsychological investigation follows from the description of the type of damage done by psychological torture methods as it was provided above. Traumatic effects on the brain will be revealed in behavioral changes. Neuropsychologists specialize in brain-behavior relations and commonly use batteries of tests in order to measure behavior under controlled conditions and to compare that performance to a sample of individuals who have similar characteristics, the so-called "normative sample." Thus, if a prisoner who alleges that he was tortured complains that he has had memory problems since that time, one might give him a test, in the same way that a cardiologist may give someone a stress test when they complain of chest pain.

As imaging techniques have advanced rapidly and allow ever more sophisticated inspection of brain processing, the need for neuropsychological testing as an indirect measure of extent and localization of lesions has diminished. Direct imaging evidence of cerebral correlates of trauma has been increasingly made possible through recent scientific advances (see Catani, Chapter 10). What remains relevant for traditional neuropsychological investigations of torture, however, is the description and measurement of functional capacities and deficits that result from injury or disease. Thus, the deficits described by Hebb in subjects who had undergone sensory deprivation were documented by administration of cognitive tests. Likewise, any functional deficits in cognitive processing, memory, and a victim's ability to plan, organize, and carry out sequences of behavior can be documented in this manner.

Neuropsychological assessment has areas of overlap and differences from psychiatric, neurological, and psychological assessment. Compared to a neurological examination, the neuropsychologist focuses more on higher cortical functions, which typically get a less detailed assessment in typical neurological examination. Neurological examination tends to be relatively brief and focused on gross sensory-motor functioning and medical diagnostic tests for signs of central nervous system abnormality. Psychiatric examinations, on the other hand, focus on behavioral history and observation, with a greater focus on signs and symptoms of psychopathology. Psychiatrists carry out a less detailed assessment of higher cognitive functions, no assessment of sensory-motor and perceptual functions, and no objective testing. Clinical psychologists may include objective testing, which is of advantage, but may have less understanding of the biological underpinnings and possible somatic causes of symptoms than the other disciplines. However, which individual discipline may contribute more to the understanding of sequelae from torture in any particular case depends both on the nature of the injuries and the skill and knowledge base of the examiner.

From the neuropsychological perspective, all behavioral functions depend on an intact brain, and among the functional domains we examine are motor control and behavior, sensory processing, attention, concentration, memory, verbal comprehension and fluency, visual-spatial processing and problem solving, calculation, abstract reasoning, and executive functioning. Different pathological conditions are associated with particular patterns of impairment in one or more of these domains. The procedures neuropsychologists use are more or less specifically sensitive to particular domains and/or have a high predictive value with regard to the presence of brain impairment in general. Neuropsychological investigations can yield rather specific and detailed objective findings and are therefore desirable in any situation in which functional impairments in cognition and memory are suspected as a result of torture. In spite of this reality, the discipline of neuropsychology has been underrepresented in the documentation and rehabilitation of torture.[14]

A significant limitation of traditional neuropsychological testing in the context of torture, however, is found in any cross-cultural examination context and in any situation that deviates significantly from a standardized assessment environment. Administration of a test battery may not be feasible in many situations of current detention or imprisonment. Whenever examiners have to assess individuals who do not have at least 6–8 years of formal education, many neuro-psychological tests have questionable validity. If any norm-referenced interpreta-tion of test results is undertaken, proper norms must exist. Linguistic and cultural competency is also required of the examiner. There are many instances in which the assessment of a torture victim cannot satisfy one or more of these conditions and therefore procedures are limited to interview and observation.

A case description of a neuropsychological examination of a victim of torture is provided in a prior publication.[15] To summarize in brief, the case involved an asylum seeker from South Asia with a severe traumatic brain injury (TBI) from torture that required subsequent surgery and resulted in a state of dementia and PTSD, which required detailed assessment to understand in its complexity. The patient had previously been diagnosed as suffering from a psychotic mental illness by a community psychiatrist and given treatment with antipsychotic medi-cation. However, neuropsychological investigation demonstrated that what was thought to be a delusional paranoia was more accurately understood as extreme fear of all authority figures as a result of having been tortured and left for dead by the police, combined with a severely compromised cognitive capacity as a result of the TBI. This was a case in which the severity of the injury warranted the use of neuropsychological procedures even in a cross-cultural context where no test norms existed.

For a scenario of psychological torture without such severe TBI, however, this type of cross-cultural assessment might not have yielded valid, interpretable results above and beyond what a psychiatric or clinical psychological evaluation may provide. Case studies with educated individuals by linguistically competent examiners would be required for a demonstration of the utility of such investiga-tions following psychological torture. The qualitative interpretation of brief and somewhat controversial tests, such as the Bender Gestalt Test, may in some cases be illuminating (see Fields, Chapter 8) but may be challenged on methodological grounds. Even without such individual investigations, however, a body of litera-ture has existed for decades now that documents the serious neuropsychological consequences of isolation, sensory deprivation, and other techniques. These lessons are sufficient evidence to be leveled against any attempts to legalize such mistreatment.

CONCLUSION

Torture of all kinds changes the victim's brain functioning. These changes may be more obviously structural, i.e., based on brain tissue damage, in the case of traumatic brain injury, or they may be more functional in nature. In both instan-ces, neuropsychological evaluation can be important in the effective investigation of torture. From a holistic point of view, and based on understanding brain-behavior relations, the apparent distinctions between physical and psychological torture methods begin to lose their apparent importance. It may be hoped that this point of view can raise awareness and contribute in the struggle against the impunity and attempted legalization of psychological torture methods. There is no greater excuse for damaging brains and minds by the types of cruelty referred to as "enhanced interrogation methods" than there is for beating a prisoner about the head with a stick. Neuroscience in general, and neuropsychology in particular, can help to make this clear.

NOTES

1. The 2007 Annual Convention of the American Psychological Association, for example, was the stage for fierce controversy among psychologists as to whether psychologists were responsible for designing and/or executing mental torture at detention sites for "enemy combatants." Some psychologists held a demonstration outside the convention, and panels on the subject of psychologists' participation in interrogations became standing-room-only events that drew hundreds of participants.

2. United Nations (2001). *Istanbul Protocol. Manual on the effective investigation and documentation of torture and other cruel, inhuman or degrading treatment or punishment.* Office of the High Commissioner for Human Rights. New York and Geneva.

3. Physicians for Human Rights & Human Rights First (2007). *Leave No Marks. Enhanced Interrogation Techniques and the Risk of Criminality.* Library of Congress Control Number 2007934152.

4. *Leave No Marks,* p. iii.

5. Alfred McCoy (2006). *A Question of Torture: CIA Interrogation from the Cold War to the War on Terror.* New York: Henry Holt.

6. Bowden, M. (2003). "The Dark Art of Interrogation." *Atlantic Monthly,* October 2003.

7. Selye, H. (1978). *The Stress of Life.* New York: McGraw-Hill.

8. Miles, S. (2007). "Medical Ethics and the Interrogation of Guantanamo 063." *The American Journal of Bioethics* 7(4): 5.

9. Grassian, S. (1983). "Psychopathological Effects of Solitary Confinement." *American Journal of Psychiatry* 140: 1450–1454

10. Hebb, D.O. (1955). "Drives and the C.N.S." *Psychological Review* 62: 243–254.

11. Lagouranis, T. (2007). *Fear Up Harsh.* New York: Penguin.

12. Miles, Steven (2006). *Oath Betrayed: Torture, Medical Complicity, and the War on Terror.* Random House.

13. Jacobs, U., Evans, B.F. & Patsalides, B. (2001). Principles of Documenting Psychological Evidence of Torture, Parts I and II. Torture Part II. *Torture 11* (3 and 4), 85–90, 100–102; see also Notes 2 and 14.

14. Jacobs, U., & Iacopino, V. (2001). "Torture and Its Consequences: A Challenge to Clinical Neuropsychology." *Professional Psychology: Research and Practice* 32 (5), 458–464.

15. See Note 7.

CHAPTER 10

THE TORTURED BRAIN

Claudia Catani, Frank Neuner, Christian Wienbruch, and
Thomas Elbert

The World Medical Association, an international organization that governs professional standards and ethics for physicians, defines torture as

> the deliberate, systematic or wanton infliction of physical or mental suffering by one or more persons acting alone or on the orders of any authority, to force another person to yield information, to make a confession, or for any other reason.[1]

Compared to this definition, the nature and purpose of torture has changed during the last century.[2] In the modern world, torture is typically used covertly and extrajudicially as part of a process of state-sponsored violence against minority ethnic, religious, or other communities. Much more than to yield information or confessions, torture is primarily used to deliberately and systematically dismantle one's identity and humanity. Its central purpose is to destroy a sense of community, eliminate leaders, and create a climate of fear in the individual victim as well as in the community. It has become obvious that the main objective of torture is not to inflict physical wounds or injuries; on the contrary, the objective is to leave psychological wounds. Indeed, even the real purpose of physical torture, which does bear physical scars, is to have a major impact on the long-term psyche of an individual. This has been proven in several studies which investigated the mental health and well-being of torture survivors even years after being exposed to torture.[3, 4] In most of the studies addressing psychological long-term consequences of torture, the investigated samples typically had experienced psychological as well as physical torture. For example, Basoglu and colleagues[3] examined a sample of 55 torture survivors in Turkey and found very similar prevalence rates for both psychological torture (blindfolding, being stripped naked, threats of more torture, threats of death) and physical techniques (electrical torture, beatings of the body, beatings of the soles of the feet).

It has only been recently that scientists have begun to investigate whether physical and psychological torture are distinct in terms of their relative psychological impact. In response to a controversy about reports of human rights abuses by the U.S. military in Guantánamo Bay, Iraq, and Afghanistan, Basoglu and coworkers carried out a cross-sectional survey examining the relative cumulative impact of physical vs. nonphysical torture[5] in a sample of 279 survivors of torture from different Balkan countries. The related question was whether or not the detention and interrogation procedures described in the reports qualify as torture. The noteworthy finding of the study was that psychological torture methods and humiliating treatment were comparable to physical torture in terms of distress and the victim's lack of control. Most importantly, it was found that physical torture and psychological torture incidences were similar in terms of the severity of mental suffering they cause. An interesting side note of the study was that it was not possible to compare two distinct groups of survivors (a group of physical torture survivors compared to nonphysical torture survivors) since nearly all participants reported both types of torture. These findings, therefore, support the assumptions that: (1) physical and psychological torture almost always occur simultaneously; and (2) a distinction between these two qualities of torture is unnecessary when discussing long-term effects on mental health.

Based on these notions, we will review findings of psychological consequences and altered brain dynamics in victims of torture regardless of the quality of torture experienced by them. In particular, neurobiological variables assessed in survivors of torture are not to be considered correlates of torture events per se, but rather brain correlates of chronic traumatization induced by extremely stressful and life-threatening experiences.

TORTURE: EXTREME TRAUMATIZATION AND ITS PSYCHOLOGICAL SEQUELAE

We have already stated that torture typically has a strong impact on the psychological condition of the victim, since it represents an act designed to psychologically damage an individual. From a clinical perspective, torture clearly represents a traumatic event according to the DSM-IV criteria for Posttraumatic Stress Disorder (PTSD). Both the required objective (e.g., death threat), as well as the subjective criteria (e.g., fear or helplessness) are fulfilled in situations in which an individual is a victim of torture. As a consequence, PTSD has become a main focus of epidemiological research with torture survivors, and several studies have shown an extremely high prevalence rate for this anxiety disorder, often accompanied by Major Depressive Disorder (for a review, see [6]). The main characteristics of PTSD are symptoms of involuntarily reexperiencing the traumatic event, avoiding reminders of the experience, and persistent hyperarousal. Symptoms are so frequent and severe that they lead to a significant functional impairment.

Basoglu and coworkers [3] conducted a particularly interesting study in a comparison of torture survivors with a group of matched non-tortured political activists in Turkey. A key finding was that torture survivors had significantly more symptoms of PTSD and anxiety/depression than the comparison subjects. The authors concluded that torture has long-term psychological effects independent of consequences related to uprooting, refugee status, or other traumatic life events that typically characterize a politically repressive environment. In another study, Silove and colleagues [4] examined the role of torture as a causal factor of PTSD in a sample of Tamil refugees living in Australia. The results showed that torture was the strongest predictor of PTSD in a multiple regression analysis. De Jong and coworkers[7] studied community samples in four countries that had recently been experiencing internal conflict. They found elevated rates for PTSD in all of these countries together with a significant relationship between torture and risk of PTSD. Data from our own workgroup show a similar picture. We have investigated different populations of refugees and asylum seekers in Germany and Italy, as well as large samples of survivors of organized violence in war-torn countries all over the world. In nearly all of these populations, torture has been the most frequent traumatic experience and the main factor related to the development of chronic PTSD.[8, 9]

In view of the high prevalence rates of trauma-related disorders in torture survivors, one might ask oneself, "What exactly makes torture such an important contributor to the development of PTSD?" The answer to this question is found by looking at the research on potential predictors of PTSD in survivors of torture. Again, Basoglu's various studies have addressed this issue and found that the subjective experience of torture, rather than objective characteristics such as the use of physical techniques and the amount of physical pain, is the most important determinant of subsequent stress-related disorders.[3, 5, 10, 11] In particular, the subjective appraisal of the torture event as being uncontrollable and unpredictable was repeatedly shown to be associated with higher perceived distress during torture and a greater likelihood of developing PTSD. This finding does, once again, support our initial notion that experiences of psychological and physical torture both have the same detrimental effects on the survivor's mental health, since both methods share the same crucial feature: exposing a person to an uncontrollable and unpredictable life-threatening situation of extreme stress.

Another factor that accounts for elevated PTSD rates in torture survivors, as well as other victims of organized violence, is the so-called "dose effect" of traumatic exposure. Epidemiological studies conducted by our workgroup[12] as well as other research teams[13, 14] have shown that with the growing number of traumatic event types, the portion of individuals with PTSD increases near-linearly, a finding that is true for both adult and child survivors of organized violence.[15] Considering that torture survivors typically are exposed to a variety of traumatic event types, includ-ing arrests, interrogations, and—most of all—episodes of various kinds of torture, the high prevalence rates of PTSD found in this population is not at all surprising.

TRAUMA AND MEMORY

Many of the current theories of PTSD[16, 17, 18] explain the development and the symptomatology of PTSD on the basis of memory representations of the traumatic event. The theories differ with regard to the number of proposed representations of the traumatic event in memory, ranging from two[16] to four[17]. All theories propose a dissociation between nondeclarative ("fear structure," "hot memory," "sensory-perceptual representation," "situationally accessible memory") and declarative ("autobiographical memory," "verbally accessible memory," "cold memory") representations. At the core of this assumed dissocia-tion is the observation of the memory-related clinical features of PTSD.

The autobiographical context memories, or "cold memories,"[19] contain knowl-edge about periods of one's life and specific events in the context of time and space. The sensory-perceptual representations, or "hot" memories, comprise emotional and sensory memories of all modalities. Cold memories (e.g., "on March 24 at 4:30 PM, I was attending the University of Diyarbakir") are usually connected with hot, sensory memories (e.g., black-masked, gun, voice of soldier) as well as with cognitive (e.g., "I can't do anything"), emotional (e.g., fear, horror), and physio-logical elements (e.g., racing heart, fast breathing, shivering). In individuals who are not affected by trauma or fear, hot memories are linked with autobiographic, declarative memories. However, in traumatized persons, the autobiographical memory is characterized by a significant distortion that is, in particular, visible in the failures of PTSD patients to narrate their traumatic experiences. As a conse-quence, sensory and emotional memories are activated by environmental stimuli without being related to autobiographic, declarative items (i.e., dates and places of autobiographical occurrences) and those autonomous hot memories form a fear network. Contrary to recollections of everyday events, flashbacks are experienced as if the event is occurring at that moment.[18] They do not fit the perception of subjective time but seem to be without context in time and space.

An example of a memory representation of a traumatic event, in this case a scene of psychological torture (mock execution), is outlined in Figure 10.1. The fear network is characterized by a great number of very strong interconnec-tions between the single memory items. The activation of a single item (e.g., see-ing a soldier or starting to sweat) will cause the entire network to be activated. Since the sensory-perceptual representation of this traumatic event is not tied to corresponding autobiographical context information, once the recollection of the torture scene is triggered, it will result in a "here and now" perception and the traumatized survivor may experience a flashback.

Figure 10.1
Example of a Memory Representation of a Torture Experience (Mock Execution)

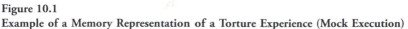
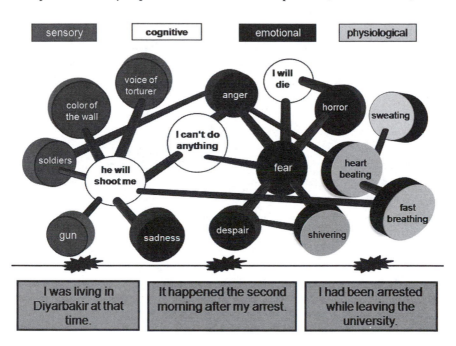

The sensory-perceptual network (fear structure) includes sensory, cognitive, emotional, and physiological elements. The boxes below represent the autobiographical memory fragments that are completely disconnected from the sensory information (fear network).

The model described here assumes that the fear network acts as an example of how the human brain responds to traumatic life events in terms of plasticity, or changing neural networks. As outlined below, there is an important body of literature, in particular data from research with rodents as well as neuroimaging findings in PTSD, arguing in favor of the proposed model. However, a definite validation of the theoretical assumption presented here still provides a challenge for future neuroscientific research. Our workgroup is addressing this specific challenge by investigating neural correlates of PTSD symptomatology in survivors of torture and organized violence.

THE TRAUMATIZED BRAIN

The neurobiological correlate of autobiographical memory cannot be identified as a single brain structure. Rather, long-term storage of autobiographic and other declarative knowledge depends on widespread neocortical neuronal activity. The hippocampus is a brain structure that plays a major role in the construction of memories that contain autobiographic information, including the temporal and spatial context of an event.[20] Research with rodents showed that both the function and the structure of the hippocampus are strongly affected by stress hormones. Exposure to glucocorticoids increases the activity of the hippocampus, but if a certain threshold is exceeded, the activity declines again. Under very high levels of stress, the functioning of the hippocampus is severely impaired. It is assumed that very high doses of adrenal steroids can even cause permanent and irreversible atrophy of the hippocampus.[21, 22]

Consistent with these findings, several neuroimaging studies have found decreased hippocampal volumes in PTSD.[23, 24] However, it is not yet clear as to whether the hippocampal volume reduction in individuals with PTSD is a consequence of the excessive exposure to adrenal steroids during the traumatic event, or whether it rather reflects a pre-trauma vulnerability for PTSD.[25] The results of studies that measured the hippocampus volume in PTSD patients are inconsistent, and the explanation of the findings is still a matter of debate. Nevertheless, the fact that this structure, which relates to the encoding of spatiotemporal information, is vulnerable to stress strongly supports the assumption that a malfunction of the hippocampus during severe stress might be responsible for the distortion of the autobiographical memory.

With respect to the storage of the sensory-perceptual representations of past events, neuroimaging studies suggest the complex involvement of brain areas considered to be responsible for visuospatial processing and emotion (limbic structures, especially posterior cingulate including the surrounding cortex as well as parietal cortex), and preparation for action (motor cortex).[26] Studies of neural mechanisms of fear conditioning offer ideas about the coding of fearful memories.[27] Based on animal studies, the suggestion here is that the amygdala, an ancient brain area located in the center of the brain, plays a crucial role in fear responses and fear conditioning. Contrary to the hippocampus, which shows decreased functioning under high levels of stress, the functioning of the amygdala seems to be enhanced as stress increases.[28, 29, 30] This finding supports the theory that a dissociation of stress effects occurs in the hippocampus and amygdala and can, therefore, provide the neurobiological framework for the assumed dissociation of hot and cold memory systems during and after a traumatic event. Furthermore, the hyperresponsiveness of the amygdala under extreme stress may cause an excess of fear conditioning to a large variety of stimuli during a traumatic event, and thus account for the assumption of unusually large fear structures in PTSD patients. Despite these findings, neuroimaging studies with PTSD patients yielded less consistent results with respect to amygdala activity. As summarized in a review by Bremner,[31] some studies support the assumption of an increased amygdala activity during symptom provocation in PTSD patients, whereas data of other studies do not speak in favor of this notion.

Instead of merely focusing on the amygdala as the crucial brain in fear responses, a more promising approach has been the investigation of the mediating role of medial prefrontal cortical areas and, in particular, their relationship to amygdaloid activity in stress and anxiety-related disorders. As shown by Bremner in his review on functional neuroanatomical correlates of traumatic stress,[31] data arguing for a dysfunction in medial prefrontal cortex (including anterior cingulate) in PTSD patients are more univocal than evidence for deficits in the hippocampus and amygdala. The strongest evidence derives from imaging studies involving symptom provocation in patients with PTSD. A failure of activation and decreased function in various subregions of medial prefrontal cortex/anterior cingulate in traumatized patients compared to healthy controls were repeatedly found during exposure to traumatic scripts[32, 33] or to combat-related pictures.[34] The results of neuroimaging studies are mostly consistent in showing that, in PTSD, the amygdala is hyperresponsive and medial prefrontal regions are hyporesponsive, and that activity in these regions is reciprocally related.[35] Given that the medial prefrontal cortex is well connected to the amygdala in primates[36] and is involved in the extinction of fear conditioning through inhibition of the amygdala, the lack of activation of prefrontal areas in PTSD patients can explain the inappropriate fear responses and the diminished extinction of the conditioned trauma related fear in these individuals.

NEUROBIOLOGICAL STUDIES WITH TORTURE SURVIVORS

Despite the large number of neuroimaging studies with traumatized patients published during the last years, research on functional or structural brain alterations in survivors of torture is still scarce. In addition to the work conducted by our workgroup at the German Outpatient Clinic for Traumatized Refugees, to our knowledge there is only a single published study on neurobiologic alterations in a group of torture survivors. Using single photon emission computed tomography, Mirzai and coworkers[37] examined brain activity through the regional cerebral blood flow in eight survivors of torture with PTSD compared to eight healthy controls. The main outcome of the study was a markedly enhanced heterogeneousness of the measured blood flow in the patient group, in particular in the temporoparietal region. However, given the small sample size, findings should be interpreted with caution and seen as preliminary. In a single-case study, Fernandez and colleagues[38] examined a patient with war- and torture-related PTSD with a positron emission tomographic scanner during a condition of symptom provocation (exposure to war sounds) and a baseline (rest) condition. Exposure to the reminders of trauma resulted in a decreased cerebral blood flow in the insula and the prefrontal cortex as well as in an increase in activity in the cerebellum and supplementary motor cortex. Activity in frontal areas was negatively correlated to heart rate during provocation as well as baseline conditions.

The authors concluded that symptom provocation in torture-related PTSD may alter neural activity in brain territories involving memory, emotion, and attention as well as motor control. In particular, the abnormalities seen in the frontal cortices during anxiety provocation were in line with evidence from previously published evidence from neuroimaging studies in PTSD[39, 40] and were assumed to reflect loss of emotional control and a failure to extinguish fear-conditioning.

ABNORMAL SLOW WAVE ACTIVITY IN TORTURE SURVIVORS

In our workgroup, we use magnetic source imaging procedures to map abnormal slow wave activity[41] in refugees with PTSD as well as schizophrenic and depressive patients.[42, 43] Abnormal slow wave rhythms (delta range 1.5–4 Hz) in the brain have been found to be related to brain pathology or dysfunctional neural tissue. In one of the first studies to describe torture victims from a neuroscience perspective, we used slow wave mapping to examine functional alterations in torture victims with a current diagnosis of PTSD and elevated dissociation scores compared to a matched control sample.[44] Severely traumatized persons, such as torture victims, often describe dissociative experiences during or immediately after trauma exposure (peritraumatic dissociation), but also later on (posttraumatic dissociation). Several studies have found peritraumatic dissociation to be a predictor for the later development of PTSD.[45, 46] Abnormal slow wave mapping results of our study showed that torture survivors had significantly more abnormal slow waves in the left ventral region than the culturally matched control group. Furthermore, the number of dissociative experiences was positively related to the density of abnormal slow wave generators in the left ventral region of the anterior cortical structures and to the left hemisphere as a whole. The inverse relationship was found for the right hemisphere as a whole and for the right anterior superior areas. Statistically partialling out the level of posttraumatic stress disorder did not influence these relationships, suggesting that the level of dissociation contributes a separate component above and beyond PTSD symptoms to abnormal brain activity.

Recently, Kolassa and colleagues[47] carried out a similar study with 97 refugees with PTSD, many of whom were victims of torture, again mapping generators of slow waves produced within circumscribed brain regions. Compared to a group of healthy controls, PTSD patients showed a higher focus of slow waves in the left temporal and the right frontal brain areas. The peak of abnormal slow wave generators was seen in the left intrasylvian cortex, suggesting a possible dysfunction of the left insula in traumatized survivors of organized violence and torture. The left insula has been ascribed a key role both in expressing affective and speech processing, and insular dysfunction could play a key role in the decoupling of emotional from language centers, leading PTSD survivors to be caught in the speechless terror of their intrusive memories. The enhanced slow wave activity in the right frontal cortex found in the present study is in line with the large body of literature on structural and functional abnormalities in the prefrontal cortex, including the anterior cingulated cortex, in PTSD patients. As summarized above, current models suggest that the prefrontal cortex, and the anterior cingulate in particular, play a major role in fear extinction through their inhibitory effects on the amygdala.[35] Thus, the findings of Kolassa and colleagues[47] provide additional evidence for the assumption that a dysfunctional prefrontal cortex may lead to diminished extinction of conditioned fear and, together with a hyperresponsive amygdala, to enhanced fear responses and hyperarousal symptoms, such as those seen in survivors of extreme trauma.

To date, more than 100 torture victims seen at our specialized outpatient clinic for refugees in Germany have been examined for functional alterations in brain activity. Findings of a comparison between slow wave activity in this group and in a healthy control sample are outlined in Figure 10.2. Traumatized torture survivors generally show a specific pattern of slow wave activity in prefrontal and temporal brain areas.

AFFECTIVE PICTURE PROCESSING IN TORTURE SURVIVORS

As outlined above, the key feature of a traumatized mind is a distortion of the memory representation for the traumatic experiences as characterized by the dissociation between the declarative "cold" memory and the "hot" fear network. Therefore, the challenge for research is to detect neurophysiological correlates of a fear network. In recent years, the use of affective pictures as stimulus material

Figure 10.2
Statistical Difference Maps Plotted on a Standard Brain Showing T-Test Differences of 98 PTSD Patients (Mostly Torture Survivors) vs. 97 Healthy Control Subjects

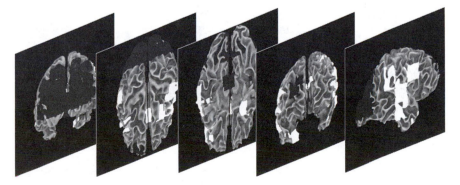

White areas indicate higher ASWA relative to controls (prefrontal and temporal focus); regions marked in gray indicate lower ASWA relative to controls.

has become a standard paradigm for studying brain responses to emotional cues. Lang and coworkers have developed the International Affective Picture System (IAPS),[48] a set of calibrated photographic slides that includes normative ratings of pleasure and arousal associated with each picture. This set of affective pictures is employed by an extended body of researchers worldwide in important cognitive, psychophysiological, and biobehavioral studies with different clinical populations.

In a first study,[49] we implemented a visual paradigm to investigate cortical activation patterns during the processing of high arousal (pleasant and unpleasant) as compared to low (neutral) arousal pictures presented for two seconds. A schematic illustration of the experimental design is provided in Figure 10.3.

In addition to magnetocortical data, we examined subjective ratings, heart rate, and startle responses in 15 survivors of torture and organized violence with PTSD, 15 schizophrenia inpatients, and 10 healthy control subjects. PTSD patients showed a differential sensitivity for high arousal pictures during the early time windows (140–220 ms after picture presentation). Moreover, PTSD patients displayed more reactivity to emotionally arousing pictures during later stages of visual stimulus processing (350–490 ms after picture presentation), which are thought to reflect enhanced cortical facilitation in attentional processes. Heart rate responses differed significantly among PTSD patients and control subjects showing sustained heart rate acceleration for highly arousing unpleasant pictures in traumatized survivors of torture and organized violence. The author concluded that the increased of this peripheral marker may be related with the activation in higher-order cortical networks.

Figure 10.3
Arousing and Neutral Pictures were Selected from the International Affective Picture System

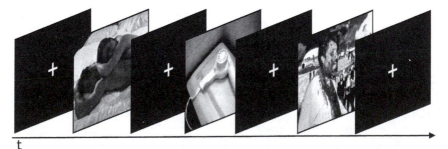

t

Highly arousing pleasant pictures included erotic couples and happy families; low-arousing neutral pictures included neutral faces and household objects; high-arousing unpleasant pictures comprised of mutilated bodies, aimed guns, and scenes of attack and threat. IAPS pictures were presented for 2000 ms with an intertrial interval (black screen) varying randomly between 4 and 10 s.

In a second study, we applied the rapid serial visual presentation paradigm[50] whereby stimuli from the International Affective Picture System are presented in very fast succession (three or five pictures per second) to traumatized torture victims and to various clinical and nonclinical control groups. With this paradigm, we detected important deviations in the processing of affective stimuli as soon as 60–120 ms after stimulus onset,[51] as illustrated in Figure 10.4. In both healthy controls and traumatized individuals, the emotional material activated the visual cortex and associated areas. However, the prefrontal and orbitofrontal areas and the cingulate gyrus were also activated in traumatized refugees.

This widespread early activation triggered by affective (not necessarily trauma-related) stimuli can be interpreted as a correlate of a rapid activation of a fear structure. These findings further suggest that torture, like any other massive experience, dramatically alters the functional organization of the brain: an enlarged fear network is activated not only by trauma-related, but generally by highly arousing aversive cues. Similar to what is known from neuroimaging studies with PTSD patients, the present data suggest that the medial and orbitofrontal cortical structures lose their ability to regulate the hyperresponsive fear

Figure 10.4
Thirteen Torture Victims with PTSD were Compared to 13 Control Subjects

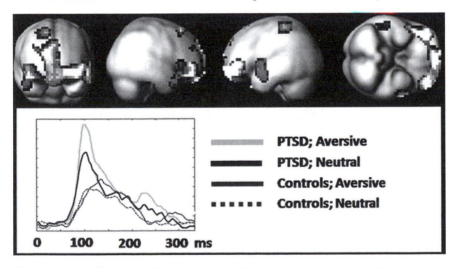

The curves below illustrate the global field power of neuromagnetic responding to either aversive or neutral pictorial stimuli in the time interval from 0 to 300 ms post stimulus. Areas of significant group differences in response to the arousing pictures in the 60–110-ms time interval are marked in the averaged MR-scans above. While both groups activate posterior regions in response to the visual stimuli, only torture victims respond with an immediate activation of regions in the frontal lobe related to action disposition, i.e., emotional responding.

structures, thus providing evidence for a dysfunctional interplay between amygdala and frontal cortex in a traumatized brain.

SUMMARY AND FUTURE CHALLENGES

The body of literature summarized in this chapter argues for functional brain changes in torture survivors with PTSD that can be associated with an altered memory organization as a consequence to the exposure of extreme trauma. To date, there are only a few studies examining neurobiological alterations in survivors of organized violence and torture. However, the data suggest that torture experiences can be regarded as an extreme form of traumatization and that there is a high probability such experiences will lead to severe psychological disturbances (PTSD) and to related dysfunctional brain processes. Both the abnormal slow wave activity in fronto-temporal networks, as well as the augmentation in early and late activation in response to emotional stimuli in torture survivors, support the assumption of a dysfunctional memory representation of the traumatic torture experience. Due to the consequences of the repeated exposure to extreme stress, the interplay between key brain structures in prefrontal, temporal, and limbic brain areas responsible for memorizing "hot" and "cold" autobiographical information as well as for processing new emotional input is disturbed. The dissociation of hot and cold memories, accompanied by an enlarged fear network, can explain the clinical features of torture survivors with PTSD. Affected individuals experience upsetting intrusions and flashbacks, and are entrapped in speechless terror and continuous fear which lacks the context of space and time.

So far, too few scientific steps have been taken to understand the clinical symptoms and related brain alteration in torture victims. A challenge for the future is to better clarify whether neurobiological findings in survivors of torture may be seen as a correlate of the resulting psychiatric diagnosis (PTSD), or whether they occur as a direct long-term consequence of the traumatic torture experience, independent of the associated psychological disorder.

As a concluding remark, we note that there is a definite need for more neuroscientific studies with survivors of torture. Taking into account the high incidence of torture on a global level on the one side, and on the other the recent boom of research and publications in the field of neurobiology of trauma, where increasing numbers of survivors of sexual violence, combat violence, or traffic accidents are examined, the scarcity of comparable studies with torture survivors is to be considered even more unsatisfactory. Of course, the use of neuroimaging and psychophysiological machinery with traumatized survivors of torture might represent a special challenge given the often extreme level of fear and, in many cases, the diverse culture background in affected individuals, some of whom are not familiar with neurological or neuroradiological assessments. Nevertheless, a joint effort of clinicians and neuroscientists should be made towards thorough and comprehensive assessments of torture survivors that allow for a clearer understanding of the long-term psychological problems, as well as the related dysfunctional brain processes. The few findings we have to date already point towards an urgent need for targeted interventions for affected individuals. A greater amount of evidence-based knowledge about the consequences of torture experiences will be indispensable in order to develop and implement adequate therapeutic approaches that meet the specific needs and impairments of traumatized survivors of torture.

REFERENCES

1. World Medical Association (1975). *A declaration on human rights*. Tokyo: Author.
2. Turner, S.T. (2004). Emotional Reactions to Torture and Organized State Violence. *PSTD Research Quarterly*, 15(2).
3. Basoglu, M., Paker, M., Paker, O., et al. (1994). Psychological effects of torture: a comparison of tortured with nontortured political activists in Turkey. *Am J Psychiatry*. 151(1), 76–81.
4. Silove, D., Steel, Z., McGorry, P., Miles, V., Drobny, J. (2002). The impact of torture on post-traumatic stress symptoms in war-affected Tamil refugees and immigrants. *Compr Psychiatry*, 43(1), 49–55.
5. Basoglu, M., Livanou, M., Crnobaric, C. (2007). Torture vs other cruel, inhuman, and degrading treatment: is the distinction real or apparent? *Arch Gen Psychiatry*. 64(3), 277–285.
6. Campbell, T.A. (2007). Psychological assessment, diagnosis, and treatment of torture survivors: a review. *Clin Psychol Rev*, 27(5), 628–641.
7. de Jong, J.T., Komproe, I.H., Van Ommeren, M., et al. (2001). Lifetime events and posttraumatic stress disorder in 4 postconflict settings. *Jama*, 286(5), 555–562.
8. Gäbel, U., Ruf, M., Schauer, M., Odenwald, M., Neuner, F. (2006). Prävalenz der Posttraumatischen Belastungsstörung (PTSD) und Möglichkeiten der Ermittlung in der Asylverfahrenspraxis. *Zeitschrift für Klinische Psychologie und Psychotherapie*, 35(1), 12–20.
9. Danese, E. (2007). Indagine epidemiologica su esperienze traumatiche relative alla violenza organizzata ed altri eventi avversi: conseguenze sulla salute mentale di rifugiati e richiedenti asilo nel Nord Italia. MA Thesis, University of Padova.
10. Basoglu, M., Mineka, S., Paker, M., Aker, T., Livanou, M., Gok, S. (1997). Psychological preparedness for trauma as a protective factor in survivors of torture. *Psychol Med.*, 27(6), 1421–1433.
11. Basoglu, M., Paker, M., Ozmen, E., Tasdemir, O., Sahin, D. (1994). Factors related to long-term traumatic stress responses in survivors of torture in Turkey. *Jama*. 272(5), 357–363.
12. Neuner, F., Schauer, M., Karunakara, U., Klaschik, C., Roberts, C., Elbert, T. (2004). Psychological trauma and evidence for enhanced vulnerability for posttraumatic stress disorder through previous trauma among West Nile refugees. *BMC Psychiatry*, 4:34.
13. Shrestha, N.M., Sharma, B., Van Ommeren, M., et al. (1998). Impact of torture on refugees displaced within the developing world: symptomatology among Bhutanese refugees in Nepal. *Jama*, 280(5), 443–448.

14. Silove, D., Sinnerbrink, I., Field, A., Manicavasagar, V., Steel, Z. (1997). Anxiety, depression and PTSD in asylum-seekers: associations with pre-migration trauma and post-migration stressors. *Br J Psychiatry,* 170, 351–357.

15. Catani, C., Jacob, N., Schauer, E., Mahendrarajah, K., Neuner, F. (2007). Family violence, war, and natural disasters: A study of the effect of extreme stress on children's mental health in Sri Lanka, *paper submitted for publication.*

16. Brewin, C.R. (2001). A cognitive neuroscience account of posttraumatic stress disorder and its treatment. *Behav Res Ther,* 39(4), 373–393.

17. Dalgleish, T. (2004). Cognitive approaches to posttraumatic stress disorder: the evolution of multirepresentational theorizing. *Psychol Bull.,* 130(2), 228–260.

18. Ehlers, A., Clark, D.M. (2000). A cognitive model of posttraumatic stress disorder. *Behav Res Ther,* 38(4), 319–345.

19. Metcalve, J., Jacobs, W.A. (1996). "Hot-system/cool-system" view of memory under stress. *PTSD Research Quarterly,* 17(2), 1–3.

20. Tulving, E., Markowitsch, H.J. (1998). Episodic and declarative memory: role of the hippocampus. *Hippocampus,* 8(3), 198–204.

21. McEwen, B.S. (2000). The neurobiology of stress: from serendipity to clinical relevance. *Brain Research,* 886(1–2), 172–189.

22. Kolassa, I.T., Elbert, T. (2007). Structural and functional neuroplasticity in relation to traumatic stress. *Current Directions in Psychology,* in press.

23. Bremner, J.D., Vythilingam, M., Vermetten, E., et al. (2003). MRI and PET study of deficits in hippocampal structure and function in women with childhood sexual abuse and posttraumatic stress disorder. *Am J Psychiatry,* 160(5), 924–932.

24. Stein, M.B., Koverola, C., Hanna, C., Torchia, M.G., McClarty, B. (1997). Hippocampal volume in women victimized by childhood sexual abuse. *Psychol Med.,* 27 (4), 951–959.

25. Gilbertson, M.W., Shenton, M.E., Ciszewski, A., et al. (2002). Smaller hippocampal volume predicts pathologic vulnerability to psychological trauma. *Nat Neurosci,* 5(11), 1242–1247.

26. Bremner, J.D. (2002). Neuroimaging studies in post-traumatic stress disorder. *Curr Psychiatry Rep,* 4(4), 254–263.

27. LeDoux, J.E. (1995). Emotion: clues from the brain. *Annu Rev Psychol.,* 46, 209–235.

28. Pitman, R.K., Shalev, A.., Orr, S.P. (2000). Posttraumatic stress disorder: Emotion, conditioning and memory. In: Gazzaniga M.S., ed. *The new cognitive neurosciences* Vol 2. Cambridge: MIT Press.

29. Vyas, A., Bernal, S., Chattarji, S. (2003). Effects of chronic stress on dendritic arborization in the central and extended amygdala. *Brain Res,* 965(1–2), 290–294.

30. Vyas, A., Mitra, R., Shankaranarayana Rao, B.S., Chattarji, S. (2002). Chronic stress induces contrasting patterns of dendritic remodeling in hippocampal and amygdaloid neurons. *J Neuroscience,* 22(15), 6810–6818.

31. Bremner, J.D. (2003). Functional neuroanatomical correlates of traumatic stress revisited 7 years later, this time with data. *Psychopharmacol Bull,* 37(2), 6–25.

32. Shin, L.M., McNally, R.J., Kosslyn, S.M., et al. (1999). Regional cerebral blood flow during script-driven imagery in childhood sexual abuse-related PTSD: A PET investigation. *Am J Psychiatry,* 156(4), 575–584.

33. Shin, L.M., Orr, S.P., Carson, M.A., et al. (2004). Regional cerebral blood flow in the amygdala and medial prefrontal cortex during traumatic imagery in male and female Vietnam veterans with PTSD. *Arch Gen Psychiatry,* 61(2), 168–176.

34. Liberzon, I., Taylor, S.F., Amdur, R., et al. (1999). Brain activation in PTSD in response to trauma-related stimuli. *Biol Psychiatry,* 45(7), 817–826.

35. Shin, L.M., Rauch, S.L., Pitman, R.K. (2006). Amygdala, Medial Prefrontal Cortex, and Hippocampal Function in PTSD. *Ann NY Acad Sci,* 1071(1), 67–79.

36. Ghashghaei, H.T., Barbas, H. (2002). Pathways for emotion: interactions of prefrontal and anterior temporal pathways in the amygdala of the rhesus monkey. *Neuroscience,* 115(4), 1261–1279.

37. Mirzaei, S., Knoll, P., Keck, A., et al. (2001). Regional cerebral blood flow in patients suffering from post-traumatic stress disorder. *Neuropsychobiology,* 43(4), 260–264.

38. Fernandez, M., Pissiota, A., Frans, O., von Knorring, L., Fischer, H., Fredrikson, M. (2001). Brain function in a patient with torture related post-traumatic stress disorder before and after fluoxetine treatment: a positron emission tomography provocation study. *Neurosci Lett, 2*97(2), 101–104.

39. Rauch, S.L., van der Kolk, B.A., Fisler, R.E., et al. (1996). A symptom provocation study of posttraumatic stress disorder using positron emission tomography and script-driven imagery. *Arch Gen Psychiatry,* 53(5), 380–387.

40. Shin, L.M., McNally, R.J., Kosslyn, S.M., et al. (1997). A positron emission tomographic study of symptom provocation in PTSD. *Ann N Y Acad Sci,* 821, 521–523.

41. Wienbruch, C. (2007). Abnormal slow wave mapping (ASWAM)—A tool for the investigation of abnormal slow wave activity in the human brain. *J Neurosci Methods,* 163(1), 119–127.

42. Wienbruch, C., Moratti, S., Elbert, T., et al. (2003). Source distribution of neuromagnetic slow wave activity in schizophrenic and depressive patients. *Clin Neurophysiol,* 114(11), 2052–2060.

43. Rockstroh B.R., Wienbruch C, Ray W.J., Elbert, T.R. (2007). Abnormal oscillatory brain dynamics in schizophrenia: a sign of deviant communication in neural network? *BMC Psychiatry.* August 30; 7(1), 44.

44. Ray, W.J., Odenwald, M., Neuner, F., et al. (2006). Decoupling neural networks from reality: dissociative experiences in torture victims are reflected in abnormal brain waves in left frontal cortex. *Psychol Sci,* 17(10), 825–829.

45. Marmar ,C.R., Weiss, D.S., Schlenger, W.E., et al. (1994). Peritraumatic dissociation and posttraumatic stress in male Vietnam theater veterans. *Am J Psychiatry, 1*51(6), 902–907.

46. Marx, B.P., Sloan, D.M. (2005). Peritraumatic dissociation and experiential avoidance as predictors of posttraumatic stress symptomatology. *Behav Res Ther,* 43(5), 569–583.

47. Kolassa, I.T., Wienbruch, C., Neuner, F., et al. (2007). Imaging brain correlates of trauma: altered cortical dynamics after repeated traumatic stress. *BMC Psychiatry,* submitted.

48. *The International Affective Picture System: Digitized Photographs* (1999). Gainesville, FL.

49. Saleptsi, E. (2005). *MEG Correlates during Affective Stimulus Processing in Posttraumatic Stress Disorder.* Dissertation, Department of Psychology, University of Konstanz.

50. Junghöfer, M., Bradley, M.M., Elbert, T.R., Lang, P.J. (2001). Fleeting images: a new look at early emotion discrimination. *Psychophysiology,* 38(2), 175–178.

51. Junghöfer, M., Schauer, M., Neuner, F., Odenwald, M., Rockstroh, B., Elbert, T. (2003). Enhanced fear-network in torture survivors activated by RSVP of aversive material can be monitored by MEG. *Psychophysiology,* 40, Suppl. 51.

CHAPTER 11

THE CASE OF MOHAMMED AL QAHTANI

Gitanjali S. Gutierrez, Esq.

I am a lawyer with the Center for Constitutional Rights (CCR), a New York–based international human rights organization, and have been representing Mohammed al Qahtani since October 2005. He is a Saudi citizen who has been detained in United States custody since January 2002 at the Guantánamo Bay Naval Station, Guantánamo Bay, Cuba (Guantánamo).

At his father's request, CCR filed a habeas petition in U.S. federal court on Mr. al Qahtani's behalf in October 2005. As a result of a court order, I have conducted 10 client interviews with Mr. al Qahtani at Guantánamo beginning in December 2005. Other than a few meetings with representatives from the International Committee of the Red Cross (ICRC), these attorney-client interviews have been Mr. al Qahtani's first and only contact since January 2002 with people who are not military personnel or other government representatives. At times, the U.S. military has forced us to conduct our meetings in the same type of cell in which Mr. al Qahtani was held in isolation for months and subjected to severe sleep deprivation and other aggressive interrogation techniques. U.S. military intelligence personnel have also lied repeatedly to Mr. al Qahtani and denied him the most fundamental human rights. As a result of his physical and psychological torture, the conditions surrounding our meetings, and his ongoing suffering from the effects of his torture and ongoing inhumane conditions, I have focused extensively upon the difficult task of establishing a trusting attorney-client relationship.

At Guantánamo, Mr. al Qahtani was subjected to a regime of aggressive interrogation techniques, known as the "First Special Interrogation Plan," that were authorized by U.S. Secretary of Defense Donald Rumsfeld. These techniques were implemented under the supervision and guidance of Secretary Rumsfeld and the commander of Guantánamo, Major General Geoffrey Miller. The methods included, but were not limited to, 48 consecutive days of severe sleep deprivation and 20-hour interrogations, forced nudity, sexual humiliation, religious humiliation, physical force, prolonged stress positions and prolonged sensory overstimulation, and threats with military dogs.

During our meetings in 2006 and 2007, Mr. al Qahtani discussed the abuses perpetrated against him during interrogations by U.S. personnel. No one questions whether Mr. al Qahtani was subjected to aggressive interrogation techniques. Numerous documents from the U.S. military and other agencies describe the specific methods of interrogation used against Mr. al Qahtani as well as U.S. government officials' awareness and authorization of, and involvement in, Mr. al Qahtani's torture and inhumane treatment. Most notably, a military intelligence interrogation log was leaked from Guantánamo that detailed a six-week period of Mr. al Qahtani's interrogation. Other government documents include an internal memorandum reporting his treatment as potential prisoner abuse and government documents disclosed through Freedom of Information Act (FOIA) litigation.

These aggressive techniques, standing alone and in combination, resulted in severe physical and mental pain and suffering. To this day, Mr. al Qahtani has not received any therapeutic medical evaluation of or treatment for the physical or psychological injuries from his interrogations. He continues to suffer from ongoing psychological pain and suffering arising from his torture and cruel, inhuman, and degrading treatment.

Mohammed's nightmare began when the U.S. military transferred him to Guantánamo in January 2002. Interrogation teams from at least three separate agencies or programs questioned Mr. al Qahtani during the first year and a half of his imprisonment: the Defense Department's Criminal Investigation Task Force (CITF);[1] a military intelligence interrogation team; and agents from the Federal Bureau of Investigation (FBI). Each of these entities rely upon different interrogation guidelines, and as Mr. al Qahtani's interrogations progressed, CITF personnel increasingly objected the most vocally within the military to the aggressive interrogation tactics used by military intelligence interrogators.

When he first arrived at Guantánamo, military personnel began interrogating Mr. al Qahtani, applying the routine tactics in use at Guantánamo during that time. By July 2002, agents from the FBI also started interrogating Mr. al Qahtani, but appear to have used traditional FBI interrogation methods.

By some point in early September 2002, military intelligence personnel at Guantánamo began planning a new, more aggressive interrogation regime for Mr. al Qahtani. They wanted to apply the training tactics used in the "SERE" program, the Survival, Evasion, Resistance and Escape training program for U.S. Special Forces. The SERE program is designed to teach U.S. soldiers how to resist torture techniques if they are captured by enemy forces. In Guantánamo, though, military intelligence officials wanted to use the training methods as interrogation techniques against Mr. al Qahtani and others. The SERE training program involves forms of torture such as religious and sexual humiliation, and water boarding. As a first step in implementing this new interrogation program, military intelligence personnel from Guantánamo attended SERE training at Fort Bragg, North Carolina on September 16–20, 2006.[2] In response to these developments, the CITF leaders memorialized in writing in September 2002 orders prohibiting their agents from engaging in coercive interrogations, especially those involving SERE techniques.[3]

After a meeting with Vice President Dick Cheney and senior lawyers from the Bush administration visiting Guantánamo on September 25, 2002,[4] and after CITF officials had raised numerous objections to the legality of the methods, Major General Michael Dunlavey, the commander of the Guantánamo detention center, sent a request up the chain of command on October 11, 2002 for approval for an interrogation plan for Mr. al Qahtani that included 19 techniques outside the traditional guidelines for military interrogations.

These techniques included:

1. *Category I:* Yelling, deception, use of multiple interrogators, misrepresenting the identity of the interrogation (as if from a country with a reputation for harsh treatment of prisoners);

2. *Category II:* Stress positions (such as standing for up to four hours), use of falsified documents or reports, isolation for 30 days or longer, interrogation in places other than the interrogation booth, deprivation of light and sound, hooding, interrogation for up to 20 hours straight, removal of all comfort items (including religious items), switching from hot food to military meals ready to eat, removal of clothing, forced grooming and shaving of facial hair, use of phobias (such as fear of dogs) to induce stress; and

3. *Category III:* Uses of scenarios to persuade the detainee that death or pain is imminent for him or his family, exposures to cold or water, use of mild non-injurious physical contact, use of a wet towel or water boarding to simulate drowning or suffocation.

Prior to formal approval of these techniques, however, military personnel at Guantánamo were already subjecting Mr. al Qahtani to severe interrogation. From August 2002 through October 2002, the military held Mr. al Qahtani in total isolation in a cell with constant bright lights. In October 2002, military dogs were also used in an aggressive manner to intimidate him. As a result of this treatment, an FBI Deputy Director reported to the Army that in November 2002 he observed a detainee, later identified as Mr. al Qahtani, exhibiting symptoms of "extreme psychological trauma":

> In September or October of 2002 FBI agents observed that a canine was used in an aggressive manner to intimidate detainee [redacted] and, in November 2002, FBI agents observed Detainee [redacted] after he had been subjected to intense isolation for over three months. During that time period, [redacted] was totally

isolated (with the exception of occasional interrogations) in a cell that was always flooded with light. By late November, the detainee was evidencing behavior consistent with extreme psychological trauma (talking to non-existent people, reportedly hearing voices, crouching in a corner of the cell covered with a sheet for hours on end). It is unknown to the FBI whether such extended isolation was approved by appropriate DoD authorities.[5]

By early November 2002, Southern Command, the U.S. military command unit overseeing Guantánamo, issued preliminary approval of the aggressive techniques proposed by Major General Dunlavey.[6] In response to the preliminary approval, the CITF leaders prepared an alternative interrogation plan proposal on November 22, 2002, noting that the aggressive techniques sought by military intelligence interrogators were "possibly illegal."[7] As described in detail below and in an interrogation log leaked from Guantánamo, military intelligence interrogators began using systematic, aggressive interrogation techniques against Mr. al Qahtani pursuant to the preliminary approval on November 23, 2002.[8] By November 27, 2002, FBI officials, the third investigative agency at Guantánamo, had also prepared a legal analysis warning that several of the proposed tactics could constitute torture.[9]

Despite these controversies and protests about the military intelligence interrogation tactics, on December 2, 2002, Secretary Rumsfeld approved 16 of the aggressive interrogation techniques for use against Mr. al Qahtani.[10] The memorandum authorized techniques, used alone or in tandem, such as forced nudity; stress positions; religious humiliation (removal of religious items and forcible shaving of beards and hair); isolation of up to 30 days with extensions possible after command approval; light and sound deprivation; exploitation of phobias (such as fear of dogs); and "mild" physical contact. He only approved one tactic in Category III, "mild non-injurious physical contact." By December 14, 2002, General Miller had proposed "standard operating procedures" for the use of SERE techniques against detainees during interrogations.[11]

At the end of November 2002, Mr. al Qahtani was not provided with any break in the isolation or his interrogations, nor treatment for his symptoms of "extreme psychological trauma" observed by the FBI deputy director. Instead, on or around November 23, 2002, through January 11, 2003, Mr. al Qahtani was subjected to an official interrogation regime known as the "First Special Interrogation Plan."[12] Details of the First Special Interrogation Plan emerged when a military interrogation log for Mr. al Qahtani was leaked from Guantánamo. The log describes a six-week program of physical and psychological interrogation methods that involved prolonged sleep deprivation; painful stress positions; physical abuses; sexual, physical, psychological and religious humiliation; the use of military dogs; and sensory overstimulation. According to some news accounts, during his entire interrogation period, Mr. al Qahtani endured a total of at least 160 days of severe isolation in a cell constantly flooded with light, with much of this time also including interrogations using aggressive tactics as part of the First Special Interrogation Plan.

During client meetings, Mr. al Qahtani provided his description of some of the methods used against him during interrogations in 2002 and 2003, methods that have been corroborated by official government documents:

- Severe sleep deprivation combined with 20-hour interrogations for months at a time;
- Severe isolation;
- Religious and sexual humiliation;
- Threats of rendition to countries that torture more than the United States;
- Threats made against his family, including female members of his family;
- Strip searching, body searches, and forced nudity, including in the presence of female personnel;
- Denial of the right to practice his religion, including prohibiting him from praying for prolonged times and during Ramadan;
- Threatening to desecrate the Koran in front of him;
- Placing him in stress positions for prolonged times;
- Placing him in tight restraints repeatedly for many months or days and nights;
- Threats by military dogs;
- Beatings;
- Exposure to low temperatures for prolonged times;
- Exposure to loud music for prolonged times;
- Forcible administration of frequent IVs by medical personnel during interrogation, which Mr. al Qahtani described as feeling like "repetitive stabs" each day.

The use of some of these methods against Mr. al Qahtani are described in detail below.

SLEEP DEPRIVATION

Mr. al Qahtani reports being subjected to severe sleep deprivation, often permitted only to sleep four or fewer hours at a time, over prolonged periods of time. U.S. military authorities imposed this sleep deprivation through the use of interrogations lasting 20 hours; shifting Mr. al Qahtani to a new cell throughout the night; imprisoning him in cells with 24-hour lighting; altering his sleep patterns by only allowing him to sleep during the day; and creating disruptive noise to wake him up. In order to facilitate 20-hour interrogations, if Mr. al Qahtani began to fall asleep from exhaustion, military police or interrogators would forcibly make him stand and sit, pour water on him, or otherwise physically abuse him. The interrogators also worked in three teams consisting of a linguist and at least two interrogators. They conducted one interrogation shift after another to keep the interrogators refreshed and active while Mr. al Qahtani continued to deteriorate from exhaustion.

Mr. al Qahtani's description of his sleep deprivation is supported by government documents and information provided to the media by military personnel. According to findings in the Schmidt Report, for example, between November 23, 2002, and January 16, 2003, Mr. al Qahtani was interrogated for 18 to 20 hours per day for 48 days.[13] Thus, during this particular two-month period of the First Special Interrogation Plan, military authorities subjected Mr. al Qahtani to extreme interrogation techniques, while simultaneously allowing him only four hours of sleep per day. In addition, military authorities subjected Mr. al Qahtani to frequent sleep disruption during 2002 and 2003, when interrogators moved him from one cell to another throughout the night in order to alter his sleep patterns.[14]

Mr. al Qahtani has not received any medical assessment of the physiological impact of his sleep deprivation. He has experienced, however, symptoms of prolonged sleep deprivation that have caused severe pain and suffering. The cumulative effect of at least the two months of severe sleep deprivation combined with these other methods was to reduce Mr. al Qahtani's blood pressure and general health to the point that he required hospitalization. As a result of this torture, Mr. al Qahtani began hallucinating and hearing voices; he urinated on himself multiple times; and he frequently broke down into tears.

SEVERE ISOLATION COMBINED WITH SENSORY DEPRIVATION/OVERSTIMULATION

For 160 days within his first two years of imprisonment, military authorities held Mr. al Qahtani in severe isolation, in which he could not communicate with other detainees in any fashion.[15] During these times, he was imprisoned in cells or a section of the prison camp apart from other prisoners. The only other human beings he had contact with were the interrogation teams and military guards. Then for the next several years, he was imprisoned in Camp 5, a maximum security prison consisting entirely of isolation cells. Apart from a few letters he received from his family through the ICRC, Mr. al Qathani was also isolated from the outside world and his family from January 2002 through December 2005, when he received his first lawyer visit. Prior to meeting with me, Mr. al Qahtani was completed dependent upon his interrogators for any information, including information concerning his family.

While in isolation in 2002 and 2003, military officials also subjected him to sensory deprivation techniques, such as holding him in prolonged semidarkness and denying him access to sunlight for weeks or months. At other times, Mr. al Qahtani faced prolonged exposure to sensory overload techniques while suffering from sleep deprivation. Officials frequently played loud music in the interrogation room (referred to as "white noise" in the interrogation log), for periods ranging from 20 minutes to three hours. At times, officials would yell at Mr. al Qahtani or ridicule him while the blaring music was playing. Occasionally, the white noise technique was used multiple times in one day. In addition to the psychological and physical stress caused by the white noise method, Mr. al Qahtani repeatedly protested that listening to this music was against his religion.

As described above, these interrogation techniques, particularly the isolation, had a severe impact upon Mr. al Qahtani, as shown by the observations of the FBI official who stated that Mr. al Qahtani was exhibiting symptoms of severe psychological trauma after three months of isolation.

RELIGIOUS, SEXUAL, AND MORAL HUMILIATION

One of the most widely reported aspects of Mr. al Qahtani's interrogation was the use of sexual, religious, and moral humiliation. In general, there is extensive evidence of U.S. interrogators using humiliation, often with religious or sexual elements, as a method of interrogation in numerous military detention facilities. Many of the humiliating techniques deliberately degrade the Islamic faith of detainees, violating taboos relating to contact with women, pornography, and homosexuality.

Because U.S. personnel's humiliation of Muslim and Arab detainees has taken a variety of forms, it is difficult to articulate a generalized and all-encompassing description of what constitutes "humiliation" in the context of U.S. interrogations. Instead, the use of humiliation by U.S. interrogators is best understood by considering illustrative examples, such as: forced nudity, sometimes for prolonged periods and in stress positions; female interrogators straddling male detainees, invading the personal space of detainees or otherwise being used in the humiliation of detainees; or placing leashes on detainees and making them act like dogs.

More specifically, Mr. al Qahtani was subjected to combinations of all of these tactics. While the Schmidt Report and the Interrogation Log contain numerous details of Mr. al Qahtani's interrogation, it is important to note that these sources are limited in terms of the incidents that they report, the level of description used (the interrogation log in particular is very sparse and often euphemistic in its descriptions) and the time period covered. Despite these limitations, it is nonetheless clear that the humiliation of Mr. al Qahtani formed a central part of the interrogation plan, and that interrogators subjected him to various types of treatment that involved humiliating him, particularly denigrating, either explicitly or implicitly, his religious beliefs.

Humiliating treatment designed to degrade Mr. al Qahtani's religious beliefs included: constructing a shrine to bin Laden and informing Mr. al Qahtani that he could pray only to bin Laden;[16] applying "forced grooming" tactics, including forcibly shaving Mr. al Qahtani's beard;[17] commandeering the call to prayer as a "call to interrogation";[18] and interrupting Mr. al Qahtani's prayer or attempting to control or deny his right to pray.[19] In addition, many other aspects of his treatment were designed to implicate his culture or religious beliefs, such as techniques involving dogs and techniques involving contact with female interrogators.

With respect to expressly sexual humiliation, reports indicate that the use of sexual humiliation by U.S. interrogators against Mr. al Qahtani took a number of forms. However, identifying these incidents with precision is difficult due to the opaque and euphemistic language used in the interrogation log, and these incidents are understandably difficult for Mr. al Qahtani to discuss while still imprisoned by the perpetrators. The Schmidt Report describes a number of incidents in which "female military interrogators performed acts designed to take advantage of their gender in relation to Muslim males" and notes that these techniques fell under different types of officially sanctioned and euphemistically named interrogation techniques, particularly "Futility"[20] and "Invasion of Space by a Female."

The interrogation log explicitly documents several instances where Mohammad al Qahtani is subjected to sexual humiliation techniques:

1. There are at least 10 separate instances in which the interrogation log reports that interrogators used a technique labeled "invasion of space by a female" or that Mr. al Qahtani is repulsed, angered, or otherwise bothered by a female interrogator invading his personal space. The details of what this involved are generally lacking.[21] "Invasion of Space by a Female" is used to describe a number of tactics, from a female interrogator straddling Mr. al Qahtani and molesting him while other military guards pin his body to the floor against his will, to a female interrogator rubbing his neck and hair, often until Mr. al Qahtani resists with force and is subdued by military guards;

2. There are documented instances of forced nudity;[22]

3. "Dance instruction":

   a. In one incident, a mask was placed on Mr. al Qahtani and he was forced to undergo "dance instruction" with a male interrogator;[23]

   b. In another incident, he was forced to wear a towel "like a burqa" and undergo "dance instruction" with a male interrogator;[24]

4. The interrogators made sexual insults and sexually offensive comments about Mr. al Qahtani and about his female family members, specifically his mother and sisters,[25] and;

5. Mr. al Qahtani was forced to either wear[26] or to look at and study[27] pornographic pictures. Interrogators required him to memorize details of the pornographic pictures and answer questions as a means to "test" his willingness to cooperate and to end other abusive interrogation practices.

In addition to explicit sexual and religious humiliation, other aspects of Mr. al Qahtani's treatment and detention were also morally humiliating and a denial of his human dignity. This included forcing him to urinate in front of U.S. personnel in either a bottle or in his pants while in restraints[28] and then subsequently denying him the opportunity to clean himself, including before his prayers. Military authorities also deprived him of privacy in his living conditions, specifically during showers when both female and male personnel were present.[29] On at least one occasion during an interrogation, he was also stripped and forcibly given an enema while military police restrained him in the presence of multiple U.S. personnel. He was also subjected to the following treatment: "On 20 Dec 02, an interrogator tied a leash to the subject of the first Special Interrogation Plan's chains, led him around the room, and forced him to perform a series of dog tricks."[30]

Although not concluding that Mr. al Qahtani's treatment rose to the level of torture, even the military's own investigation into his interrogation, the Schmidt Report, concludes that "[r]equiring the subject of the first Special Interrogation Plan to be led around by a leash tied to his chains, placing a thong on his head, wearing a bra, insulting his mother and sister, being forced to stand naked in front of a female interrogator for five minutes, and using strip searches as an interrogation technique the AR 15-6 found to be abusive and degrading, particularly when done in the context of the 48 days of intense and long interrogations."

Without question, the regime of religious, sexual, and moral humiliation inflicted upon Mr. al Qahtani during his interrogations, alone and particularly in combination with other abuses, constituted torture that profoundly injured his personal dignity, mental health, and at times, physical health.

STRESS POSITIONS AND TEMPERATURE EXTREMES

Generally, military authorities used stress positions on detainees at Guantánamo by forcing detainees to stand in an erect position for hours at a time, sometimes with arms extended outward to the side.[31] Short-shackling involves binding a detainee's wrist to his ankle with metal or plastic handcuffs, and doubling the detainee over, either while lying on the ground or sitting in a chair.[32] Prolonged standing produces "'excruciating pain' as ankles double in size, skin becomes 'tense and intensely painful,' blisters erupt oozing 'watery serum,' heart rates soar, kidneys shut down, and delusions deepen."[33] Military officials familiar with the practice describe short-shackling as routinely employed at Guantánamo.[34]

Mr. al Qahtani reports being restrained with very tight handcuffs in painful positions for extended periods of time, both during the day and night. The Schmidt Report also states that Mr. al Qahtani was forced to stand for long periods of time.[35] As noted above, he was left in restraints on numerous occasions until he had no recourse but to urinate on himself. Moreover, he was placed in rooms with very cold temperatures and, to this day, is sensitive to cold temperatures during attorney-client meetings. General Schmidt also testified that at times Mr. al Qahtani was suffering from hypothermia.

Mr. al Qahtani was placed in painful positions for extended times during interrogations that were also accompanied by sleep deprivation, various forms of humiliation, and other abuses.

THREATS WITH MILITARY DOGS

Mr. al Qahtani reports being threatened with military working dogs on several occasions. The interrogation log corroborates Mr. al Qahtani's report, stating that: "issues ar[o]se between MPs and dog handler" on December 7, 2002. The Schmidt Report also records a past instance of an officer directing a dog "to growl, bark, and show his teeth at" Mr. al Qahtani. In addition to creating a physical danger for the detainees, military dogs were permitted to growl and threaten them as a means of exploiting cultural and individual phobias associated with dogs.

AN INCOMPLETE ACCOUNT

The interrogation log and the enclosed information do not describe everything that happened to Mr. al Qahtani. As with many victims of torture, particularly those who have yet to receive any treatment for their physical and psychological injuries, there are many other methods used against him that Mr. al Qahtani cannot yet discuss—and perhaps may choose never to discuss, including some of the methods used to humiliate and degrade his moral and personal integrity.

Additionally, Mr. al Qahtani has no memory of some of the interrogation methods used against him or events that occurred at Guantánamo, evidencing that he has not fully recovered from the trauma of his torture and still suffers from its impact. For example, according to new accounts of information leaked by intelligence personnel, Mr. al Qahtani was subjected to a "fake rendition" authorized by Secretary Rumsfeld around April 2003:

> Mr. Kahtani, a Saudi, was given a tranquilizer, put in sensory deprivation garb with blackened goggles, and hustled aboard a plane that was supposedly taking him to the Middle East.
>
> After hours in the air, the plane landed back at the United States naval base at Guantánamo Bay, Cuba, where he was not returned to the regular prison compound but put in an isolation cell in the base's brig. There, he was subjected to harsh interrogation procedures that he was encouraged to believe were being conducted by Egyptian national security operatives.
>
> The account of Mr. Kahtani's treatment given to the *New York Times* recently by military intelligence officials and interrogators is the latest of several developments that have severely damaged the military's longstanding public version of how the detention and interrogation center at Guantánamo operated. In order to carry on

the charade that he was not at Guantánamo, the military arranged it so Mr. Kahtani was not visited by the Red Cross on a few of its regular visits, creating a window of several months, said a person who dealt with him at Guantánamo.[36]

Yet, at this time, Mr. al Qahtani is unable to remember all of the details of this experience.

INVOLVEMENT OF MEDICAL PROVIDERS

In general, Mr. al Qahtani suffered severe physical and psychological injury as a result of his prolonged exposure to these and other methods used against him during interrogations. As a result, Mr. al Qahtani's weight fell from approximately 160 pounds to 100 pounds. During his attorney-client meeting, Mr. al Qahtani also exhibits the signs of an individual suffering from Posttraumatic Stress Syndrome or other trauma-related condition, including memory loss, difficulty concentrating, and anxiety. He is aware that his interrogation has left him physically and mentally injured from the abuse. He will not seek treatment from any health professional at Guantánamo, however, because of their involvement in his interrogation and torture.

Despite Mr. al Qahtani's lack of therapeutic medical treatment, medical personnel were directly and indirectly involved in his interrogations. With respect to their indirect involvement, between November 2002 and January 2003, medical personnel frequently "cleared" him for interrogations and monitored his vital signs on a daily basis. He was also hospitalized at least twice when he was close to death during interrogations at Guantánamo. On one occasion described in the interrogation log, he was rushed to a military base hospital when his heart rate fell dangerously low during a period of extreme sleep deprivation, physical stress, and psychological trauma. The military flew in a radiologist from the U.S. Naval Station in Puerto Rico to evaluate the computed tomography ("CT" or "CAT") scan. After he was permitted to sleep a full night, medical personnel cleared Mr. al Qahtani for further interrogation the next day. During his transportation from the hospital, Mr. al Qahtani was interrogated in the ambulance.

With authorization from General Miller and his superior officers, medical professionals were also directly involved in Mr. al Qahtani's interrogation. This involvement ranged from administering medical procedures, such as enemas, as punishment during interrogations to health professionals participating on Behavioral Science Consultation Teams ("BSCT teams") to advise interrogators how to increase the psychological stress on him.

CONCLUSION

Mr. al Qahtani strives each day to maintain his mental and physical health while imprisoned at Guantánamo and prevented from obtaining any independent medical treatment. He must live with the knowledge that the U.S. government has deprived him, and continues to deprive him, of the most basic of human rights. During our meetings, Mr. al Qahtani has described the fundamental nature of the rights the U.S. authorities stripped from him:

> A human being needs four things in life that were taken from me at Guantánamo. First, to honor his religion and freedom to practice religion and respect it. Two, honoring his personal dignity by refraining from humiliating a human being through beating or cursing him and bad treatment in general. Three, respect for his honor, which means not dishonoring him through sexual humiliation or abuse. Four, respect for human rights by allowing a human being to sleep and be comfortable where he is; to be in a warm shelter; to have security for his life; to have sufficient food and beverage; to have means to relieve himself and clean his body; to have humane medical treatment; and to know that his family is safe from threats or harm. Again, all of these rights were taken from me.

NOTES

1. CITF's primary mission was to conduct interrogations for purposes of criminal prosecution via military commissions. In contrast, military intelligence personnel sought information concerning al Qaeda activities and operations for purposes of tactical intelligence.

2. Dedman, Bill. *Can "20th Highjacker" Ever Stand Trial? Aggressive Interrogation at Guantanamo May Prevent His Prosecution,* MSNBC.COM, October 26, 2006, http://www.msnbc.msn.com/id/15361462/ (*Aggressive Interrogation*).

3. Dedman, *Aggressive Interrogation.*

4. Dedman, Bill. *Battle over Tactics Raged at Gitmo,* MSNBC.COM, October 24, 2006, http://www.msnbc.msn.com/id/15361458/ (*Battle over Tactics*).

5. Letter re: Suspected Mistreatment of Detainees, from T.J. Harrington, Deputy Assistant Director, Counterterrorism Division, FBI, to Major General Donald R. Ryder, Criminal Investigation Command, Department of the Army, July 14, 2006.

6. Prior to this time, a military dog was used to threaten Mr. al Qahtani on October 1, 2002. *See* Dedman, *Aggressive Interrogation.*

7. Dedman, *Aggressive Interrogation.*

8. Dedman, *Aggressive Interrogation.*

9. Dedman, *Aggressive Interrogation.*

10. See Action Memo Approved by Donald L. Rumsfeld, December 2, 2002.

11. Dedman, *Aggressive Interrogation.*

12. Army Regulation 15-6 Final Report, Investigation into FBI Allegations of Detainee Abuse at Guantanamo Bay, Cuba Detention Facility (April 1, 2005) ("Schmidt Report").

13. Schmidt Report at 17; *see also* Interrogation Log of Mohammed al Qahtani.

14. See Schmidt Report at 27; Lewis, Neil A. "Broad Use of Harsh Tactics Is Described at Cuba Base," *N.Y. Times,* October 17, 2004 (*Fresh Details*) (describing this method as: "[A]n inmate was awakened, subjected to an interrogation in a facility known

as the Gold Building, then returned to a different cell. As soon as the guards determined the inmate had fallen into a deep sleep, he was awakened again for interrogation after which he would be returned to yet a different cell. This could happen five or six times during a night").

15. According to several reports, Mr. al Qahtani was held in isolation for 160 days, during which he was subjected to a variety of other interrogation methods, including 20-hour long interrogations combined with severe sleep deprivation. *See* Schmidt Report at 20.

16. Interrogation Log, 01/02/2003.

17. It is unclear how often this occurred. The Interrogation Log documents it explicitly twice: "Detainee's head and beard were shaved with electric clippers. Detainee started resistance when beard was shaved and MPs had to restrain. Shaving was halted until detainee was once more compliant. LTC P supervised shaving. No problems occurred. Photos were taken of detainee when the shaving was finished" (12/03/2002). "Detainee's head and beard were shaved with electric clippers. Detainee started to struggle when the beard was touched but quickly became compliant" (12/18/2002). "Lt G entered the interrogation booth and gave detainee an even shave. The detainee did not resist" (12/20/2002). "Source received haircut. Detainee did not resist until the beard was cut. Detainee stated he would talk about anything if his beard was left alone. Interrogator asked detainee if he would be honest about himself. Detainee replied 'if God wills.' Beard was shaven" (01/11/2003). Military authorities forcibly shaved Mr. al Qahtani in violation of his religious beliefs and practices as recently as the end of 2005, prior to his first meeting with me.

18. "Upon entering the booth, lead played the call to prayer with a special alarm clock. Detainee was told, 'this is no longer the call to prayer. You're not allowed to pray. This is the call to interrogation. So pay attention'" (12/12/2002).

19. Numerous instances are recorded. For example, "When control entered booth, detainee stated in English 'Excuse me sergeant, I want to pray.' Control said 'Have you earned prayer? I know you have a lot to ask forgiveness for, but I already told you that you have to earn it.' Detainee says 'Please, I want to pray here' (pointing to floor next to his chair). Control responds no" (11/28/2002). "Detainee allowed to pray after promising to continue cooperating" (12/06/2002). "Detainee's hands were cuffed at his sides to prevent him from conducting his prayer ritual" (12/14/2002).

20. Both of the following incidents, used on the General Detainee Population, were characterized as use of the "Futility" technique: "a female interrogator approached a detainee from behind, rubbed against his back, leaned over the detainee touching him on his knee and shoulder, and whispered in his ear that his situation was futile, and ran her fingers through his hair" (Schmidt Report at 7). And, "In March 2003, a female interrogator told a detainee that red ink on her hand was menstrual blood and then wiped her hand on the detainee's arm" (Schmidt Report at 8). In the context of the Special Interrogation Plans, female interrogators straddled detainees, massaged the detainee's back and neck, and "invaded the private space of the detainee" (Schmidt Report at 15–16). The Schmidt Report identified the following techniques used on Mr. al Qahtani: (1) "On 06 Dec 02, the subject of the first Special Interrogation Plan was forced to wear a woman's bra and had a thong placed on his head during the course of the interrogation;" (2) "On 17 Dec 02, the subject

of the first Special Interrogation Plan was told that his mother and sister were whores;" (3) "On 17 Dec 02, the subject of the first Special Interrogation Plan was told that he was a homosexual, had homosexual tendencies, and that other detainees had found out about these tendencies"; (4) "On 20 Dec 02, an interrogator tied a leash to the subject of the first Special Interrogation Plan's chains, led him around the room, and forced him to perform a series of dog tricks"; (5) "On 20 Dec 02, an interrogator forced the subject of the first Special Interrogation Plan to dance with a male interrogator" (6) "On several occasions in Dec 02, the subject of the first Special Interrogation Plan was subject to strip searches. These searches, conducted by the prison guards during interrogation, were done as a control measure on direction of the interrogators"; (7) "On one occasion in Dec 02, the subject of the first Special Interrogation Plan was forced to stand naked for five minutes with females present. This incident occurred during the course of a strip search;" (8) "On three occasions in Nov 02 and Dec 02, the subject of the first Special Interrogation Plan was prevented from praying during interrogation"; (9) "Once in Nov 02, the subject of the first Special Interrogation Plan became upset when two Korans were put on a TV, as a control measure during interrogation, and in Dec 02 when an interrogator got up on the desk in front of the subject of the first Special Interrogation Plan and squatted down in front of the subject of the first Special Interrogation Plan in an aggressive manner and unintentionally squatted over the detainee's Koran" (10) "On seventeen occasions, between 13 Dec 02 and 14 Jan 03, interrogators, during interrogations, poured water over the subject of the first Special Interrogation Plan head."

21. (1) "The detainee was bothered by the presence and touch of a female" (12/04/ 2002); (2) "Detainee became irritated with the female invading his personal space" (12/ 05/2002); (3) "The approaches employed [included] Invasion of Space by a Female" (12/06/2002); (4) "Detainee was repulsed by the female invasion of his personal space" (12/09/2002); (5) "Detainee became very annoyed with the female invading his personal space" (12/10/2002); (6) "SGT L started "invasion of personal space" approach" and "The detainee is still annoyed with the female invasion of space" (12/12/2002); (7) "He attempts to resist female contact" (12/19/2002); (8) "He was laid out on the floor so I straddled him without putting my weight on him" (12/21/2002); (9) "Female interrogator used invasion of personal space and detainee cried out to Allah several times" (12/23/ 2002); (10) "Detainee spoke in English when the female interrogator invaded his personal space" (12/25/2002).

22. For example, the Interrogation Log states, "The detainee was stripped searched. Initially he was attempting to resist the guards. After approximately five minutes of nudity the detainee ceased to resist. He would only stare at the wall with GREAT focus. His eyes were squinted and stuck on one point on the wall directly in front of him. He later stated that he knew there was nothing he could do with so many guards around him, so why should he resist. He stated that he did not like the females viewing his naked body while being searched and if felt he could have done something about it then he would have" (12/20/2002).

23. "In order to escalate the detainee's emotions, a mask was made from an MRE box with a smiley face on it and placed on the detainee's head for a few moments. A latex glove was inflated and labeled the 'sissy slap' glove. This glove was touched to the detainee's face periodically after explaining the terminology to him. The mask was placed back on the

detainee's head. While wearing the mask, the team began dance instruction with the detainee. The detainee became agitated and began shouting" (12/12/2003).

24. "A towel was placed on the detainee's head like a burka with his face exposed and the interrogator proceeded to give the detainee dance lessons. The detainee became agitated and tried to kick an MP. No retaliation was used for the kick and the dance lesson continued" (12/20/2002).

25. "Detainee appeared to have been disturbed by the word homosexual. He did not appear to appreciate being called a homosexual. He denies being a homosexual. He also appeared to be very annoyed by the use of his mother and sister as examples of prostitutes and whores" (12/17/2007).

26. (1) "While walking out, detainee pulled a picture of a model off (it had been fashioned into a sign to hang around his neck)" (12/19/2002); (2) "Upon entering booth, lead changed white noise music and hung pictures of swimsuit models around his neck. Detainee was left in booth listening to white noise" (12/23/2002); (3) "Control entered booth, changed music playing, and hung binder of fitness models around detainee's neck" (12/24/2002); (4) "Detainee was eating his food (given by the previous team). Lead walked into booth turned on white noise and put picture binder of swimsuit models over detainees neck" (12/26/2002).

27. (1) "He appeared disgusted by the photos of UBL and a variety of sexy females. Detainee would avoid looking at all of the photos shown to him" (12/17/2002); (2) "Interrogators had detainee look at pictures of women in bikinis and identify if the women were the same or different. Detainee refused to look at girls and began struggling. A few drops of water were sprinkled on his head to gain compliance" (12/19/2002); (3) "Detainee listened to white noise while interrogators added photos of fitness models to a binder. Once completed, the interrogators began showing the photos and asking the detainee detailed questions about the photos" (12/20/2002); (4) "New interrogation shift enters the booth and begins 'attention to detail' approach. Detainee looks at photos of fitness models and answers questions about the photos" (12/21/2002); (5) "Lead began the 'attention to detail' theme with the fitness model photos. Detainee refused to look at photos claiming it was against his religion. Lead poured a 24 oz bottle of water over detainee's head. Detainee then began to look at photos" (12/22/2002); (6) "The 'attention to detail' approach began. Lead pulled pictures of swimsuit models off detainee and told him the test of his ability to answer questions would begin. Detainee refused to answer and finally stated that he would after lead poured water over detainees head and was told he would be subjected to this treatment day after day" (12/23/2002); (7) "Control entered the booth and began the 'attention to detail' lesson for the night. The detainee still would not accurately answer questions about the fitness models and control stated that the lesson would continue the next day" (12/24/2002); (8) "Lead entered the booth and began attention to detail approach. Detainee missed 3 of 10 questions. He has learned to provide more details and provides enough information to substantiate his answers" (12/26/2002); (9) "Detainee was taken to bathroom and walked 10 minutes. The 'attention to detail' theme was run with the fitness model photos" (12/27/2002).

28. "Detainee again said he has to go to bathroom. SGT R said he can go in the bottle. Detainee said he wanted to go to the bathroom because it's more comfortable.

SGT R said 'You've ruined all trust, you can either go in the bottle or in your pants.' Detainee goes in his pants" (11/25/2002).

29. "Detainee given shower, brushed teeth, and given new uniform. The detainee was very shy and asked several times to cover himself with his trousers or a towel while in the shower" (12/21/2002).

30. Schmidt Report. This is documented in the interrogation log as follows: "Told detainee that a dog is held in higher esteem because dogs know right from wrong and know to protect innocent people from bad people. Began teaching the detainee lessons such as stay, come, and bark to elevate his social status up to that of a dog. Detainee became very agitated." Then: "Dog tricks continued and detainee stated he should be treated like a man. Detainee was told he would have to learn who to defend and who to attack. Interrogator showed photos of 9-11 victims and told detainee he should bark happy for these people. Interrogator also showed photos of Al Qaida terrorists and told detainee he should growl at these people" (12/20/2002).

31. See Bazelon, Emily, et al., *What Is Torture? An Interactive Primer on American Interrogation,* Slate.com, May 26, 2005, at http://www.slate.com/id/2119122/.

32. See Bazelon (2005).

33. See Bazelon (2005) (citations omitted).

34. Lewis, *Fresh Details.*

35. Schmidt Report at 21.

36. See Lewis, *Fresh Details.*

CHAPTER 12

THE CASE OF SALIM HAMDAN (DECLARATION OF DARYL MATTHEWS)

Daryl Matthews

DARYL MATTHEWS, M.D., Ph.D., hereby declares and states as follows:

1. I am over the age of eighteen (18) years. The following is true and correct to the best of my knowledge. I have personal knowledge of the matters stated herein and, if called upon to testify, could competently testify thereto.

2. My qualifications to render expert psychiatric opinions include my education and training and my professional experience, set forth in detail in my curriculum vita, which is attached as Appendix A.[1]

3. I received my M.D. degree in 1973 from the Johns Hopkins University School of Medicine. My postgraduate medical education included a residency in psychiatry at Johns Hopkins Hospital from 1973 to 1976 and a fellowship in forensic psychiatry at the University of Virginia Schools of Law and Medicine. I am board certified in psychiatry and forensic psychiatry by the American Board of Psychiatry and Neurology, serve as an Examiner for that Board, and as a member of the Board's Forensic Psychiatry Examination Committee.

4. I have held faculty positions in medicine and public health at the Johns Hopkins University, Boston University, The University of Virginia, and the University of Arkansas, and am currently Professor of Psychiatry and Director of the Forensic Psychiatry Program at the John A. Burns School of Medicine at the University of Hawaii.

5. I have conducted psychiatric evaluations of more than 1,000 patients or forensic examinees, hundreds of them within the confines of jails, prisons, and similar facilities. These have included scores of facilities in 12 states, of all security levels, operated by local, state, civilian federal, and military authorities.

6. My evaluations and expert opinions have been admitted into evidence in more than 500 legal proceedings, including commitment hearings, civil trials, and criminal trials. I have been admitted to testify as an expert at trial by state and federal courts and military courts-martial in 20 jurisdictions.

7. My sources of information in this matter are:

(a) Affidavit of Mr. Salem Ahmed Salem Hamdan, (translated by Mr. Charles Schmitz), of February 9, 2004, and

(b) Representations made to me by Mr. Hamdan's attorney, LCDR Charles Swift.

8. According to his affidavit and his attorney, Mr. Hamdan is approximately 34 year-old married Yemini male, father of two children ages 4 and 2, who is currently confined at the U.S. Naval Base, Guantanamo Cuba.

9. Since December 2003 Mr. Hamdan has been confined alone in a cell, in a house that is guarded by a single non-Arabic-speaking guard. A translator is rarely available. He receives 60 minutes of exercise outdoors three times a week, only at night.

10. Mr. Hamdan has met his attorney, but he has not been charged with any offense. He has been told that he is facing trial before a military commission, but does not know when this is to occur. He understands that, even if acquitted, he potentially faces indefinite confinement at the discretion of the U.S. government.

11. Mr. Hamdan has described his moods during his period of solitary confinement as deteriorating, and as encompassing frustration, rage (although he has not been violent), loneliness, despair, depression, anxiety, and emotional outbursts. He asserted that he has considered confessing falsely to ameliorate his situation. LCDR Swift has described Mr. Hamdan's condition to me, as observed during their meetings, as initially agitated and withdrawn, with a brightening mood as the visit proceeds, but ending with Mr. Hamdan begging him not to leave.

12. Mr. Hamdan's past history includes the death of both parents before he was 12 years old, followed by periods of non-supervision and homelessness.

13. The medical literature has described the harmful mental effects of solitary confinement at least since 1854; the recent literature confirms their presence. Adverse effects include hypersensitivity to external stimuli, hallucinations, perceptual distortions, derealization experiences, depression, anxiety, mood liability, difficulties in concentration and memory, paranoid thinking, and problems with impulse control. The extent of these appears to vary with the length of solitary confinement and the degree of isolation experienced. There is evidence that some prisoners suffer long term psychological damage as a result of such confinement.

14. It is my opinion, to a reasonable medical certainty, that Mr. Hamdan's current conditions of confinement place him at significant risk for future psychiatric deterioration, possibly including the development of irreversible psychiatric symptoms. Additionally the conditions of his confinement make Mr. Hamdan particularly susceptible to mental coercion and false confession in conjunction with his case.

15. The conditions of confinement described by Mr. Hamdan and his legal counsel may also cause deterioration to the point of significant impairment of his ability to assess his legal situation and assist defense counsel. His array of pre-isolation stressors place him at particularly high risk, as does the psychological stress of the uncertainty he faces over his lack of charges and about the nature and duration of his future confinement.

16. It is my medical opinion that a release from solitary confinement and a return to the general population combined with a definite advisement as to potential charges and proceedings would significantly mitigate the risk of mental impairment/coercion in Mr. Hamdan's case.

17. These opinions were reached without my conducting a personal examination of Mr. Hamdan due to government restrictions preventing access to Mr. Hamdan for all but cleared persons.

I declare under penalty of perjury under the laws of the State of Washington that the foregoing is true and correct to the best of my knowledge and belief.

Daryl Matthews (Signed), March 31, 2004.

NOTES

Editor's Note: This declaration was part of the case Lieutenant Commander Charles Swift, resident of the State of Washington, next friend of Salim Ahmed Hamda, Petitioner v. Geoffrey Miller et al., Respondents, filed at the United States District Court, Western District, Seattle, Washington.

1. Editor's Note: This Appendix is not included in this volume.

INDEX

Abourezk, James, 33
Abu Ghraib detention center, 70, 127;
    detainee abuse at, 18, 78, 96
Afghanistan, 11, 75, 174; detention center
    in, 93
Agency for International Development
    (AID), 29
Air Force, U.S., 12, 25, 48, 76; School of
    Aviation Medicine, 43, 58. *See also*
    Survival-Evasion-Resistance-Escape
    (SERE) program
Al Qaeda, 11, 52, 97, 121. *See also* bin
    Laden, Osama
Algerian War, 141
Allen, Morse, 50, 57
Altman, Neil, 74
American Civil Liberties Union (ACLU),
    94, 103
American Medical Association (AMA), 72,
    82–83, 99, 100, 102, 110n84, 157n5
American Psychiatric Association, 71–72,
    102; prohibitions of direct participation,
    99–100
American Psychological Association (APA),
    40, 47, 51, 78, 85, 142; ethical standards
    of, 60, 61, 71; Ethics Code, 72, 80–81,
    157n5; moratorium resolution by, 75;
    Psychological Ethics and National

Security (PENS) Task Force, 72–73, 79,
    98; Resolution Against Torture and
    Other Cruel, Inhuman, or Degrading
    Treatment or Punishment, 73, 74, 81
Amnesty International, 70, 94, 142,
    159n10
amygdala, 145, 178–79, 181
Anderson, Jack, 33
anterior cingulate cortex, 179, 181
anxiety, cultivation of, 5, 7, 15
anxiety disorders, xiv. *See also* Posttraumatic
    Stress Disorder (PTSD)
APA. *See* American Psychological
    Association
Archives of General Psychiatry, 41
Argentina, torture victims in, 142, 152,
    154, 156, 159n10
Army, U.S., 25, 94, 95, 101; brainwashing
    and, 150; (Green Beret) Mobile Training
    Teams, 9, 24, 33, 34, 35; interrogation
    manual, 103; Medical Research Board,
    56; Military Intelligence, 58
Arnold, M. B., 145, 153
arousal patterns. *See* hyperarousal, in
    PTSD
Arrigo, Jean Maria, 72
ARTICHOKE (CIA project), 25–26, 46,
    50, 57

ABOUT THE EDITOR AND CONTRIBUTORS

Claudia Catani, PhD, is a psychologist with expertise in mental health disorders related to traumatic stress as a consequence of organized and domestic violence and is currently postdoctorate researcher at the Department of Clinical Psychology at the University of Konstanz. She is board member of the international NGO *vivo*—victim's voice (http://www.vivo.org), an organization working to overcome and prevent traumatic stress and its consequences within the individual as well as the community, safeguarding the rights and dignity of people affected by violence and conflict. Dr. Catani's research activities include extensive field work in different post-war countries (Afghanistan, Somalia, Sri Lanka) addressing the epidemiology of mental health problem in the aftermath of war and the treatment of posttraumatic stress disorder in adults and children with Narrative Exposure Therapy. Dr. Catani also has a major research interest in psychophysiological correlates of emotional elaboration and neurophysiological indicators of stress reactions and post-traumatic stress disorder. Currently, she is employing Magnetoencephalography (MEG) to investigate alterations of neural network indicators through narrative treatment in torture victims.

Thomas Elbert, Professor of Clinical Psychology and Neuropsychology at the University of Konstanz, Germany, studied Psychology and Physics at the Universities of Munich and Tübingen (PhD, 1978). His publications focus on the self-regulation of the brain, and on cortical organization, neuroplasticity and their relation to behaviour and psychopathology. Together with his colleagues, from *vivo*, Elbert has contributed to the development of Narrative Exposure Therapy

(NET), a culturally universal short-term intervention for the reduction of traumatic stress symptoms in survivors of organized violence, torture, war, rape, and childhood abuse. This treatment has been field-tested in war-torn areas. Elbert has worked in crisis regions in East-Africa, Sri Lanka and Afghanistan.

Rona M. Fields, PhD, is a psychologist with expertise in violence and terrorism and is currently a visiting scholar at Howard University, Washington, DC, and is the Founder and Director of Associates in Community Psychology, a clinical and consulting practice in Washington, DC. She graduated with honors in psychology from Lake Forest College in Lake Forest, Illinois, and did graduate work at the University of Illinois in Champaign-Urbana and Loyola University of Chicago, where she achieved a master's in psychology. She holds a doctorate from the University of Southern California. Fields did extensive research on torture in Northern Ireland and Portugal and Portuguese Africa during the 1974–76 period of the Revolutionary Government, and was appointed to the Amnesty International Medical Commission in the Campaign to Abolish Torture in 1973, as well as held a visiting fellowship at the Peace Research Institute in Oslo and the International Peace Research Association. She was a co-founder of the Socialwissenschaftliche Insstitut fur Katastrophen und Umfallforschung in Kiel. Fields authored *Northern Ireland: Society under Siege, The Future of Women, Society on the Run,* and *The Armed Forces Movement and the Portuguese Revolution.* Her most recent book, *Martyrdom: The Psychology, Theology and Politics of Self Sacrifice* was published by Praeger in 2004.

R. Matthew Gildner is a doctoral student in the Department of History at The University at Texas at Austin, where he is specializing in modern Latin America. While his current research focuses on the cultural and racial politics of Bolivia's 1952 National Revolution, his interests also include U.S. diplomatic history, transnational approaches to the Cold War, and human rights. He is the recipient of a Fulbright Fellowship as well as the American Historical Association's Albert J. Beveridge Grant in the History of The Western Hemisphere. He presently lives and works in La Paz, Bolivia.

Stuart Grassian, MD, is a psychiatrist with extensive experience in evaluating the psychiatric effects of stringent conditions of confinement, including involvement in a number of major class action lawsuits around the country. His work has been cited in a number of significant legal decisions, including cases in both federal and state courts. Dr. Grassian has experience with a wide variety of concerns associated with the effects of such confinement, including the problem of "volunteerism" in death penalty cases, impairment of the Sixth Amendment rights of pretrial detainees, and issues concerning prisoners accused or convicted of politically motivated crimes, including '60s radicals and accused terrorist detainees.

Gitanjali S. Gutierrez, Esq., was the first habeas attorney to meet with clients at the base and currently travels regularly to the military prison for client. She is counsel for Mohammed al Qahtani, a Saudi citizen detained in Guantánamo, who was subjected to a regime of "aggressive" interrogation techniques and Majid Khan, a U.S. resident and citizen of Pakistan who was transferred to Guantánamo in September 2006 from secret detention in CIA black sites. She also represents a Libyan citizen, Abu Abdul Ra'ouf Qassim, who is challenging the military's efforts to transfer him from Guantanamo to the dictatorship of Colonel Moammar Qadhafi where he faces torture or persecution. Gutierrez joined the Center for Constitutional Rights (CCR) on August 1, 2005. She has been working on legal challenges to Guantánamo since 2003, first as a CCR cooperating attorney and public interest fellow, and then as a CCR staff attorney beginning in 2005. She was a member of the legal team in *Rasul v. Bush* before the Supreme Court in 2004 and is part of the legal team litigating the *Al Odah v. Bush* appeal presently before the Supreme Court.

Uwe Jacobs, PhD, has been working with Survivors International (SI) for the past 12 years and has developed and implemented a variety of programs for survivors. He is both a clinical neuropsychologist and a psychotherapist. He is an expert on the psychological and neuropsychological assessment of asylum seekers and has written and published guidelines on this topic (see SI publications at http://www.survivorsintl.org). Dr. Jacobs drafted the chapters on the psychological and neuropsychological sequelae of torture for the currently existing international guidelines for the examination of torture published by the UN High Commissioner (Istanbul Protocol) and for the handbook on assessment of asylum seekers by Physicians for Human Rights. Prior to becoming Director of SI, Dr. Jacobs developed other programs for disadvantaged populations. He founded and directed the Homeless Assessment Program through the Wright Institute, Berkeley. He served as the psychological consultant in developing the Life After Exoneration Project (LAEP), a national program for wrongfully convicted ex-prisoners. Dr. Jacobs has also published in the area of psychotherapy process research. Dr. Jacobs has served as an Adjunct Faculty at the Wright Institute, Berkeley since 1997 and maintains an independent practice.

Terry A. Kupers is board-certified in psychiatry, a Distinguished Fellow of the American Psychiatric Association, and a Fellow of the American Orthopsychiatric Association. He is on the staff of Alta Bates Medical Center, is Contributing Editor of Correctional Mental Health Report, and is an editorial advisor for the journals Free Associations, Men and Masculinity, Psychology of Men & Masculinity. In 2005, Dr. Kupers received the Exemplary Psychiatrist Award from the National Alliance on Mental Illness (NAMI). His forensic psychiatry experience includes testimony in several large class action litigations concerning jail and prison conditions, sexual abuse, and the quality of mental health services inside correctional facilities. He is a consultant to Human Rights Watch. His diverse interests are reflected in the titles and subject matter of his four books, the books he edited, and the articles he has authored.

Jonathan H. Marks, Associate Professor of Bioethics, Humanities, and Law at the Pennsylvania State University; Barrister and Founding Member, Matrix Chambers, London. The author is Director of the Bioethics and Medical Humanities Program at the Pennsylvania State University's main campus at University Park. He also holds a joint appointment in the Department of Humanities at the College of Medicine in Hershey.

Daryl Matthews, MD, PhD, is Professor of Psychiatry and Director of Forensic Psychiatry at the John A. Bursn School of Medicine, University of Hawai'i at Manoa. His research interests include multiple homicide, murder-suicide, cultural issues in forensic psychiatry, forensic psychiatry and international human rights law. He is the author of *Disposable Patients: Situational Factors in Emergency Psychiatric Decisions* and a coauthor of *Reproductive Pasts, Reproductive Futures: Genetic Counseling and its Effectiveness,* as well as of *Cultural Competency in Forensic Psychiatry.* Dr. Matthews has served as a psychiatric consultant to the U.S. Army and has been called to give advice about the Guantánamo Bay Detention Center.

Alfred W. McCoy is the J.R.W. Smail Professor of History at the University of Wisconsin-Madison. After earning his PhD in Southeast Asian history at Yale in 1977, his writing on this region has focused on two topics—the political history of the modern Philippines and the politics of opium in the Golden Triangle. His first book, *The Politics of Heroin in Southeast Asia* (1972), originally sparked controversy when the CIA tried to block its publication, but is now regarded as the standard work on the subject of illicit narcotics. It has been in print for over 30 years, and been translated into nine languages—most recently Thai and German. His history of the Philippine officer corps, *Closer Than Brothers* (1999) examines the impact of the CIA's torture training upon the Philippine armed forces. Most recently, *A Question of Torture: CIA Interrogation, From the Cold War to the War on Terror* (2006), which is also available in German, continues his exploration of the covert netherworld and its influence upon U.S. foreign policy. His forthcoming book on Philippine police during the twentieth century will draw together the main two strands in his research, the covert netherworld and modern Philippine history, to explore the transformative power of police, information, and scandal in the shaping of both the Philippine republic and the U.S. national security state.

Frank Neuner, PhD, is Assistant Professor for Clinical Psychology and Psychotherapy at the University of Konstanz. He has conducted several studies about epidemiology and treatment of posttraumatic stress disorders in refugee communities and populations affected by war and natural disasters. He has contributed to the development and ongoing evaluation of Narrative Exposure Therapy. Currently he investigates brain changes through psychotherapy in victims of torture.

Almerindo E. Ojeda, PhD, is the Founding Director of the UCDavis Center for the Study of Human Rights in the Americas (CSHRA). CSHRA is an academic research center founded in the Spring of 2005 through a grant from the UCDavis Committee of Research, after which it received a grant from the University of California Office of the President. The mission of CSHRA is to gather information about human rights in the American continent, to interpret it form cross-cultural perspectives, to develop legal instruments appropriate to human rights protections, to create relevant curricula, and to enhance human rights across the American continent through enlightened action. Currently, CSHRA is engaged in two research projects: The Guantanamo Testimonials Project and the Neurobiology of Psychological Torture. Almerindo Ojeda is a Professor of Linguistics at the University of California at Davis, where he specializes in formal syntax and semantics. He is the author of *Linguistic Individuals.*

Brad Olson, PhD, is a community, social, and personality psychologist. He is research faculty at Northwestern University in the Foley Center for the Study of Lives and in the Human Development and Public Policy Program. His research areas include public policy, community action, nonviolence, human rights, substance abuse and the narrative study of lives. He is a founder of the Coalition for an Ethical Psychology, and was chair of the Divisions for Social Justice (DSJ), a collaborative of 12 divisions within the American Psychological Association working on social justice issues within psychology.

Gilbert Reyes, PhD, is the Series Editor for Praeger's Trauma and Disaster Psychology Series and the lead editor of the four-volume *Handbook of International Disaster Psychology,* published by Praeger in 2006. Dr. Reyes has consulted with the International Federation of Red Cross and Red Crescent Societies (IFRC) in a variety of situations and has provided mental health support for people affected by disasters in the United States. He also consults with the Terrorism and Disaster Center of the National Child Traumatic Stress Network regarding the psychosocial needs of children and families displaced by massive disasters such as Hurricane Katrina. He serves on the Steering Committee of Psychologists for Social Responsibility and as the Disaster Relief Chair for the Division of Trauma Psychology of the American Psychological Association. Dr. Reyes is a licensed clinical psychologist and the Associate Dean for Clinical Training at Fielding Graduate University in Santa Barbara, California.

Stephen Soldz is a clinical psychologist, psychoanalyst and public health researcher. Currently he is Professor and Director of the Center for Research, Evaluation, and Program Development at the Boston Graduate School of Psychoanalysis. He founded the Coalition for an Ethical Psychology, one of the organizations leading the struggle to change American Psychological Association policy on psychologists and interrogations and is Co-chair of the Psychologists for Social Responsibility End Torture Action Committee. Dr. Soldz is coeditor of *Reconciling Empirical Knowledge and Clinical Experience: The Art and Science of Psychotherapy* (2000), and has numerous professional publications in the areas of psychotherapy research, personality, substance abuse, tobacco control, research methodology, and the ethics of interrogations. He is on the editorial boards of several journals, including Psychotherapy Research and the Journal of Research Practice. Recently he has written social commentary for numerous web sites including Znet, CounterPunch, OpEdNews, Dissident Voice, Common Dreams, and Scoop and published the Psyche, Science, and Society blog.

Christian Wienbruch received a diploma (masters) in Geophysics in 1990 from the University of Münster. From 1991 until 1997 he worked with MEG at the Institute for Experimental Audiology at the University of Münster where he received a doctor in medical science (PhD) in 1996 for his work on source localization of methohexital induced spike activity in patients suffering from intractable temporal lobe epilepsy. In 1997 he joined the Clinical Psychology department at the University of Konstanz where he began to work on the relevance of MEG in clinical psychiatry and clinical psychology—for example, ADHD, schizophrenia, PTSD, tinnitus, and developmental disorders.